D0127825

Mrs. Cook's Kitchen
Basics & Beyond

Enjoy!

Suzy

Mrs. Cook's Kitchen

Basics & Beyond

by

Gay Cook

WHITECAP BOOKS

Vancouver | Toronto

Copyright © 2000 by Gay Cook
Whitecap Books
Vancouver | Toronto

All rights reserved. No part of this publication
may be reproduced, stored in a retrieval system,
or transmitted in any form or by any means,
electronic, mechanical, photocopying, recording
or otherwise, without prior written permission
of the publisher.

The information in this book is true and complete to the
best of our knowledge. All recommendations are made
without guarantee on the part of the authors or Whitecap
Books Ltd. The authors and publisher disclaim any liability
in connection with the use of this information. For additional
information, please contact Whitecap Books Ltd., 351 Lynn
Avenue, North Vancouver, BC V7J 2C4

Edited by Alison Maclean
Proofread by Elizabeth McLean
Book design by Enki, New York
Photographs by Michael Kohn
Food Styling by Sue Henderson

Printed and bound in Canada

Canadian Cataloguing in Publication Data
Cook, Gay, 1930-
    Mrs. Cook's kitchen

    Includes index.
    ISBN 1-55285-014-5

    1. Cookery. I. Title.
TX714.C6543 2000   641.5'12   C00-910075-X

The publisher acknowledges the support of the Canada
Council for the Arts and the Cultural Services Branch
of the Government of British Columbia for our publishing
program. We acknowledge the financial support of
the Government of Canada through the Book Industry
Development Program for our publishing activities.

Contents

Acknowledgments vi

Introduction 1

The Well-Equipped Kitchen 3

Appetizers 11

Wine, Beer & Other Beverages 26

Soups 34

Salads 46

Breads 61

Eggs & Cheese 83

Pasta, Pizza, Grains & Legumes 98

Fish & Seafood 120

Poultry 132

Beef, Veal, Lamb & Pork 147

Vegetables. 168

Sweets, Cakes, Cookies, Pies & Tarts 192

Menus 233

Glossary 238

Index 242

Acknowledgments

There are many people I wish to thank for their patience and input in fulfilling my dream to publish this book.

My abiding thanks go to my whole family — my late husband Bob, my son Don, my daughter Kelly, my sisters, Jean Pigott (and all her family) and Grete Hale. Their inspiration and their ability to put up with my strong opinions about food were vital. As well, they acted as willing victims as they tasted, tested and consumed the results of my culinary pursuits.

My gratitude to Claire Aubrey for her patience, enthusiasm and the countless hours she gave in organizing my dreams for the cookbook; Rosanne Kang, a mentor and friend who had faith in this cookbook and the talent to be its artistic director; Michael Kohn, for his exceptional photography; Sue Henderson, for her gifted food styling; Cindy Yabar, who gave much time to testing the recipes, and her family who had the job of eating the final products; Dorothy McGill, Liz Smith and Cindy Katz for generously taking the time to test recipes in their homes; Maureen Prentice for her Irish Soda Bread recipe, and Cindy Azar for her work preparing the manuscript.

Many thanks to Vince Piazza of Ottawa Bagel and Delicatessen for his advice on cheese varieties; Jill Snider, manager of Robin Hood Kitchens of Robin Hood Multifoods; Nicole Beauchamp, head of communications and promotion of the Chicken Farmers of Canada; Jane Jordan, owner of the All Your Kitchen Needs store, who gave invaluable information on kitchen equipment and props for the photos; Mark Hayhoe of Hayhoe Mills for his input on flour; the Spagnoli family of the Osgoode Orchard for their input on apples; Corinne Dawley, home economist at The Beef Information Centre, and the Jordash restaurant equipment company for the loan of props for the photographs.

Special thanks to Don Cook, Veronique Rivest, Michael Botner and Tim Collins for their advice on wines.

Introduction

I love to cook and I love to help people love the kitchen as much as I do.

The kitchen is a place where you can come alive and enjoy an adventure in learning about cooking, whether it's trying a new recipe, inventing a dish with leftovers, or adding a new spice to an old favorite.

Working with food uses all our senses. We see, hear, smell, taste and feel the ingredients. That's why cooking is an instinctive art form — not a science bound by absolute quantities, times and temperatures.

I was lucky to come from a home where meals played an important role. Our family life was centered around the dining table and it was not unusual to have to set extra places for family and friends who would drop in for a friendly talk and a plate of food.

My dad ran a family-owned bakery with a catering and restaurant business in Ottawa and the neighboring city of Hull, Quebec. When Dad came home from work, it was normal for us to discuss (after he had finished the main course) what was happening in the business, our day at school, or politics. Everyone's opinion was welcome and I cherish the memory of our mealtime conversations.

My sisters and I started working in the family business during our high school days. We began by packing cookies on the assembly lines and progressed to making dozens of sandwiches in the catering department. I loved Saturdays when, dressed in my black uniform with my little white lace apron, I would board a catering van and head out to catering jobs. I always volunteered for the country weddings so I could avoid meeting my friends from the city! We also learned the financial ropes that included taking in the daily deposits from the delivery drivers. The bakery was in our blood.

I had always wanted to be a chef, but it was not then an acceptable profession for women. So instead, I enrolled in the first class of the Hotel, Resort and Restaurant Administration course at the Ryerson Polytechnic University in Toronto in 1953. Afterwards, I took advantage of my parents' connections to secure positions working as a cook in homes throughout Europe and the Americas. This held wonderful experiences for me as I had to deal humbly with my culinary mistakes — I thought I knew it all. I also learned much about the different foods and traditions of each country.

My husband, Bob, and I were living in Washington, DC, when I began catering from our first home. I remember our young son Don and daughter Kelly doing everything from cleaning shrimp to accidentally sitting on freshly made meringues that were for a catered dinner party! Later, I opened a "hands-on" cooking school while we were living in Toronto and a second school when we moved to Ottawa. Today, I am a food columnist at the *Ottawa Citizen* and freelance food writer at several other publications.

Our family sold the bakery, catering and restaurant businesses over 20 years ago and we went into the business of manufacturing frozen convenience foods. Today we have three factories in Toronto where we make appetizers, frozen entrées, meat pies and desserts under the Savarin and Coming Home brand names and private labels sold throughout North America. I am pleased that my family is in the convenience food business, even though I am in the business of cooking from scratch. They go hand in hand as they both play a role in our lives today.

During my cooking school days, it meant a great deal to see people from all walks of life gain confidence in making soups, kneading dough, rolling pastry and learning that you can cook a meal from scratch, quickly and easily. I taught basics about food preparation, including the necessity for fresh ingredients and the best use of butter, herbs and salt to enhance flavor. This cookbook is the culmination of all my years of food experience. The recipes have been collected lovingly throughout a lifetime involved with food. Each recipe is introduced with a tip on its use, its history or its personal association. I offer tips on methods, equipment, techniques and ingredients written for the "undergraduate" cook. I don't assume that the reader has an intricate or specialized knowledge. I do, however, assume that the reader loves food.

Many people have missed growing up at their mother's elbow in the kitchen, leaving gaps in their culinary knowledge. I hope to make the timid cook a little bolder and the experienced cook even more adventurous—to help every cook realize that recipes are only a set of guidelines, not a set of rules.

So here we go on a fun journey through the world of food — no seat belts required!

The Well-Equipped Kitchen

Equipping a kitchen can be an overwhelming task. My advice is to begin the process with a few quality items that will last a long time.

Utensils, back row, from left: whisk, rasp, wooden spoon, metal spatula, metal lifter

Front row, from left: ladle, rubber spatula, scissors, potato masher, brass skimmer

Knives: Giving You an Edge in the Kitchen

When buying your knives, remember that good ones will last for a lifetime. The knives that my husband and I bought when we were first married made a dent in our budget, but they are still working hard for me every day.

To help you select the right knives, here's a little background information: high-carbon stainless steel knives are best because they maintain a sharp edge and are easy to clean. The most expensive knives are forged from a single piece of steel tapering to a sharp point. The thick end, or tang, extends right through the handle to prevent it from working loose. Knives of lesser quality are machine-stamped and have thinner blades that do not extend through the handle.

To care for your knives, keep them clean and sharp. Warm water and a soft cloth are best for cleaning. Never use abrasive cleansers or a dishwasher that could cause your knives to scratch or split at the handle. Sharp knives are essential to reduce cutting accidents and sharpening them is easy if you do it regularly. To get a sharp edge on your knives, first have them sharpened on a whetstone by a professional and thereafter you can do it yourself or continue to get professional help.

If you're going to sharpen your knives yourself, you need to get a whetstone, a block of natural or synthetic stone available at hardware or kitchen stores. To use a whetstone, lightly wet the gritty side with water or mineral oil and place the stone on a folded cloth to keep it steady. Hold the handle of the knife with one hand and, with the fingers of the other hand, hold down the blade on a slight angle on the flat side of the blade near the tip. Push the blade away from you, moving from the tip to the handle, across the stone. Then turn the knife over and pull the blade toward you, from the handle to the tip. Repeat 5 times. Turn the stone over to the smooth side and repeat the procedure 3 times.

To maintain sharp edges on your knives, use a sharpening steel: hold the steel at a right angle to your body and draw the knife blade down the length of the steel at a 20° angle. Repeat this action, drawing the blade down the back of the steel. Repeat the entire procedure 5 or 6 times. It is very important to use the sharpening steel on your knives after each use to maintain this edge.

From top: whetstone, steel sharpener, carving knife, 10" (25 cm) chef's knife, serrated knife, 8" (20 cm) chef's knife, and utility knife

Pans, from top: steel omelet pan, cast iron grill pan, cast iron griddle pan, cast aluminum skillet, and cast iron skillet (frying pan)

Cookware: The Big Choice

There are many types of pots and pans, but the most important consideration is their ability to hold and conduct heat efficiently. If possible, they should also have non–heat-conductive handles. Here is a brief rundown of the different kinds of cookware available:

- Stainless steel pots and pans are durable, non-reactive and scratch resistant, making them an excellent choice. You should look for cookware with an outer layer of stainless steel enclosing 3 to 7 layers of copper, aluminum or other heat-conductive alloy.

- Copper pots are the best heat conductors, but they must be lined with stainless steel or tin to prevent a reaction with food. Stainless steel will never wear out, but a tin lining will need to be replaced eventually. Copper cookware is beautiful and very expensive.

- Cast iron pans have been used for centuries. They distribute heat evenly and hold it well. They are also inexpensive and I love them. You do need to season cast iron every so often by covering the cooking surface with a thin film of vegetable oil and baking the pan in a moderate oven for 1 hour. This ensures that the cast iron doesn't rust and the surface is practically nonstick.

- Enameled cast iron has the same qualities as cast iron, but you don't need to season it. Enameled pots look great, but they do have a tendency to chip.

- Cast aluminum is a good choice because it is lighter than cast iron with many of the same qualities. It doesn't have the superb heat conduction of cast iron, but it's a practical alternative.

- Aluminum used to be popular, although it has drawbacks if it's unlined: it pits easily, discolors and reacts with acidic and alkaline foods.

- Nonstick pans are not recommended because you cannot achieve the color and flavor so important in savory cooking without high heat. Nonstick pans can't be used on high heat because the coating on the cooking surface could release chemicals into the food. However, nonstick is fine for use in bakeware.

Bakeware: What's Best

Bakeware is not essential for a kitchen, but it will encourage you to bake, which will encourage visitors! I've learned from experience that the heavier the baking pan, the better it bakes. Most are made from aluminum, nonstick metal and glass. I have never liked glass since you can't get the fast heat required for making pastry, but I do like heavy-gauge aluminum. While nonstick is fine for muffin and cake tins, it's not a good choice for pie plates, since the nonstick surface can be scratched when you cut into the pie.

When you're buying cookie sheets, get ones that are heavy enough not to bend when baking. My favorite are the heavy aluminum sheets with no rims. Because they have 2 layers of metal sandwiching a layer of air, they bake cookies and breads evenly.

The Lists

I have divided kitchen tools and equipment into 3 lists for simplicity's sake: The Essentials, The Extras and The Luxuries. When setting up a kitchen, follow the guide for essentials and acquire the extras and luxuries later.

The Essentials

- Chef's knife, 10 inches (25 cm), wide, weighted blade for chopping or slicing, a versatile tool
- Serrated knife, 8 inch (20 cm), for slicing bread and tomatoes, worth the investment
- Carving knife, 10 inch (25 cm), with a long, thin, flexible blade for accurate carving
- Paring knife, 3–4 inch (7.5–10 cm)
- Utility knife, 5–6 inch (12.5–15 cm)
- Skillet, 10 inch (25 cm), with a long handle and sloping sides
- Saucepans, 4 cup (1 L) and 6 cup (1.5 L), with tight-fitting lids
- Blender, inexpensive, purées everything from milkshakes to soups
- Heavy-duty electric mixer
- Colander, for draining and straining
- Corkscrew
- Cutting board, hardwood maple is best
- Grater
- Rasp, metal carpenter's tool for finer grating and zesting
- Turner or flipper, metal or coated, solid or slotted
- Measuring spoons, imperial and metric
- Measuring cups for dry ingredients, imperial and metric

- Measuring cups for liquid, imperial and metric
- Mixing bowls, small, medium and large
- Pepper mill
- Spatulas, rubber or heat resistant, small and large
- Spoons, wooden, for mixing and stirring
- Spoons, metal, slotted and plain, for stirring and serving
- Whisks, small, medium and balloon, for sauces, beating eggs, whipping cream
- Can opener

The Extras

- Grill pan, for cooking meat, poultry and fish, low-fat cooking
- Small skillet, 6 or 7 inch (15 or 17.5 cm), for scrambled eggs, omelets, crêpes
- Griddle, flat cast iron pan with a raised edge, for pancakes, tortillas, pizza
- Large saucepans, 8 cup (2 L) to 20 cup (5 L)
- Dutch oven, 6-quart (6 L), cast iron or heavy stainless steel with lid is best
- Roasting pan, 16 x 13 x 3 inch (40 x 32.5 x 7.5 cm), heavy-duty is an excellent investment
- Baking pan, 15 x 10 x 3/4 inch (38 x 25 x 2 cm), useful for rolled cake or roulade

- Cake pans, round set of 2, 8 or 9 inch (20 or 22.5 cm)
- Cake pan, square, 8 x 8 inch (20 x 20 cm)
- Cake pan, rectangular, 11 x 7 inch (27.5 x 17.5 cm)
- Pie plate, 8 or 9 inch (20 or 22.5 cm)
- Muffin tins, nonstick, medium and mini sizes
- Baking dish, shallow, of ovenproof glass, glazed earthenware or ceramic, 3 or 4 inches (7.5 or 10 cm) deep
- Hand-held mixer, great for mixing small amounts right in the saucepan, bowl or pitcher
- Food processor, a good investment
- Wire mesh lifter, for removing foods from hot oil or water
- Bulb baster, for basting meats and poultry
- Citrus juicer
- Cookie cutters, various shapes and sizes
- Funnels, various shapes and sizes
- Garlic press
- Potato masher
- Salad spinner
- Cooling racks, metal
- Pastry bag, with various metal tips for decorating
- Pastry brushes, short- and long-handled
- Pastry cutter

The Extras (cont.)

- Thermometers, 3: meat, candy and oven
- Rolling pins, wooden is best
- Spatula, metal, for frosting cakes
- Timer, choose one with a long ring
- Tongs, metal, with a locking ring to keep them closed
- Parchment paper

The Luxuries

- Sauté pan, straight-sided, great for fried chicken or stews
- Stockpot, 6 quart (6 L) to 20 quart (20 L), for stocks, corn, lobsters
- Tart or flan pan, 9 inch (22.5 cm), with removable bottom
- Bundt pan, 10 inch (25 cm), or tube pan, with removable center tube
- Loaf pans, various sizes
- Ceramic soufflé dish, straight-sided, 1/2-cup (125-mL) ramekins to 4-quart (4-L) dishes
- Whetstone, or honing stone, for sharpening knives
- Cherry/olive pitter
- Food mill
- Kitchen scale, with imperial and metric measures
- Melon baller
- Nutmeg grater
- Potato ricer
- Zester, for citrus peel

Appetizers

Appetizers say "welcome," whether to one friend or a roomful of guests.

In this chapter, I have tried to offer recipes that are delicious, colorful and simple to make.

An appetizer before dinner is often a debatable subject. To have or not to have? Serving an appetizer is meant to tweak but not kill the appetite before dinner. You put much effort, time and money into the meal, so you want your guests to nibble on only a few light tidbits while sipping an apéritif. These tidbits could include bruschetta, mushroom pâté with homemade Melba toast or tapenade-stuffed cherry tomatoes.

Apéritifs are drinks to stimulate the appetite for the upcoming meal. These include dry or sweet rich-tasting sherry or herb-infused vermouth, both of which are fortified wines. Others include chilled, crisp and fruity Sauvignon Blanc from the New World, Pinot Gris, sparkling wines or a champagne. A young fruity red wine like a Chianti or Beaujolais can be delightful. Appetizers with a spicy flavor go well with chilled beer. As you learn more

about food, your ability to marry apéritifs with appetizers will improve.

We had a little rule in our house: when we gave a dinner party we never offered "hard" drinks before the meal because they deaden the taste buds, while wine-based drinks stimulate the tasting ability. A test is in the first two bites of a succulent steak. After that the sensation is gone as the fats coat the taste buds. The acidity in wine cleanses the taste buds and a sip between bites revives the taste of the steak or whatever foods are being eaten.

When preparing a buffet table which includes several courses, vary the heights of presentation for visual appeal and to help set those juices flowing. The array could include flow-ers, low and high pedestal serving plates, large and small baskets or bowls and platters. Good choices could include a Broccoli/Cauliflower Head, a Vegetable Tree with dips, Mushroom or Liver Pâté, a Glazed Whole Ham, or a cake on a pedestal.

Tapenade

MAKES 3/4 CUP (175 ML)
PREPARATION: 20 MINUTES

This black olive pâté from Provence can be served with breads, tossed in salads or with vegetables, or used as a stuffing for cherry tomatoes. The best olives are sold in bulk packed in brine or oil, but I suggest you taste-test them in the store—a good shop will be happy to let you do that.

1 cup	250 mL	black olives, pitted
3–4	3–4	canned anchovy fillets
or 1 tbsp	15 mL	anchovy paste
1/4 cup	50 mL	drained capers
1 tbsp	15 mL	lemon juice, or add to taste
3 tbsp	45 mL	olive oil
1/2 tsp	2 mL	freshly ground black pepper

Place the olives in a food processor or blender with the anchovies, capers, lemon juice and oil. Purée to a finely chopped paste. Season with pepper, but do not add salt as both olives and anchovies tend to be salty.

> To pit olives, use cherry pitter or lightly crush with a rolling pin and remove the stones.

Mushroom Pâté

MAKES 4 TO 6 SERVINGS
PREPARATION: 10 MINUTES
COOKING: 5 MINUTES

This light and easy pâté marries toasted walnuts with the woodland taste of mushrooms—it's also great for wraps or sandwiches.

1/4 cup	50 mL	chopped walnuts or pecans
8 oz	250 g	portobello or brown mushrooms, washed, drained
2 tbsp	25 mL	butter
1/4 cup	50 mL	finely chopped onions
1 or 2	1 or 2	garlic cloves, minced
2 tsp	10 mL	lemon juice, or to taste
3/4 tsp	4 mL	salt
		pinch cayenne pepper

To toast the walnuts, heat a skillet over medium-high heat, add the nuts and stir until an aroma rises; set aside. Discard the tough ends of the mushroom stems, place the mushrooms and nuts in the processor and process until finely minced. Remove and reserve.

Reheat the skillet over medium-low heat, add the butter and sweat the onions and garlic, covered for 5 minutes, stirring several times. Raise the heat to high, stir in the mushroom/nut mixture and sauté for 1 minute, stirring often. Remove from the heat. Stir in the lemon juice, salt and cayenne pepper. Cool in a small serving bowl.

Chicken Liver Pâté with Brandy

MAKES 1 1/2 CUPS (375 ML)
PREPARATION: 15 MINUTES
CHILLING: 1 TO 2 HOURS

This rich-tasting pâté is great for a buffet or as a spread for sandwiches or wraps. I think it is best when puréed to a smooth consistency.

8 oz	250 g	chicken livers, fat or membranes removed
1 tbsp	15 mL	butter
1	1	small onion, chopped
1	1	garlic clove, chopped
1/4 cup	50 mL	butter, cut into pieces
1 tsp	5 mL	salt
1/2 tsp	2 mL	freshly ground black pepper
1/4 tsp	1 mL	freshly grated nutmeg
2 tbsp	25 mL	brandy

Heat the first amount of butter in a small skillet over low-medium heat and sweat the onion and garlic, covered, for 5 minutes. Raise the heat to medium-high, add the livers and sauté until they are no longer pink inside, turning often. Cool for 5 minutes.

Purée the mixture in a processor or blender until smooth. Add the butter pieces as the mixture is processing, then the salt, pepper and nutmeg to taste, and finally the brandy. Pour the mixture into a serving dish or several small ramekins. Chill until firm and bring to room temperature 30 minutes before serving. Serve with sliced French baguette, Melba toast or water biscuits. This recipe can be made 5 to 6 days ahead, if you wish.

Homemade Melba Toast or Pita Wedges

MAKES: 48 MELBA TOAST OR 32 TO 48 PITA WEDGES
PREPARATION: 15 MINUTES
COOKING: 10 TO 12 MINUTES

Thin, homemade slices of bread or pita wedges are easy to toast until crisp and are so much tastier than the commercial product for dips or pâtés.

| 1/2 loaf | 1/2 loaf | unsliced bread, partially frozen |
| or 4 | 4 | 6-inch (15-cm) pita or pocket breads |

Remove the crusts of the bread, if desired, and thinly slice (freezing will make this easier) about 1/8 inch (.5 cm) thick. Cut each slice into 4 triangles. If you're using pitas, cut them in half, gently separate the pockets and cut each half into 4 or 6 wedges. Place the bread triangles or pita wedges on a baking sheet and toast in a preheated 375°F (180°C) oven for 10 to 12 minutes or until crisp and golden. Store in a closed container.

Oysters on the Half Shell with Lemon Wedges

ALLOW 2 TO 3 OYSTERS PER PERSON
PREPARATION: 20 TO 30 MINUTES

Oysters from cold waters retain their wonderful flavors best when served raw on the half shell. My favorite seasoning is a little freshly ground black pepper, fresh lemon juice and perhaps a dash of hot sauce.

If you're planning to serve oysters on the half shell, ask the fishmonger for some extra crushed ice for the presentation. If you are not opening the oysters immediately, freeze the crushed ice for later use and keep the oysters cold and moist by placing them in a large open plastic bag with a damp cloth covering them. Keep in the refrigerator but do not close the bag— they will last up to a day.

When shelling oysters, wash them thoroughly to remove loose bits of shell and grit. To open, it's best to use a blunt-tipped oyster knife. Place the oyster on the work surface, cupped side down. Hold it with a thick towel on the side opposite the slit that forms the hinged opening. Insert the knife into the hinge, press in and wiggle the knife as you twist open, being careful not to lose any of the juice. Set the oyster in its shell on ice for presentation, with lemon wedges in a bowl, or placed attractively on the ice with the oysters.

Shucking oysters (see opposite)

Shrimp with Cucumber Herb Sauce

MAKES 4 TO 6 SERVINGS
PREPARATION: 6 MINUTES
COOKING: 2 TO 3 MINUTES

Shrimp cooked in seawater or well-salted water are delicious and tender, especially when served with this cucumber sauce or with clarified butter and lemon.

1 qt	1 L	cold water
1–2 lbs	.5–1 kg	large or medium shrimp with shells
4 tsp	20 mL	salt

Cucumber Herb Sauce

1/2	1/2	seedless cucumber, cut into chunks
		zest and juice of 1/2 lemon
3 tbsp	45 mL	mayonnaise or yogurt cheese
2 tbsp	25 mL	chopped fresh dill or cilantro, or 1 tbsp (15 mL) dried
1/2 tsp	2 mL	salt, or to taste

In a food processor or blender, process the cucumber until finely minced. Press the cucumber with a rubber scraper and drain off some of the juice. Place the cucumber in a bowl and stir in the lemon rind, juice, mayonnaise or yogurt cheese, and herbs. Add salt to taste.

Add the cold water to a saucepan containing the shrimp and salt. Place the pan on medium-high heat and bring to a boil. When the shrimp are a bright pink, 2 to 3 minutes, drain them immediately. Remove the shells, but leave the tails on. Serve with Cucumber Herb Sauce or clarified butter (page 130) and lemon wedges.

To make yogurt cheese, put plain yogurt in a sieve lined with cheesecloth or paper towel. Set over a bowl to drain for 20 minutes, or overnight in the refrigerator. The longer it drains, the thicker and creamier it gets.

Whole Artichokes with Lemon Mayonnaise Sauce

MAKES 4 TO 6 SERVINGS
PREPARATION: 20 MINUTES
COOKING: 30 TO 45 MINUTES

When an artichoke is cooked whole and each leaf is dipped into a zippy sauce, it's a unique treat. Artichokes are the flower heads of a thistle that grows in a warm, dry climate. The "hearts" are the edible core topped with an inedible fuzzy choke and surrounded by tough outer leaves, each with a spike at the end. They are a difficult food to match with wines, but my choice is a crisp, grassy Sauvignon Blanc.

6–8	6–8	fresh artichokes, with 1-inch (2.5-cm) of stem removed
1 tbsp	15 mL	salt
3 tbsp	45 mL	lemon juice or vinegar

Lemon Mayonnaise Sauce

1/3 cup	75 mL	mayonnaise, homemade or commercial
2 tbsp	25 mL	fresh lemon juice
1 tbsp	15 mL	chopped fresh herbs such as tarragon, dill or basil
1/4 tsp	1 mL	salt, or to taste

Combine all the ingredients in a small bowl.

Use a sharp knife to cut 2 inches (5 cm) off the top of each artichoke. Use scissors to snip off the thorny ends of remaining leaves. Half fill a large saucepan with water, add the salt and the lemon juice and bring to a gentle boil. Add the artichokes and weigh them down with a plate until they are fully immersed. Cook for 30 to 40 minutes until the tip of a sharp knife easily penetrates the core at the bottom of the artichoke. Remove and invert the artichokes on a rack to drain.

To remove the chokes, spread the outside leaves open and pull out the purple "funnel"—it lifts out easily. Spoon out the hairy choke from the cavity and discard. Replace the funnel, if desired.

Serve the artichokes at room temperature with the Lemon Mayonnaise Sauce. It can be served separately or you can remove the funnel and pour the sauce into the cavity, which makes an attractive presentation.

Tomato Bruschetta

MAKES 4 TO 6 SERVINGS
PREPARATION: 12 MINUTES

The combination of fresh tomatoes and basil is ideal—a taste made in heaven, particularly during the growing season. The secret is in carefully making and flavoring the tomato concassé. Although it's expensive, using real Parmigiano-Reggiano makes this delicious and authentic.

12	12	prepared Crostini (page 19)
4 or 5	4 or 5	plum tomatoes
1 tsp	5 mL	wine vinegar
		sprinkling of salt and freshly ground black pepper
6–8	6–8	fresh basil leaves cut into thin slices
1 oz	30 g	piece of Parmigiano-Reggiano cheese, for shaving or 1/4 cup (50 mL) freshly grated Parmesan

To make concassé, cut the tomatoes in half crosswise and squeeze each half to remove the seeds and juice. Cut the tomato pulp into small cubes and toss with the vinegar, salt and pepper. Stir in the basil. Top each warm crostini with a spoonful of tomato mixture. Use the slicer section in a grater or a vegetable peeler to shave a few slices of Parmigiano-Reggiano, or sprinkle some Parmesan over each bruschetta. Serve within 10 minutes.

Gorgonzola Bruschetta

MAKES 4 TO 6 SERVINGS
PREPARATION: 10 MINUTES

Gorgonzola, one of Italy's masterpieces, is a robust blue-veined cheese that makes this bruschetta deliciously rich.

12	12	prepared Crostini (below)
4 oz	120 g	Gorgonzola cheese, brought to room temperature
1 tbsp	15 mL	extra-virgin olive oil
1/4 tsp	1 mL	freshly ground black pepper
2 tsp	10 mL	chopped fresh rosemary needles
1 tbsp	15 mL	rosemary needles for garnish

In a small bowl, mash the cheese with a fork and stir in the oil, pepper and rosemary. Place a mound on each crostini and garnish with 1 or 2 rosemary needles.

Crostini

MAKES 4 TO 6 SERVINGS
PREPARATION: 8 MINUTES

The simple flavors of extra-virgin olive oil and garlic on toasted bread are special.

12 slices	12 slices	day-old Italian or French or country-style bread
1 or 2	1 or 2	garlic cloves, peeled, split lengthwise, slightly squashed
1/4 cup	50 mL	extra-virgin olive oil for brushing sprinkling of salt

If the bread slices are large, cut them in half or into rounds with a cookie cutter before you broil, or barbecue just until the bread is golden on both sides. Watch carefully, as the bread will brown easily. Drizzle or brush the oil on one side and rub with garlic. Lightly sprinkle with salt on the garlic side. Serve while still fresh and warm.

Fresh Vegetable Tree (Crudités)

MAKES 20 TO 25 SERVINGS
PREPARATION: 2 HOURS

This makes a stunning eye-catcher on a buffet table. Fresh vegetables in all colors of the rainbow are attached with toothpicks to a tall Styrofoam cone, or to a fresh cabbage or cauliflower head and served with a variety of dips. Or, the vegetables can be mounded separately on a tray or in a basket with dips placed nearby. Most vegetables should be raw, but I find that broccoli and cauliflower taste best when blanched briefly.

1	1	cauliflower head, washed
2	2	broccoli heads, washed
1	1	bunch radishes, washed
2 cups	500 mL	cherry tomatoes, washed
1	1	red pepper, seeded, cut into 1/2-inch (1-cm) strips
1 cup	250 mL	black olives
1	1	bunch parsley, thick stems removed
1	1	12-inch (30-cm) Styrofoam cone and 1 box of toothpicks
		1 recipe Chèvre Cheese Dip or Roasted Red Pepper Dip (page 21)

Cut the cauliflower and broccoli into small florets with 1-inch (2.5-cm) stems. In a medium saucepan bring water to a full boil and drop in the cauliflower florets; return to the boil and cook for 1 minute. Drain in a colander. Cool in ice water. Drain. Repeat for the broccoli florets.

Remove the tips of the radishes but leave 1/2-inch (1 cm) green stems. To make radish roses, use a vegetable peeler or small sharp knife to peel thin strips from the tip almost to the stem, about 1/2-inch (1 cm) wide. Do not detach. Continue all the way around each radish. Drop into ice water for 30 minutes so the strips branch out like the petals of a rose.

To affix the vegetables and olives, start at the top of the cone, alternating textures and colors as you go. Use small bunches of parsley to cover any visible cone. This procedure can be done several hours ahead, but wrap the vegetable tree with moistened paper towels and cover with a cloth towel to retain moisture. To serve, place the tree on large serving platter with extra vegetables and olives in small clumps around the base of the cone. Serve with Chèvre Cheese Dip or Roasted Red Pepper Dip.

Chèvre Cheese Dip

MAKES ABOUT 1 1/4 CUPS (300 ML)
PREPARATION: 10 MINUTES

5 oz	150 g	soft chèvre (goat cheese)
1/2 cup	125 mL	plain yogurt
1 or 2	1 or 2	garlic cloves, minced
1 tsp	5 mL	dill, fresh or dried
2 tbsp	25 mL	brandy or sherry
1/2 tsp	2 mL	salt, or to taste

Whisk the cheese, yogurt, garlic and dill until smooth. Season with the brandy or sherry and salt to taste.

Roasted Red Pepper Dip

MAKES 1/2 CUP (125 ML)
PREPARATION: 15 MINUTES

2	2	large fresh red bell peppers
2	2	garlic cloves, peeled, minced
1/4 cup	50 mL	mayonnaise or yogurt cheese (page 16)
1 tbsp	15 mL	red wine vinegar
1/2 tsp	2 mL	salt, or to taste
1/8 tsp	.5 mL	hot red pepper sauce, or to taste

Roast the peppers on a grill or under a broiler until the skin is completely charred—the blackening intensifies the flavor. Cool, then peel off the charred skin, discard the seeds and purée in a food processor or blender. Whisk together with garlic, mayonnaise and vinegar. Season with salt and the hot pepper sauce.

Mexican Tortilla Chicken or Beef Wraps

MAKES 8 SANDWICH WRAPS OR 32 BITES
PREPARATION: 30 MINUTES

This recipe makes delightful little bites for an informal meal or delicious sandwich wraps — the possibilities are endless. Lightly toasting tortillas before making the wraps rids them of that "doughy" taste and texture.

2	2	Barbecued Chicken Legs (page 134)
or 8 oz	250 g	Marinated Flank Steak (page 152)
4	4	12-inch (30-cm) or 8, 6-inch (15-cm) flour tortillas
1 cup	250 mL	Guacamole (page 23)
1 cup	250 mL	Fresh Tomato Salsa (page 23)
3–4	3–4	green onions, finely sliced

If you're using barbecued chicken, pull the meat off the chicken legs and tear into strips. If you're using steak, cut it into thin strips.

To toast the tortillas, heat a large, dry skillet, griddle or grill pan on medium heat. Place a tortilla on the pan for 30 seconds. Turn and heat until the tortilla is lightly golden but not crisp—that makes them too difficult to roll. The tortilla will bubble, but that is a good sign it is toasting.

To assemble, lay the tortillas on a work surface and spread each one with guacamole. Distribute equal amounts of chicken or steak across the center of each tortilla, then spoon on the salsa and sprinkle with the green onions. Roll the tortilla tightly to make wraps. Wraps may be made several hours ahead, covered and chilled. To serve the wraps, place the rolled wraps seam-side down on a cutting board and cut in half on the diagonal. For bites, cut into diagonal 1/2-inch (1 cm) slices.

Guacamole

MAKES ABOUT 1/2 CUP (125 ML)
PREPARATION: 10 MINUTES

Avocados play an important role in Mexican cuisine, in dips, salads or topping hot dishes. I like to choose avocados with dark green pebbly skin such as the Haas variety. I prefer their flavor to that of the bright green avocados with smooth skins.

1	1	ripe avocado, halved, pit removed
1 tbsp	15 mL	fresh lemon or lime juice
1	1	garlic clove, finely chopped
1/2 or 1	1/2 or 1	jalapeno pepper, chopped
1/4 cup	50 mL	finely chopped fresh cilantro
1/4 tsp	1 mL	salt, or to taste

Spoon the avocado out of the skin into a bowl and mash with a fork until it is slightly lumpy. Stir in the lemon or lime juice, garlic, jalapeno and cilantro. Taste for salt. If you are not using the guacamole immediately, cover it tightly to keep the air from causing the avocado to darken. Keep chilled and if the mixture does darken, just stir it. Guacamole will keep for 4 days.

Fresh Tomato Salsa

MAKES ABOUT 11/2 CUPS (375 ML)
PREPARATION: 10 MINUTES

Salsa means "sauce" in Spanish. It is served at most meals in Mexican homes or restaurants and it's steadily gaining popularity as a condiment in North America.

2	2	medium tomatoes, finely chopped
1/2	1/2	medium onion, finely chopped
1/4–1/2	1/4–1/2	jalapeno pepper, finely chopped, or to taste
1/2 tsp	2 mL	salt, or to taste
1–2 tsp	5–10 mL	fresh cilantro, leaves only, chopped

Combine all the ingredients in a blender or food processor, pulsing it on and off so the salsa remains chunky. Leave for 30 minutes to mingle the flavors.

Vietnamese Salad Rolls with Peanut Sauce

MAKES 20 ROLLS
PREPARATION: 40 MINUTES

These delightful nutritious finger foods can be made several hours ahead. Turn them into fun party fare, with your guests choosing their own fillings and wrapping them in the moistened rice paper. This parchment-like paper is made from rice dough, dried in the sun on bamboo mats and then softened in warm water just before using. The rolls can also be fried to make spring rolls.

1 qt	1 L	cold water
4 tsp	20 mL	salt
8 oz	250 g	medium shrimp with shells
4 oz	120 g	narrowest dried rice stick noodles
10	10	lettuce leaves
2–3	2–3	garlic chives, if available, cut into 2-inch (5-cm) slivers
1 1/2 cups	375 mL	finely shredded carrots and/or cucumber
1/2 cup	125 mL	fresh cilantro and/or mint and/or basil leaves
20	20	6-inch (15-cm) rice paper wrappers
		1 recipe Peanut Sauce (page 25)

Bring the water, salt and shrimp to a boil in a saucepan over medium-high heat. Drain immediately and cool. Remove the shells and black vein of the shrimp and cut each shrimp in half lengthwise.

Cook the noodles in boiling water for 4 minutes. Drain and rinse under cold water.

Dry the lettuce on a tea towel and cut it into quarters. Put the prepared shrimp, noodles, lettuce, chives, carrots or cucumber, cilantro and mint or basil in individual bowls.

To assemble the salad rolls, soak an individual rice paper in warm water for 10 seconds and place it on a clean work surface. Choose a little of the fillings and place them in the center of the wrap. The last step is to fold in the top and bottom and sides of the rice paper and roll it up tightly. Chill for 10 minutes or longer, covered with a towel. If desired, cut in half on the diagonal. Serve with Peanut Sauce for dipping.

Peanut Sauce

MAKES ABOUT ¾ CUP (175 ML)
PREPARATION: 5 MINUTES

1 or 2	1 or 2	garlic cloves, minced
3 tbsp	45 mL	fish sauce
2 tbsp	25 mL	freshly squeezed lime juice
¼–½ tsp	1–2 mL	ground hot red pepper, or 1 small fresh hot red pepper, minced
¼ cup	50 mL	unsweetened peanut butter
¼ cup	50 mL	water

Combine the garlic, fish sauce, lime juice, red pepper, peanut butter and water.

Let the mixture rest at least 10 minutes to allow the flavors to mingle.

Ceviche with Corn or Avocado

MAKES 4 TO 6 SERVINGS
PREPARATION: 10 MINUTES
MARINATING: 6 TO 8 HOURS

This is a traditional South American dish, sometimes spelled "seviche." Although this method of preparation seems unusual at first, it's perfectly safe. It's the high acid content in lime juice that does the trick—it actually "cooks" the protein in fish and shellfish.

1 lb	500 g	white fish and/or shrimp or scallops
½ cup	125 mL	fresh lime juice
⅓ cup	75 mL	fresh lemon juice
½–1	½–1	jalapeno, finely chopped
1 tsp	5 mL	salt, or to taste
6	6	leaf or Boston lettuce leaves, washed, towel dried
1 tbsp	15 mL	finely cut fresh chives
⅓ cup	75 mL	corn kernels or 1 ripe avocado, peeled and sliced
2 tbsp	25 mL	chopped fresh cilantro

If you're using shrimp, peel them and if you're using large scallops, cut them in half. In a china or glass bowl, combine the fish and shellfish with the lime and lemon juices, jalapeno and salt. Marinate for several hours or overnight in the refrigerator, covered.

Cut off the thick stems out of the lettuce leaves. Serve the ceviche on the lettuce and garnish with chives, corn or avocado slices and cilantro.

Wine, Beer & Other Beverages

Whether you're enjoying a casual meal or hosting a dinner party, beverages are a convivial addition.

They may serve as stimulants for the appetite, complements to food, or even as a morning wake-up or bed-time relaxer.

Water is one of the best thirst quenchers and it never conflicts with the flavors in food. Organically based drinks, such as wine made from grapes or beer made from grains and hops, bring out the best in food.

Milk-based and fruit beverages or herb-infused drinks can be refreshing or soothing. However, it's important to ensure that drinks do not overpower foods. For example, orange juice conflicts with the simpler flavor of fish or veal. Soft drinks are best enjoyed between meals, as they are made with chemically based flavors and interfere with the taste of food.

Learning to appreciate wine has been an exciting experience for me. My parents didn't drink wine with meals and my husband, Bob, and I started our married life enjoying Blue Nun (a sweet, inexpensive German wine). Although we moved up the scale from those early experiments, the world of wine appreciation opened up for us when our son, Don, became a wine consultant and sommelier. Don traveled the world to learn about the wine industry and then settled in California to work for the family-run winery, Gallo of Sonoma.

Wine and food marry beautifully when their flavors complement or contrast with each other. Remember that long cooking with wine adds flavor to a dish, but sacrifices the wine's own character. Wine added at the last moment retains its true flavor and makes it easy to match with food— just serve the same wine you used to cook dinner!

Here, with help from Don, is a short list of suggested food and wine pairings:

White Wines

Pinot Blanc, Riesling and Sauvignon Blanc are dry, fragrant, clean and fresh-tasting, with citrus and apple fruit flavors. These wines are best served chilled and go well with appetizers, cheese, baked or sautéed vegetarian dishes and baked or roasted poultry.

Chardonnay is often aged in oak barrels to develop into a richly flavored wine. It has a lower acid level, which acts as a foil for nutty or tropical fruit flavors. Chardonnay is also an excellent match with fish or poultry in cream sauce, or grilled, and with pasta and game dishes.

With spicy food, you can choose to serve an aromatic and perfumed Muscat, or sweet Gewurztraminer.

Champagne and sparkling wines are traditionally served at the beginning or the end of a meal. These wines act as a contrast to heavy, rich, or spicy food and they cleanse the palate.

Red Wines

Spicy red Zinfandels from California and sturdy Chiantis can stand up to Mexican and Mediterranean foods as well as barbecued meats and tomato-based pasta sauce.

Pinot Noir is a wonderful wine with just about any cuisine. Like Pinot Noir, Merlot has low tannin, which results in low bitterness, with a soft but intense fruit flavor. Serve a Merlot with poached fish, braised game, or roasted poultry.

Cabernet Sauvignon, Rhône wines and Syrah (Shiraz in Australia) feature rich texture and color with a deep berry and peppery flavor. They have a bitterness that goes well with beef, game or lamb dishes with strong flavors and herb seasonings.

Beer

The basic rule of thumb about cooking with beer is neatly expressed by the owner of the award-winning Cafe Henri Burger, in Quebec. Says Robert Bourassa: "Beer can replace wine in most dishes in which you want less acidity, more sweetness and nuttiness." Today, "cuisine à la bière" is becoming more popular, especially in North America. Of course, drinking beer is a matter of personal taste.

A friend and beer writer, Jamie MacKinnon, helped me to see the possibilities for cooking with beer. Once I got started, there was no stopping the culinary creativity: marinades, barbecue sauces, a new depth of flavor in soups and stews, even batter for frying fish. If you haven't realized the many uses for this wonderful beverage, try it instead of milk in pancake batter, biscuits, bread and desserts.

In a multi-course meal, serve beer for drinking in the following order: light to dark and light-bodied to full-bodied. Big-flavored and bitter beers marry well with complex and spicy foods, such as curry, while more subtly flavored foods require simpler beers, such as cream ales and pilsners.

The Perfect Pot of Tea

MAKES 4 CUPS (1 L)
PREPARATION: 6 MINUTES

There are 1,500 different types of tea found in three categories: black tea, black blended tea and green tea. They all come from the same variety of bush grown in tropical and subtropical countries. It's the processing treatment of the leaves and leaf buds that gives tea its character. The leaves are dried and allowed to ferment to make black tea, but green tea is not fermented. Herbal teas are made from herbs, flowers or fruits and are caffeine-free. Great black teas include Darjeeling and the aromatic Jasmine from China with real jasmine flowers added. Earl Grey and English Breakfast are famous blends.

During my stay in England, I learned how to brew a pot of tea that made tea-drinking a real pleasure! It must always begin with fresh cold water because it has a higher percentage of oxygen, the element that brings out the flavor in tea. The water should just come to a boil (if water boils hard, the oxygen content is lowered), be poured quickly over the tea, preferably in a china pot, and left to steep for a few minutes. For green tea, the water should be just below the boil. Always use a teapot in proportion to the amount of tea you are making.

When buying tea, look for quality. Loose tea is usually less expensive than tea bags. Store all tea in an airtight container as it loses flavor when exposed to air.

4 1/2 cups	1.125 L	fresh cold water, filtered if possible
2	2	tea bags or 4 tsp (20 mL) loose tea

Bring the water just to the boil. Heat the teapot with 1/2 cup (125 mL) hot water and drain. Add the tea bags and pour in the boiling water. Cover and leave to infuse for 3 to 5 minutes. This increases the flavor and reduces the caffeine. If using loose tea, sieve the tea into each cup. Serve with milk or lemon and sugar.

The Perfect Cup of Coffee

MAKES 4 CUPS (1 L)
PREPARATION: 6 TO 8 MINUTES

To brew the perfect cup of coffee, it is essential to grind your own coffee beans. The top quality arabica bean grows in mountainous, subtropical climates. The robusta bean, used in mass-produced commercial coffees, grows at sea level.

The first step towards that great cup of coffee is to choose only freshly roasted, aromatic beans, buy them in small quantities (a 2- or 3-week supply) and store them in a tightly sealed china or metal container. Avoid storing in the refrigerator or freezer where the beans will absorb moisture and flavors. The beans should be ground, just before brewing, in a mill that shreds them between metal discs, thus enhancing the flavor. You can also use a coffee grinder that chops the beans with whirling blades, but this method causes them to overheat and lose flavor. Beans need to be ground to different degrees of fineness, depending on the method used to make the coffee.

My preferred way to make coffee is the drip method, using finely-ground coffee in a paper, cloth or gold mesh filter, with the water slowly poured over the grounds. I also like the plunger method, which forces the floating grounds to the bottom of the pot. The only disadvantage is that it can't be placed over direct heat. The percolator method was once popular, but it repeatedly filters boiling coffee over the grounds, making a bitter-tasting coffee. Espresso coffee came to our shores from Italy. It's made using extra-fine grounds under steam pressure in a metal espresso maker.

To make drip or plunger coffee: Use 1 1/2 to 2 tbsp (20 to 25 mL) freshly ground coffee to each cup of water.

Drip method: Place the ground coffee in the filter. Bring fresh cold water just to a boil, and slowly pour it over the coffee grounds in the filter.

Plunger method: Place the ground coffee in the pot and pour in the boiling water. Slowly force the floating coffee grounds to the bottom of the pot with the plunger and leave to infuse for 5 minutes. Remove the plunger and enjoy!

Serve the fresh coffee immediately or keep in a thermos as it deteriorates quickly when kept on direct heat.

Hot Chocolate

MAKES 3 CUPS (750 ML)
PREPARATION: 10 MINUTES

Making hot chocolate is quick and easy and much less expensive than commercially prepared mix. Adding chopped chocolate makes it rich and delicious. If possible, use higher quality Dutch cocoa.

2 tbsp	25 mL	cocoa
2 tbsp	25 mL	granulated sugar, or to taste
2 2/3 cups	650 mL	milk
1 sq	1 sq	semi-sweet chocolate or 1 oz (30g), chopped
2 or 4	2 or 4	large marshmallows (optional)

In a saucepan, combine the cocoa and sugar. Whisk in the milk and add the chopped chocolate. Place on medium heat, whisking often, until bubbling around the edge. Pour into mugs and top with a marshmallow, if desired.

You can also make this recipe in a microwave, using a microwave-safe bowl. Follow the method to the point of heating and put the bowl into the microwave on medium-high heat for 2 to 3 minutes. Whisk the mixture a couple of times during the microwaving.

Hot Mulled Cider

MAKES 4 TO 6 SERVINGS
PREPARATION: 15 MINUTES

This recipe is great on a chilly night and it can be made into hot mulled wine by replacing the cider with dry red wine. For larger groups, leave the orange whole, stud it with cloves, and add it to the cider or wine.

6 cups	1.5 L	fresh apple cider
1	1	3-inch (7.5-cm) cinnamon stick
3–5	3–5	whole cloves
1	1	orange, thinly sliced
1–2 tbsp	15–25 mL	sugar (optional)

In a large saucepan, combine the cider, cinnamon, cloves, orange slices and sugar, if using. Cover and gently simmer for 20 minutes. Strain before serving.

Minted Ice Tea

MAKES 6 TO 8 SERVINGS
PREPARATION: 10 MINUTES

Freshly made iced tea is so refreshing and special that it can't be compared to powdered ice tea.

4	4	tea bags or 8 tsp (40 mL) loose tea
2	2	fresh mint sprigs
2 tbsp	25 mL	granulated sugar, or to taste
1 qt	1 L	water, just boiling
1 tbsp	15 mL	fresh lemon juice (optional)
		8 mint leaves and 8 lemon wedges, for garnish

Place the tea, mint and sugar in a 1-qt (1-L) teapot and fill with boiling water. Leave for 8 minutes. Stir and pour the tea (through a sieve if using loose tea) into a glass pitcher with a metal spoon set inside to prevent the pitcher from breaking when the hot tea is added. Avoid refrigerating the tea as the cold will turn the mixture cloudy.

Serve in glasses with ice cubes. Garnish with mint leaves and lemon wedges.

Minted Fresh Lemonade

MAKES 6 SERVINGS
PREPARATION: 25 MINUTES

Homemade lemonade is easy to make and doesn't require making a syrup. For more intense flavor, add the squeezed lemon rinds to the lemonade.

1 cup	250 mL	juice from 3 or 4 lemons, lemons reserved
1/2 cup	125 mL	granulated sugar, or to taste
4 cups	1 L	water
2–3	2–3	fresh mint sprigs, optional
		6 lemon slices and 6 fresh mint leaves, for garnish

In a glass or china pitcher, combine the lemon juice, squeezed lemons, sugar, water and mint. Allow the sugar to dissolve, stirring often, for 20 minutes.

To serve, remove the mint sprigs and lemon shells. Fill glasses with ice cubes, stir the mixture and pour into the glasses. To make the garnish, remove the pits from the lemon slices. Cut a slit in each slice from the edge to the center. Slide each slice onto the edge of a glass and add a mint leaf.

Chocolate Coffee Cooler

MAKES 6 SERVINGS
PREPARATION: 15 MINUTES

This drink is for all coffee and chocolate lovers.

2 oz	60 g	unsweetened chocolate
1 cup	250 mL	strong hot coffee
3 tbsp	45 mL	granulated sugar
3 cups	750 mL	milk
1 qt	1 L	coffee or chocolate ice cream

In a saucepan, heat the chocolate and coffee over low heat until the chocolate is melted. Add the sugar and half the milk and gently combine flavors for 10 minutes. Remove from the heat, add remaining milk and chill.

Whisk the chocolate mixture and ice cream in the chilled bowl of an electric mixer, in a food processor, or by hand, until frothy and blended. Serve immediately, in tall glasses.

Banana & Cocoa Smoothie

MAKES 2 CUPS (500 ML)
PREPARATION: 5 MINUTES

Smoothies (also called shakes) are a delicious way to use any ripe fruit.

2	2	medium bananas, each cut into 3 pieces
2 tbsp	25 mL	cocoa powder
1 tbsp	15 mL	granulated sugar or honey, or to taste
1 cup	250 mL	milk, plain yogurt or orange juice

Put the bananas into a food processor or a blender. Add the cocoa and sugar or honey to the bananas. Pour in the milk, yogurt or orange juice and process until smooth and frothy. Pour into glasses and serve as soon as possible as the smoothie begins to separate after 30 minutes.

Variations: Replace the bananas with 1 cup (250 mL) berries or mango.

Sangria Blanca

MAKES AT LEAST 12 SERVINGS
PREPARATION: 20 MINUTES PLUS 3 HOURS FOR CHILLING

This is a special summer drink to serve for casual entertaining.

3 cups	750 mL	chilled dry white wine
1/2 cup	125 mL	Cointreau or brandy
2–3 tbsp	25–45 mL	granulated sugar, or to taste
1 each	1 each	lime and lemon, cut into thin slices, pits removed
1	1	unpeeled green apple, cored, sliced thinly
1 cup	250 mL	green grapes, halved and pitted
1 1/2 cups	375 mL	club soda

In a large glass pitcher, combine wine, Cointreau or brandy, sugar and fruit. Refrigerate for at least 3 hours to mix the flavors.

To serve, add club soda to the pitcher and some ice cubes. Serve in large glasses with 2 or 3 pieces of fruit in each glass.

Eggnog

MAKES 10 TO 12 SERVINGS
PREPARATION: 25 MINUTES

This is a favorite at Christmas or New Year's Eve.

5	5	eggs, separated
1/4 cup	50 mL	granulated sugar
1/2 cup	125 mL	whisky or rum
1/4 cup	50 mL	brandy
3 cups	750 mL	milk
1 cup	250 mL	heavy or light cream
		freshly grated nutmeg

In the top of a double-boiler, combine the egg yolks with half the sugar and place over simmering water. Whisk until the mixture is pale yellow and thick. Remove from the heat and cool. Beat in the whisky or rum, brandy and milk. Chill for several hours or overnight.

To serve, beat the egg whites just until soft peaks form and beat in the remaining sugar. Fold the whites into the yolk mixture and stir in the cream. Sprinkle the nutmeg over top of the eggnog.

Soups

Soups have played an important role in my cooking classes from the start.

Nothing teaches so simply how to get comfortable in a kitchen. Making soup also emphasizes the importance of tasting your creation before you serve it. Does it need an extra pinch of seasoning? Longer cooking to deepen the flavor? From the basics, lentil soup and purées, we move on to elegant consommés to begin a fine dinner.

Experiment when you're making soup. Not much can go wrong as long as you taste often and don't allow the soup to boil over. Soups are a great way to explore different ingredients and textures — the choices are limited only by your imagination.

Here are some tips about soup-making before you start:

- Use fresh, seasonal ingredients whenever possible.
- Vegetables make the best thickeners for soup.
- Flour, rolled oats or bulgur can also be used as thickeners.
- Never boil stock, since proteins in the bones, fat, and meat will break up and disperse through the stock, making it taste fatty.
- Never add salt to stock during cooking; wait until the end to taste and season.
- Onion skins contain a natural dye that makes stock a rich deep brown.

Brown Stock

MAKES ABOUT 2 QTS (2 L)
COOKING: 5 TO 6 HOURS

*The key to obtaining a rich brown beef stock is roasting bones and vege-
tables to a deep color, then slowly simmering the stock for 5 or 6 hours to
draw out the marvelous flavors. Ask your butcher to cut up the bones.*

4 lbs	2 kg	beef or part veal knuckle or shank bones with meat
2	2	onions, skins left on, quartered
2	2	leeks, cut into 3 pieces
2	2	celery stalks, coarsely chopped
1 or 2	1 or 2	bay leaves
3 or 4	3 or 4	sprigs parsley
1 tsp	5 mL	fresh thyme, or 1/2 tsp (2 mL) dried
5	5	whole peppercorns
3	3	ripe tomatoes, or 1 cup (250 mL) canned tomatoes

Spread the bones in a roasting pan and brown in a 425°F (220°C) oven for
30 minutes, turning often. Add the vegetables and continue roasting until
they are nicely browned, about 30 minutes more.

Transfer the mixture to a stockpot. Carefully drain away any fat from the
roasting pan, leaving the flavorful browned bits, and place the pan over
medium heat. Deglaze with cold water (see Glossary), then add this liquid
to the stockpot with the bay leaf, parsley, thyme, peppercorns, tomatoes
and cold water to cover. Bring slowly to a gentle boil, reduce the heat to
medium-low, or a very gentle simmer, for 5 to 6 hours. Remove the scum
as it rises to the top. If the liquid reduces below the top of the bones,
add more water.

Strain the stock. Chill and remove any solidified fat that forms on the surface.
If desired, pour into containers and freeze.

Chicken Stock

MAKES 2 QTS (2 L)
COOKING: 2 TO 3 HOURS

Butchers offer useful packages of chicken backs, wing tips and necks for making stock. The bones can be first roasted as in the Brown Stock recipe to intensify the flavor and color.

3 lbs	1.5 kg	chicken back bones and wings, with skin
1	1	medium onion, peeled, sliced
1	1	leek, coarsely chopped
2	2	medium carrots, coarsely chopped
2	2	celery stalks, coarsely chopped
1 tsp	5 mL	fresh thyme leaves
3 or 4	3 or 4	sprigs parsley
3 qts	3 L	cold water or enough to cover bones

Combine the chicken, vegetables, herbs and water in a large saucepan. Bring to a slow boil on low heat. Skim the foam as it forms and continue to simmer for 2 to 3 hours.

Strain the stock and chill. Remove the solidified fat that rises to the top. The stock can be chilled for 3 days or frozen for several months.

Vegetable Stock

MAKES 2 QTS (2 L)
COOKING: 2½ TO 3 HOURS

This is a perfect way to use vegetables to replace chicken or beef stock.

3 or 4	3 or 4	leeks, chopped
4	4	medium carrots, chopped
4	4	celery stalks, chopped
2 or 3	2 or 3	tomatoes, chopped
3 or 4	3 or 4	sprigs parsley, chopped
3	3	garlic cloves, peeled, smashed
1 or 2	1 or 2	bay leaves
2 tsp	10 mL	fresh thyme leaves or 1 tsp (5 mL) dried
1 tbsp	15 mL	cider or wine vinegar

Put all the ingredients in a large pot and add cold water to cover. Bring to a boil, reduce heat and simmer, uncovered, for 2 hours. Strain, press out as much moisture as possible from the vegetables and discard them. Taste to check the depth of flavor and, if it is not strong enough, leave the strained stock to simmer for 30 minutes or longer. The stock can be stored, covered, in the refrigerator for up to a week or frozen for several months.

Tomato Soup with Herbs

MAKES 4 TO 6 SERVINGS
PREPARATION: 10 MINUTES
COOKING: 20 TO 25 MINUTES

This soup is delicious when tomatoes are at their peak of flavor in the summer. Off-season, canned diced tomatoes are good and less watery than whole canned tomatoes.

6	6	ripe tomatoes, or 2 cups (500 mL) canned diced tomatoes
2 tbsp	25 mL	olive oil and/or butter
1	1	medium onion, sliced
1	1	medium carrot, sliced
1 tbsp	15 mL	all-purpose flour
3 cups	750 L	Chicken Stock or Vegetable Stock (page 36)
1	1	large or 2 small bay leaves
1/2 tsp	2 mL	salt, or to taste
		chopped tarragon or chives for garnish

If you are using fresh tomatoes, plunge them into boiling water for 20 seconds. Drain, cool slightly and slip off skin. Cut out the core with the tip of a sharp knife and coarsely chop the tomatoes. Dice and reserve 2 tbsp (25 mL) tomatoes for garnish.

In a saucepan, heat the oil and/or butter and cook the onion and carrot, covered, on low heat for 5 minutes to sweat out the flavors. Stir in the flour and cook for 1 minute, then whisk in the stock and add the diced tomatoes and bay leaf. Cover and gently cook on medium heat for 20 minutes. Remove the bay leaf and purée the soup in a blender or processor. Season to taste.

To serve, reheat, and garnish with reserved tomatoes and a sprinkling of herbs.

Spicy Lentil Soup with Yogurt

MAKES 4 TO 6 SERVINGS
PREPARATION: 10 MINUTES
COOKING: 50 TO 60 MINUTES

Paradoxically, this recipe is equally great on a chilly day or a hot summer day. Lentils are nutritious legumes full of fiber and vitamins. Don't confuse split peas with lentils, since split peas take much longer to cook.

1 tbsp	15 mL	vegetable oil
1 tbsp	15 mL	butter
1	1	medium onion, finely chopped
1	1	medium carrot, shredded
2	2	garlic cloves, finely chopped
3 tbsp	45 mL	curry powder
1 cup	250 mL	yellow or green lentils
4 cups	1 L	Beef, Chicken or Vegetable Stock (page 35 or 36)
2 tsp	10 mL	lemon juice
1/2 tsp	2 mL	salt, or to taste
1/4 tsp	1 mL	pepper, or to taste
1/2 cup	125 mL	plain yogurt or yogurt cheese (page 16) for garnish curry powder and shredded carrot (optional)

In a heavy saucepan, heat the oil and butter together to prevent the butter from burning. Add the onion, carrot, garlic and curry powder, cover and gently cook for 5 minutes to sweat out the flavors. Pour in the lentils and stock and bring to a simmer, partially covered, for 50 to 60 minutes. Add the lemon juice and season to taste.

To serve, top with a dollop of yogurt, sprinkling of curry powder and shredded carrot, if desired.

Three Sisters Bean Soup

MAKES 4 TO 6 SERVINGS
PREPARATION: 8 TO 10 MINUTES
COOKING: 30 MINUTES

This variation on a traditional Iroquois soup was created by Cree Chef Arnold Olson, whom I had the honor to meet when I was food editor at the Ottawa Sun newspaper. The "three sisters" are squash, corn and beans, traditionally grown together so the squash and beans can wrap around the tall corn stalk. "We always dry the corn kernels and cook them in water and hard wood ash to remove the husks, thus making hominy," says Olson, a gold medal winner at the 1996 Culinary Olympics in Frankfurt, Germany, representing Canada's First Nations people.

4 oz	120 g	salt pork, diced
1	1	medium onion, diced
2	2	celery stalks, diced
1	1	carrot, diced
1	1	small butternut squash, peeled, halved, seeded and cubed
4 cups	1 L	Vegetable Stock, cold (page 36)
1	1	19-oz (540-mL) can kidney beans, drained
1	1	19-oz (540-mL) can white beans, drained
2	2	19-oz (540-mL) cans hominy, undrained

In a large saucepan on medium heat, sauté the salt pork for 5 minutes to release the fat. Add the onion, celery and carrot and sauté for 5 minutes, stirring often. Add the squash to the mixture with the stock. Bring the soup to a boil and cook until the vegetables are tender, for about 20 minutes.

Add the beans and hominy 15 minutes before serving so they don't become mushy.

Fresh Pea Soup with Mint or Dill

MAKES 4 TO 6 SERVINGS
PREPARATION: 5 MINUTES
COOKING: 12 MINUTES

This is a gorgeously colored, refreshing soup that can be served hot or cold. It's quickly made using frozen peas and is especially good with fresh mint or dill and croutons. It's your choice as to which soup texture you prefer: a blender finely purées, the food processor purées but leaves bits of husk, a food mill purées and sieves out the husk. This soup freezes well.

4 cups	1 L	frozen or fresh peas
1	1	medium onion, peeled and chopped
2¼ cups	550 mL	Chicken Stock, (page 36) or more if needed for thinning
½ cup	125 mL	milk or cream, or more if needed
		pinch granulated sugar
¼ cup	50 mL	finely chopped fresh dill or fresh mint
1 tsp	5 mL	salt, or to taste
¼ tsp	1 mL	black pepper, or to taste
½ cup	125 mL	toasted or fried Croutons (optional)

In a saucepan, bring the peas, onion and stock to a boil. Simmer for 6 to 8 minutes and purée. Stir in the milk or cream and sugar. If the consistency is too thick, thin with either stock or more milk. To serve, reheat with the dill or mint, reserving a little for garnish. Season to taste with salt and pepper. Garnish with croutons and herbs.

Croutons

PREPARATION: 2 MINUTES
COOKING: 8 TO 10 MINUTES

½ cup	125 mL	small bread cubes without crusts
1 tbsp	15 mL	butter

In a skillet, heat the butter and sauté the bread cubes, stirring constantly, until they are golden and crisp. Or, place the bread cubes on a baking sheet, drizzle with melted butter and bake in a 375°F (190°C) oven for 8 to 10 minutes, until the croutons are golden and crisp.

Gazpacho

MAKES 4 TO 6 SERVINGS
PREPARATION: 30 MINUTES
CHILLING: 1 TO 2 HOURS

Spain is the home of this popular cool-tasting soup, a concoction of wonderful fresh vegetables. Gazpacho is derived from the Arabic for "soaked bread," the secret ingredient in this delicious dish. Served with a variety of garnishes, it makes a wonderful one-dish meal for a hot steamy day, especially with a glass of crisp, dry white wine.

1	1	slice bread, crust removed
1 cup	250 mL	cold water
5	5	ripe, medium tomatoes
1	1	medium seedless cucumber, reserve 1/2 for garnish
1	1	green bell pepper, seeded, reserve 1/2 for garnish
1	1	red bell pepper, seeded, reserve 1/2 for garnish
1	1	small chili pepper
1/2	1/2	medium onion, peeled, chopped
2–3	2–3	garlic cloves, peeled, chopped
2 tbsp	25 mL	wine vinegar
4 tbsp	50 mL	olive oil
2 tsp	10 mL	salt, or to taste
1/2 tsp	2 mL	freshly grated black pepper, or to taste
1 cup	250 mL	Croutons (page 40)

In a large bowl, soak the bread in the water. Whisk to break up the bread. Cut the tomatoes in half and squeeze each half to release the seeds over a sieve. Add the juice to the bread and discard the seeds. Coarsely chop the cucumber, then purée with the squeezed tomatoes in a food processor or blender. Pour the tomato mixture into the bread mixture.

Purée the green and red peppers, chili pepper, onion and garlic in the food processor or blender and add to the tomato mixture. Stir in the vinegar and olive oil. Add more water if the soup is too thick. Add salt and black pepper. Chill the gazpacho for at least an hour.

To prepare the garnishes, cut the reserved cucumber and green and red peppers into small cubes and place them in separate serving dishes. Place the croutons in a serving dish and let the diners choose the garnishes to sprinkle on their soup.

Leek & Potato Soup

MAKES 4 TO 6 SERVINGS
PREPARATION: 12 TO 15 MINUTES
COOKING: 30 MINUTES

The combination of leek and potato is the basis of many delicious soups. It's a good idea to make this in the autumn when vegetables are the cheapest, then freeze and use it through the winter. Potatoes are a natural thickening agent for soups, with a higher starch content in the autumn and winter, so adjust the amount of liquid accordingly.

3	3	medium leeks
1 1/2 tbsp	20 mL	butter
2 or 3	2 or 3	potatoes, about 1 lb (500 g), peeled and diced
4 cups	1 L	water or Chicken Stock (page 36)
1 cup	250 mL	milk or half-and-half cream
1 tsp	5 mL	salt, or to taste
1 tbsp	15 mL	finely chopped parsley

Use only the white part of the leek and cut it lengthwise through the center without cutting through the root end. Rinse under running water to remove all grit. Slice thinly, crosswise.

In a large saucepan, melt the butter on medium-low heat and stir in the leeks. Cover and sweat for 5 minutes. Add the potatoes and sweat for another 5 minutes. Add the stock, cover and simmer for 20 minutes, until very tender.

Purée the soup in a food processor or blender. The mixture can be frozen at this point. To serve, reheat the purée with milk or cream. If the soup is too thick, thin it with more liquid. Season and garnish with parsley.

Cream of Spinach Soup: Simply add 10 oz (300 g) of spinach to the soup for the last 2 minutes of cooking time, then purée and serve as directed.

From left: Gorgonzola Bruschetta (page 19)
and Tomato Bruschetta (page 18)

Clockwise from bottom:
sherry, red wine, champagne, and white wine
(pages 26–27)

From top : Tomato Soup with Herbs (page 37), Spicy Lentil Soup with Yogurt (page 38), and Fresh Pea Soup with Mint and Croutons (page 40)

Frisée Salad with Warm Chèvre (page 54)

Vichyssoise

MAKES ABOUT 6 CUPS (1.5 L)
CHILLING: 2 HOURS OR LONGER

An elegant cold soup created by the famed Louis Diat, Chef at the Ritz-Carleton in New York City from 1910 to 1950. He named the soup for his beloved Vichy region in France.

6 cups	1.5 L	Leek & Potato Soup (page 42), chilled overnight
3/4 cup	175 mL	whipping cream, or more if needed
		salt to taste
2 tbsp	25 mL	finely sliced chives

Combine Leek and Potato Soup with cream. Season to taste. Chill and serve, garnished with chives.

Chilled Minted Cucumber Soup

MAKES 4 TO 6 SERVINGS
PREPARATION: 10 MINUTES
COOKING: 20 MINUTES

Here's another cool summer soup using fresh local cucumbers, if possible. Cooking the cucumber briefly brings out its flavor.

1	1	seedless or field cucumber, about 1 lb (500 g)
2 tbsp	25 mL	butter
1	1	onion or washed leek, sliced
4 cups	1 L	Chicken Stock (page 36) or water
1/4 cup	50 mL	packed fresh mint leaves, reserve 6 leaves for garnish
		salt and pepper to taste

The skin of seedless cucumbers is tender so they don't need to be peeled. Field cucumbers have a tough skin, so peel, but leave 1 or 2 strips of peel for color. Cut the field cucumber in half lengthwise and use a spoon to scoop out the seeds. Coarsely chop the cucumber.

Heat the butter in a medium saucepan over medium heat and sweat the onion or leek, covered, until tender, about 5 minutes. Add the cucumber, stock or water and mint. Bring to a boil, cover and cook for 10 to 12 minutes.

Purée the soup in batches in a blender or food processor. Season to taste with salt and pepper. Chill for at least 2 hours. To serve, garnish with mint.

Minestrone with Parsley Pesto

MAKES 6 TO 8 SERVINGS
PREPARATION: 20 MINUTES
COOKING: 2 HOURS

This is a meal! This classic Italian soup is thick with vegetables, slowly cooked to marry their robust flavors. The vegetables suggested here can be replaced with others in season. Leftover soup can be frozen.

8 oz	250 g	pancetta, bacon or salt pork, cut into small cubes
2–3	2–3	garlic cloves, minced
2	2	medium onions, chopped
2	2	medium carrots, chopped
1/2	1/2	fennel bulb, tough stem removed, chopped
2 cups	500 mL	Savoy cabbage or Swiss chard, chopped
1	1	28-oz (796-mL) can diced tomatoes or 5 fresh tomatoes, peeled and chopped
2 tbsp	25 mL	chopped fresh thyme or 2 tsp (10 mL) dried
2 tbsp	25 mL	chopped fresh rosemary or 2 tsp (10 mL) dried
1/8 tsp	.5 mL	crushed hot red pepper flakes, or to taste
6 cups	1.5 L	hot water or Vegetable Stock (page 36)
5 oz	150 g	fresh spinach, coarsely chopped
1 cup	250 mL	small macaroni or shells or broken spaghetti
1	1	19-oz (540-mL) can white kidney beans, drained and rinsed
1 tsp	5 mL	salt, or to taste
1/2 cup	125 mL	freshly grated Parmesan cheese
		1 recipe Parsley Pesto (page 45)

In a large saucepan, sauté the pancetta, bacon or pork for 5 or 6 minutes, stirring over medium heat until it begins to brown lightly. Reduce the heat to medium-low, stir in the garlic and onion and sweat, covered, for 5 or 6 minutes. Stir in the carrots, fennel, cabbage or chard, tomatoes, herbs and red pepper. Add the water or stock and boil. Reduce heat to a gentle simmer for 1 1/2 to 2 hours. Add the spinach, pasta and beans and continue to cook for 10 minutes until the pasta is tender. Add more water or stock if the soup is too thick. Season to taste with salt.

To serve, sprinkle with cheese and add a dollop of Parsley Pesto to each bowl.

Parsley Pesto

MAKES 1 CUP (250 ML)

2 tbsp	25 mL	pine nuts, walnuts or almonds
1 cup	250 mL	packed parsley leaves, stems removed
2–3	2–3	garlic cloves, peeled and chopped
6 tbsp	75 mL	extra-virgin olive oil
1/2 tsp	2 mL	salt, or to taste

Chop the nuts, parsley and garlic in a blender or food processor. Drizzle in the oil until a smooth paste is formed. Season to taste.

Chicken, Rice & Tofu Soup

MAKES 4 TO 6 SERVINGS
PREPARATION: 10 MINUTES
COOKING: 1 HOUR

I haven't always enjoyed tofu but I do like it in soups where it absorbs the rich flavors and melts in your mouth. This soup is perfect for anyone feeling under the weather because of the healing components — real or perceived — of ginger, chicken and tofu.

2	2	chicken legs, or 1 1/4 cups (300 mL) cooked chicken
2 tbsp	25 mL	finely grated fresh ginger
6 cups	1.5 L	cold water or 4 cups (1 L) Chicken Stock (page 36)
1/4 cup	50 mL	long- or short-grain rice
1 tbsp	15 mL	fish sauce (see Glossary)
8 oz	250 g	firm tofu cut into 1/2-inch (1-cm) cubes (optional)
1/2 tsp	2 mL	salt, if needed
2 tbsp	25 mL	chopped fresh cilantro or sliced green onion

Simmer the chicken legs and ginger in the water or stock for 35 to 40 minutes. Remove the chicken and leave it to cool for 5 minutes. When cool, pull the meat from the bones, shred it and return it to the pot. If you're using previously cooked chicken, shred it and add it now.

Add the rice to the soup and continue to simmer for 20 minutes. Stir in the fish sauce and tofu, if using, and simmer for a further 2 minutes. Taste for salt and serve, sprinkled with cilantro or onion.

Ginger is easier to grate fine if you freeze it first.

Salads

Salad ingredients are at their peak in the warmer months when the sun has ripened them.

It is possible to buy greens, tomatoes and cucumbers that have been grown indoors in a nutrient solution when garden produce is unavailable. These hydroponic vegetables are excellent and welcome during the barren winter months.

Most salads have greens as their base, either single varieties or combinations. You can now buy bagged mixed greens in supermarkets and the mesclun mix has become so popular that gardeners can even buy packets of "mesclun" seeds — containing a variety of different lettuces. When buying greens, look for those with whole, fully formed leaves that are crisp and shiny. To store them, sprinkle with a little water and enclose them in plastic bags that have small holes pricked in them for ventilation.

To prepare greens for salad, submerge them in lukewarm water then gently shake off the water and dirt. Discard tough stems, rinse the leaves in cold water and drain in a colander. Tear into bite-sized pieces, but do not cut the greens or they will bruise and turn brown. Dry in a salad spinner or on a tea towel. Place in a salad bowl, cover with a towel and chill until ready to serve.

One problem with most salads is that they are overdressed. Salad greens are delicate in flavor, so they need a dressing to enhance, not overpower. I find commercial dressings are so heavily flavored that they smother tender lettuce. Homemade vinaigrettes are the ideal dressing; they are easily made in the salad bowl and they won't compete with the lettuce's flavor.

Always toss salads just before serving. One trick I use at the table, when the salad will not be eaten immediately, is to place the greens in the bowl and the dressing in a small container on or near the bowl. When ready to serve, dribble the dressing over the salad and toss it 13 times! This is a lesson I learned in France, where my mentor insisted that it required that many tosses to properly coat each leaf — it works!

Segmenting oranges (see page 60)

Here is a basic description of the salad and dressing ingredients I prefer to use:

Greens

- Bibb, Boston, red or green leaf, and lamb's lettuce (also called corn salad or mâche) are light-textured lettuces that should be eaten immediately after they're dressed or they will wilt.

- Arugula, rocket, curly endive (also called chicory frisée), escarole, watercress, chicory and young dandelion have a light bitter taste that goes well with stronger-tasting vinaigrettes.

- Romaine, iceberg and spinach can take heavier-bodied dressings and will stay crisp longer after being tossed.

- Belgian endive has tight layers of firm, white leaves with a slightly bitter taste. Endive may also be braised or grilled.

- Collards, kale, radicchio, Napa cabbage, bok choy, broccoli raab (also called rapini), chard and red or green Savoy cabbage have pungent flavors and are best cooked tender-crisp before use.

Vinegars

- Red and white wine vinegars have a subtle flavor that is ideal for salad dressings.

- Raspberry-infused vinegar is popular in marinades and dressings, although it is perishable and should be purchased in small quantities. Drain out any sediment that forms at the bottom of the bottle.

- Herb-infused vinegar is great for salads, but the intense flavor can become tiresome — sprinkle fresh herbs on salads instead.

- Balsamic and sherry vinegars are aged in barrels for up to 12 years for a mellow, sweet and sour taste, although cheap balsamic vinegar is harshly flavored.

- Fresh citrus juices can replace vinegar to bring a fresh light taste to salads.

Oils

- Green or golden-colored extra-virgin olive oil with its full, fruity taste is made from the first cold-pressing of olives and is the finest edible oil on earth, the best for dressings.

- Olive oil comes from subsequent pressings that use heat and it is strained to remove sediment, which removes some flavor. It is better for cooking than for salads.

- Canola oil is made from rape seed and, if you can get the first extraction, it's very flavorful in dressings; otherwise use for cooking.

- Hazelnut and walnut oils have a piquant, nutty (of course) flavor and are best bought in small quantities and used cold.

- Peanut oil has a mild, sweet flavor and is useful for frying in addition to salad dressings.

- Sesame oil is light-textured with a strong flavor; even one drop in a salad is noticeable.

- Herb-flavored oils are perishable and strong-tasting, so buy in small quantities.

Mustards

An essential ingredient in salad vinaigrettes is mustard. There are three types I prefer to use:

- Dijon mustard, smooth or coarse, is my favorite because it has a creamy texture with spices and wine vinegar flavorings.

- Dried mustard made from finely ground mustard seeds is excellent as an accent in dressings, but use less of it than of Dijon, because its taste is sharper.

- German or "honey" mustard brings a sweet and sour taste that goes particularly well with cabbage salads.

Basic Vinaigrette

MAKES ABOUT 1/2 CUP (125 ML)

2 tbsp	25 mL	wine vinegar or lemon or grapefruit juice
1/4 tsp	1 mL	salt
1/2 tsp	2 mL	Dijon mustard or 1/4 tsp (1 mL) dry mustard (optional)
5 tbsp	65 mL	olive oil
1/4 tsp	1 mL	freshly ground black pepper

In a small bowl, whisk together the vinegar and salt to dissolve the salt. Add the mustard, if using, and whisk in the oil. Add the pepper at the end.

Variations: Add 1 or 2 garlic cloves, minced, or 2 tsp (10 mL) chopped fresh parsley, chives, tarragon or basil.

Balsamic Vinaigrette

MAKES ABOUT 1/3 CUP (75 ML)

1/4 cup	50 mL	balsamic vinegar
2 tbsp	25 mL	extra-virgin olive oil
		salt and freshly ground black pepper to taste

Combine the vinegar and oil in the bottom of a salad bowl. Add the lettuce, sprinkle on salt and pepper generously, then toss.

Yogurt Dressing

MAKES ABOUT 1/2 CUP (125 ML)

This dressing is delicious with chicory, spinach or romaine.

4 tbsp	50 mL	plain yogurt
2 tbsp	25 mL	olive oil
1/2 tsp	2 mL	salt
1 tbsp	15 mL	honey
1 tbsp	15 mL	white wine or cider vinegar

Whisk together the yogurt, oil, salt, honey and vinegar.

Mayonnaise

MAKES 1 CUP (250 ML)
PREPARATION: 10 MINUTES

Homemade mayonnaise may seem time-consuming but it's worth it. You can make it in a blender, which takes half the time! Keep the mayonnaise chilled and use it within a week so there is no danger of salmonella contamination.

1	1	egg yolk
1 tsp	5 mL	Dijon or 1/2 tsp (2 mL) dry mustard
1 tbsp	15 mL	lemon juice, or more if needed
3/4 cup	175 mL	cold-pressed canola, nut or olive oil
		salt and freshly ground pepper, to taste
		pinch of cayenne (optional)
		chopped fresh herbs (optional)

By hand: In a small mixing bowl, using a whisk, combine the egg, mustard and lemon juice. While continually whisking, add oil a drop at a time until the mixture begins to thicken. Gradually increase the rate to a spoonful at a time, whisking constantly. Finally, add the oil in a thin continuous stream until it is completely incorporated. Taste for salt and pepper. Add the cayenne and extra lemon juice, if desired. Stir in herbs, if using.

By food processor or blender: Add the egg, mustard and lemon juice to the machine to blend briefly. With the machine running, slowly add the oil, first in drops then slowly in a thin stream, until the mixture thickens. Add salt and pepper to taste, cayenne pepper and more lemon juice, if desired. Stir in herbs, if using.

Mayonnaise Provençal: Stir 2 minced garlic colves and 1 tbsp (15 mL) chopped fresh herbs into the prepared mayonnaise.

Creamy Potato Salad with Peas & Parsley

MAKES 4 TO 6 SERVINGS
PREPARATION: 30 MINUTES
COOKING: 25 MINUTES

Potato salad is a winner with young and old. Adding yogurt to the mayonnaise makes it less rich without sacrificing taste. Be careful not to overcook the potatoes as they will break and become mushy when tossed with the dressing.

2 lbs	1 kg	all-purpose, waxy potatoes, whole or halved
1 tbsp	15 mL	lemon juice
1/4 cup	50 mL	plain yogurt
1/2 cup	125 mL	mayonnaise
1	1	medium onion, finely chopped or 4 green onions, finely sliced
1/4 cup	50 mL	finely chopped fresh parsley
1/2 tsp	2 mL	salt, or to taste
1/4 tsp	1 mL	freshly ground pepper
1 cup	250 mL	frozen peas, defrosted, or blanched fresh peas

In a saucepan, cover the potatoes with cold salted water, cover and simmer until just tender, 20 to 25 minutes. Drain and cool for at least 30 minutes so the potatoes do not break apart. Peel, if desired, and dice or slice.

In a large bowl, mix the lemon juice, yogurt, mayonnaise, onions, parsley, salt and pepper and toss with the potatoes and peas.

This salad (minus the peas, as they lose their color in the lemon juice) can be made a day ahead, but keep it covered and chilled. To enhance the flavors, remove the salad from the refrigerator 20 to 30 minutes before serving; add the peas at that time.

Warm New Potato Salad with Tarragon

MAKES 4 TO 6 SERVINGS
PREPARATION: 5 MINUTES
COOKING: APPROXIMATELY 20 MINUTES

There is no need to peel new potatoes. The peel is tender and holds in the flavor and nutrients.

2 lbs	1 kg	new potatoes, well scrubbed
4 tbsp	50 mL	white wine vinegar
4 tbsp	50 mL	olive oil
2 or 3	2 or 3	garlic cloves, minced
3 tbsp	45 mL	sliced chives, or 4 green onions, finely sliced
2 tbsp	25 mL	chopped fresh tarragon
2 tsp	10 mL	granulated sugar
1/2 tsp	2 mL	salt, or more if needed

Place the potatoes in a saucepan of cold water, cover and cook for 20 minutes or until tender. Drain. While still warm, slice the unpeeled potatoes into 1/4-inch (.5 cm) slices or, if small, cut in half. Gently toss with the vinegar, oil, garlic, chives or onions, tarragon, sugar and salt. Serve warm.

Grated Carrot & Cumin Salad

MAKES 4 TO 6 SERVINGS
PREPARATION: 15 MINUTES

This refreshing salad goes well with spicy foods.

5 or 6	5 or 6	medium carrots, well scrubbed, unpeeled
1 1/2 tbsp	20 mL	fresh lemon juice
1 tsp	5 mL	grated lemon rind
2 tsp	10 mL	toasted cumin seeds
1/2 tsp	2 mL	salt, or to taste
2 tbsp	25 mL	finely chopped parsley or cilantro

Grate the carrots and place them in a bowl. Toss with the lemon juice, rind and cumin seeds. Add the salt and parsley or cilantro.

> To toast cumin seeds, place them in a small, dry skillet on medium heat. When the seeds begin to crackle, after about 2 minutes, remove and cool slightly.

Frisée Salad with Warm Chèvre

MAKES 4 TO 6 SERVINGS
PREPARATION: 15 MINUTES

Chicory frisée, or curly endive, has a little "nip" and, as with most greens, it is best when young and tender. You may use any lettuce you choose instead of frisée. All lettuces go well with chèvre.

1	1	small bunch frisée (curly endive)
1 1/2 tbsp	20 mL	wine vinegar
3 tbsp	45 mL	olive oil
1/2 tsp	2 mL	salt
		olive oil for brushing
5 oz	150 g	soft chèvre roll, cut into 1/2-inch (1-cm) rounds
		freshly ground black pepper
4 tbsp	50 mL	toasted pine nuts

Preheat broiler. Wash the frisée, especially at the stem end, to remove grit. Dry in a salad spinner or between towels. Tear it into bite-sized pieces and chill in a towel until serving time.

In a small bowl, whisk together the vinegar, oil and salt.

Lightly brush a rimmed baking pan with olive oil and arrange the chèvre rounds on it. Brush the cheese with oil and add a few grindings of pepper. Broil rounds about 3 inches (7.5 cm) from the heat until slightly softened, about 2 minutes.

To serve, toss the frisée with dressing and divide it among 4 or 6 salad plates. Top each serving with warm chèvre slices. Grind pepper over the cheese and sprinkle with nuts.

> To toast pine nuts, heat a small, dry skillet on medium heat and add the nuts, shaking the pan until they turn golden, about 2 minutes. Set aside.

Poached Pear with Roquefort Salad

MAKES 4 TO 6 SERVINGS
PREPARATION: 10 MINUTES
COOKING: 10 TO 12 MINUTES

Pear and Roquefort are a great combination — the sweetness of the pear contrasts wonderfully with the piquant cheese.

6–12	6–12	red or green lettuce leaves, washed, drained
3	3	firm, ripe medium-sized pears, Bartlett or Anjou
1/2 cup	125 mL	red wine or cranberry juice
3	3	green onions, finely sliced (include tender green parts)
3 oz	90 g	Roquefort cheese, crumbled
		freshly ground black pepper to taste
3 tbsp	45 mL	walnut or extra-virgin olive oil
2 tbsp	25 mL	white wine vinegar
1/4 tsp	1 mL	salt, or to taste
1/3 cup	75 mL	toasted walnut pieces

Cut away the thick lettuce stems. Place the leaves between paper towels, and chill.

Halve the pears, peel and core, using a melon baller or spoon. In a saucepan, bring the wine or juice to a simmer. Add the pears, cut side down; they should be just covered with juice. Simmer for 8 to 10 minutes or until tender when pierced with the tip of a sharp knife. Remove the pears and cool on a plate, core side up; reserve juice for another use.

In a small bowl, mix the onions, cheese and pepper with a fork. Using a teaspoon, form the mixture into small balls and place a ball in the core of each pear.

Make the vinaigrette by combining the oil, wine vinegar and salt.

To assemble the salad, place 1 or 2 lettuce leaves, depending on their size, on individual salad plates inside the frame of the plate; this shows off the salad as a frame does a picture. Place a pear half on the lettuce. Dribble with vinaigrette dressing and garnish with walnuts.

To toast walnuts, heat them in a small, dry skillet over medium-high heat, shaking the pan often until the aroma rises. Reserve.

Wilted Winter Salad

MAKES 4 TO 6 SERVINGS
PREPARATION: 30 MINUTES
COOKING: 3 TO 4 MINUTES

This delightful salad uses the strongly flavored winter greens that taste great and have a wonderful texture. Choose any 3 or 4 of the following: green or red kale, Swiss chard, collards, bok choy, green or red cabbage, Napa cabbage or radicchio.

1–1¼ lb	500–625 g	winter greens
6	6	bacon slices, cut into small pieces
½ cup	125 mL	chicken or vegetable stock, or water
3	3	garlic cloves, minced
2	2	firm, tart apples, cored and chopped
1 tsp	5 mL	salt, or to taste
2 tbsp	25 mL	olive oil
2 tbsp	25 mL	balsamic vinegar

Wash the greens well in warm water. Drain. Trim away the ends of the stems and discard. Slice the stems thinly. Keep separate from the leaves. Pile the leaves on top of each other and finely slice.

In a skillet, over medium heat, fry the bacon until crisp. Drain off the fat and reserve the bacon.

In a large saucepan, bring the stock to boil with the garlic and chopped stems. Cover, and cook for 1 or 2 minutes until tender-crisp. Remove the lid. Add the greens and apple in small amounts, turning into the stock. Cover again and cook for 1 minute or until just wilted. Toss with salt and pepper and drizzle with the olive oil, vinegar and bacon bits. Serve at room temperature.

Chicken, Mango & Grape Salad

MAKES 4 TO 6 SERVINGS
PREPARATION: 15 MINUTES
COOKING: 15 MINUTES

Mango is a tropical fruit that is at peak flavor during late spring and into summer. The skin is edible but, if desired, peel using a small, sharp knife as the skin is too tough for a vegetable peeler.

3 cups	750 mL	chicken stock
2	2	single chicken breasts with bones
1 cup	250 mL	mayonnaise
1/2 cup	125 mL	plain yogurt
1 tbsp	15 mL	curry powder
		juice of 1 lemon
1 1/2 cups	375 mL	finely diced celery
1	1	ripe peeled mango, diced
1/2 cup	125 mL	green grapes, cut in half, pits removed
1/2 tsp	2 mL	salt, or to taste
		small bunches of parsley or watercress, with stems

In a skillet, heat the chicken stock. Simmer the chicken breasts, covered, for 14 or 15 minutes. Remove the chicken and cool. Remove all meat from the bones and discard the bones and skin. Cut the chicken into thin slices about 1/2 inch (1 cm) thick and 1 inch (2.5 cm) in length. Chill.

In a large mixing bowl, blend the mayonnaise, yogurt, curry powder and lemon juice. Toss in the chicken, celery, mango and grapes. Add salt to taste. To serve, place in a salad bowl, or on a platter, and garnish with parsley or watercress.

> To dice the peeled mango, cut a small slice off the bottom to steady it and stand the fruit on a cutting board. Slice the fruit from around the pit in 3 lengthwise sections and dice each section.

Orzo Salad with Tuna & Vegetables

MAKES 4 TO 6 SERVINGS
PREPARATION: 10 MINUTES
COOKING: 10 TO 12 MINUTES

The dainty, rice-shaped orzo suits this light summer salad, but feel free to use any small pasta. I find tuna packed in oil has more flavor than the water-packed product. You can use canned salmon in place of the tuna, if you wish.

1¼ cups	300 mL	orzo
1½ qts	1.5 L	boiling water, with 2 tsp (10 mL) salt
⅓ cup	75 mL	olive oil
4 tbsp	50 mL	white or red wine vinegar
2	2	6-oz (170-g) cans chunk tuna fish, drained
2	2	tomatoes, diced
½	½	medium red onion, quartered and thinly sliced
½ cup	125 mL	green or red peppers, cut into small dice
½ cup	125 mL	finely chopped, seeded, cucumber or zucchini
¼ cup	50 mL	chopped fresh herbs — basil, mint and/or parsley
1 tsp	5 mL	salt, depending on saltiness of tuna
		generous grinding of black pepper

Add the pasta to the boiling salted water and cook for 8 to 10 minutes, just until al dente. Drain the pasta well and place it in a salad bowl. While it's still warm, toss the pasta with the olive oil and vinegar.

Break up the tuna into smaller chunks and add it to the pasta with the vegetables and herbs. Toss gently to avoid breaking up the tuna. Season to taste with salt and pepper. Let sit for 30 minutes for the flavors to blend.

Bulgur, Feta & Mint Salad

MAKES 4 TO 6 SERVINGS
PREPARATION: 20 TO 25 MINUTES
COOKING: 10 MINUTES

This salad features the flavors of Greece that blend so well together. The tangy saltiness of the crumbled feta goes perfectly with the cool mint and the nutty, chewy bulgur.

1 cup	250 mL	bulgur
2 cups	500 mL	boiling water
1 tsp	5 mL	salt
3 tbsp	45 mL	fresh lemon juice
3 tbsp	45 mL	olive oil
1 tsp	5 mL	freshly ground black pepper
1	1	green bell pepper, seeded, quartered and finely sliced
1	1	medium tomato, seeded and diced
4	4	radishes, trimmed and thinly sliced
3	3	green onions, thinly sliced
1/4 cup	50 mL	pitted and halved black olives
4 oz	120 g	feta cheese, crumbled
		salt and pepper to taste
1/3 cup	75 mL	chopped fresh mint leaves

In a saucepan, add bulgur to the boiling salted water, then cover and simmer for 10 minutes. Place the bulgur in a bowl and add the lemon juice, olive oil and pepper. Leave to cool for 10 minutes. Add the green pepper, tomato with the juice, radishes, onions, olives and feta cheese. Stir in half the mint leaves. Season with salt and pepper if needed, depending on the saltiness of the olives and feta. Garnish with remaining mint.

To seed the tomato, cut crosswise and squeeze each half into a sieve over a bowl; reserve the juice. Dice the tomato pulp.

Coconut & Orange Couscous Salad

MAKES 4 TO 6 SERVINGS
PREPARATION: 5 MINUTES
COOKING: 15 MINUTES

This fresh-tasting salad is great winter or summer. Steaming the couscous makes it fluffier.

1 cup	250 mL	quick-cooking couscous
1/2 cup	125 mL	canned coconut milk
2 tsp	10 mL	lemon juice
1/4 cup	50 mL	chopped green olives
2	2	seedless navel orange segments
		pinch cayenne pepper, or to taste
		salt, depending on saltiness of olives
2 tbsp	25 mL	chopped fresh cilantro

Place the couscous in a sieve, toss briefly under lukewarm tap water (this prevents the couscous going through the sieve) and leave for 3 minutes to swell.

In a saucepan, bring 1 inch (2.5 cm) water to a boil and place the sieve above the water. Cover and steam the couscous for about 10 minutes, stirring it several times. Remove the sieve and let the couscous cool briefly, then gently rub it through your hands to separate the clumps. Return it to the heat and steam for 5 minutes more. Fluff the couscous again and cool completely.

Place the couscous in a salad bowl and stir in the coconut milk, lemon juice, olives and orange segments. Season with cayenne pepper and salt to taste and add the cilantro.

To make orange segments, cut a thin slice off the top and bottom of the orange, then stand it upright on a cutting board. With a sharp knife, cut off the rind, including the white pith, in strips from top to bottom so no pith remains. Hold the orange in one hand and cut between the membranes to remove the segments.

Breads

Bread has always held a special place in my heart because my dad was a baker.

I can remember the whole family heading off to the bakery on Sunday because Dad wanted to go and chat with the bakers who gave up the day with their families so there would be bread to deliver on Monday morning. I can vividly remember slipping into the store-room to steal a handful of raisins, my weakness at the time.

For centuries, people have had a deep love affair with breads made from a variety of flours into every shape and taste imaginable. There are many grains, legumes and vegetables that can be ground into flour, but wheat is the only grain that contains gluten, which is why other flours require the addition of wheat flour to rise properly.

Wheat flour is made from the ground kernels of wheat. The kernels' layers of bran, endosperm and germ are ground commercially between rollers to separate the endosperm from the bran and germ. To make whole wheat flour, the endosperm and bran are reunited, but the germ is not added since it can turn rancid. In mills that grind the old-fashioned stone-ground whole wheat flour the germ is added, but the flour must be kept refrigerated.

Wheat flour can be one of four types, each differing by the amount of gluten contained in it. The types are: soft and hard winter wheat, and soft and hard spring wheat. Winter wheat has the highest gluten content and is used in commercial bakeries and in pasta production. Hard spring wheat made into all-purpose or bread flour. Soft spring wheat is ground into cake and pastry flour.

Unfortunately, most white flour is bleached chemically to remove the yellowish tinge. The good news is that white flour is enriched by law with calcium, riboflavin, iron, folic acid and phosphorous to replace nutrients lost in the milling process.

My favorite flour — one that has given me great success in yeast breads and quick-baking items — is unbleached bread flour.

Bread-Baking Tips

- Yeast is vital to help the gluten to stretch in bread dough. Test for the viability of yeast by allowing a small amount to bubble in a small bowl of lukewarm water with a pinch of sugar — if it doesn't bubble, it's inactive and should be discarded.

- Use flour at room temperature. Warm in a bowl over hot water, or in a warm oven, if necessary. If your kitchen is too warm, use cool liquids, since yeast does not react well to hot or cold conditions.

- Add salt to bread dough to help form the gluten, improve the flavor and make a good crust.

- A little fat added to the bread dough will keep the bread moist longer and allow for longer storage in the freezer.

- Powdered milk can be substituted for fresh milk: whisk 1/4 cup (50 mL) powdered milk into 1 cup (250 mL) cold water, or add the powder to the flour and add the water with other liquid ingredients.

- To knead dough, sprinkle a work surface and your hands with flour, then use the heel of your hand to press down lightly on the dough while stretching it away from you. Fold the dough over, give it a quarter turn and repeat until the dough is elastic, soft and not sticky, about 8 minutes.

- Let the dough rise slowly for better flavor and texture. I place the dough in a bowl in a plastic bag to create a cozy, moist temperature where yeast loves to grow. If your kitchen is cold, place the bowl with the dough inside a larger bowl that is partially filled with warm water and enclose both bowls in a plastic bag. Replenish the water as it cools.

- If dough over-rises, don't worry, just punch it down and let it rise again.

- Remove baked loaves from the pans immediately and cool on racks.

Baking with Baking Powder and Baking Soda

- Never shake the cup as you are measuring flour or you could end up with more flour than the recipe requires, resulting in cracks in the top of your breads and muffins.

- Never beat the batter when the flour is added, or the result will be cavities in the finished product, mix gently with a rubber spatula.

- Although it's more expensive, butter is worth every penny for its rich flavor. If you must, substitute shortening or lard, but never margarine because it contains water that will affect your baking.

- To test whether the flour you have is all-purpose or cake flour, squeeze a fistful tightly in your hand; if it clumps, it's cake flour.

Kneading bread dough (see opposite)

Baking Powder Biscuits

MAKES 16 3-INCH (7.5-CM) OR 36 1¹/₂-INCH (3.5-CM) MINI BISCUITS
PREPARATION: 10 MINUTES
BAKING: 12 MINUTES

These biscuits can be made and baked immediately or prepared, cut and chilled up to 12 hours in advance. Experiment with different flavors and shapes for an easy treat any time of day. I've found that adding cream of tartar makes these biscuits extra light. If you wish to make buttermilk biscuits, replace the milk with buttermilk, but add 1 tsp (5 mL) baking soda to the dry ingredients to neutralize the acidity. You can use a combination of butter and shortening or butter and lard, if you prefer not to use butter alone.

2 cups	500 mL	unbleached all-purpose flour or bread flour
1 tbsp	15 mL	baking powder
¹/₂ tsp	2 mL	cream of tartar, optional
¹/₂ tsp	2 mL	salt
¹/₂ cup	125 mL	cold butter
⁷/₈ cup	230 mL	milk
¹/₄ cup	50 mL	flour for dusting
		granulated sugar for sprinkling (optional)

Preheat the oven to 425°F (220°C). In a mixing bowl, combine the flour, baking powder, cream of tartar, if using, and salt. Use a pastry blender or grate the fat into the dry ingredients, tossing the flour often to keep the fat particles from sticking together. Use a fork to stir the milk through the mixture just until combined — it will be soft and moist. Turn the dough onto a lightly floured surface. Dust the dough surface and your hands with flour and gently knead 4 or 5 times, shaping into a flat circle or rectangle about 1 inch (2.5 cm) thick.

Use a cookie cutter, or a glass dipped in flour to cut out 16 3-inch (7.5-cm) biscuits or 36 1¹/₂-inch (3.5-cm) mini biscuits. Gently press the scraps together and cut out more biscuits. For square or triangle-shaped biscuits, use a knife to cut the rectangle of dough into 16 square or triangle shapes. Place the biscuits on an ungreased baking sheet, just touching. If you want crisp sides, separate biscuits slightly. Sprinkle sugar over the biscuit tops, if desired. Bake for 12 to 14 minutes, until golden.

To make drop biscuits, use two spoons to drop a mound of dough the size of muffins or mini-muffins onto the baking sheet.

Cheese Biscuits: Follow the Baking Powder Biscuit recipe, but add 1/2 cup (125 mL) grated, lightly packed medium or strong Cheddar cheese to the dry ingredients. Sprinkle 3 tbsp (45 mL) grated cheese evenly over the tops of the biscuits before baking. Do not sprinkle with sugar.

Irish Soda Bread

MAKES 8-INCH (20-CM) ROUND LOAF
PREPARATION: 12 MINUTES
BAKING: 40 TO 45 MINUTES

This loaf has been the traditional bread of Ireland for decades. I once wrote a St. Patrick's Day story with wonderful Irish recipes including this soda bread. If desired, replace half the all-purpose or bread flour with whole wheat flour.

1 cup	250 mL	currants or raisins
3 cups	750 mL	unbleached all-purpose flour or bread flour
1/2 tsp	2 mL	salt
2 tsp	10 mL	baking soda
2 tbsp	25 mL	granulated sugar
1/2 cup	125 mL	cold butter
1 1/2 cups	375 mL	buttermilk

Preheat the oven to 375°F (190°C). Soak the currants or raisins in hot water for 3 minutes. Drain and reserve. In a mixing bowl, combine the flour, salt, baking soda and sugar. Use a pastry blender or grate the butter into the dry ingredients, tossing the flour often to separate the particles of fat. Use a fork to stir the buttermilk through the mixture just until dough is formed.

Turn the dough onto a lightly floured surface and gently knead to form a smooth, round shape. Place in a floured 8-inch (20-cm) cake pan or cast iron frying pan. Cut a 1/2-inch (1-cm) deep cross in the top with a sharp knife. Bake for 40 to 45 minutes or until a toothpick inserted in the middle comes out clean. Leave to cool for 3 minutes in the pan before removing to cool on a rack.

Ginger Tea Bread

MAKES 9- X 5-INCH (22.5- X 12.5-CM) LOAF
PREPARATION: 20 TO 25 MINUTES
BAKING: 1¼ HOURS

This is a delicious loaf for special friends or guests. It's best if left for a few hours or overnight before slicing. Butter the slices, if you like, for added rich taste. Crystallized ginger is available in most bulk food sections of markets or specialty stores. Don't be surprised at the thickness of the yolk mixture when you're folding in the beaten egg whites — that's the way it's supposed to be.

4 oz	120 g	crystallized ginger, finely chopped
2 cups	500 mL	unbleached all-purpose flour or bread flour
1 tbsp	15 mL	baking powder
½ tsp	2 mL	salt
¾ cup	175 mL	butter, softened to room temperature
¾ cup	175 mL	granulated sugar
2	2	eggs, at room temperature, separated
½ cup	125 mL	vodka, white vermouth or milk

Preheat the oven to 325°F (160°C). Lightly brush a 9- x 5-inch (22.5- x 12.5-cm) loaf pan with melted butter or use nonstick cooking spray.

In a bowl, toss the ginger with a little of the flour to separate the pieces. Combine the ginger with the remaining flour, baking powder and salt.

In an electric mixer, or by hand using a wooden spoon, beat the butter and ½ cup (125 mL) sugar until creamy. Beat in the yolks until fluffy.

With a rubber scraper, lightly fold the dry ingredients through the yolk mixture, alternately with the vodka, vermouth or milk, just until moistened.

Beat the egg whites until soft peaks form, then, while still beating, sprinkle in the remaining sugar, and continue beating until stiff peaks form. Gently fold the egg whites into the yolk mixture, using a spatula to move the mixture from the bottom up to the top until combined.

Pour into the prepared pan. Make a trench along the top surface so the loaf will bake with a level top. Bake for 1 ¼ hours or until a toothpick inserted in the center comes out clean. Cool the loaf in the pan for 15 minutes before inverting to remove it. Gently turn the bread over so the bottom is on the rack to continue cooling.

Rosemary or Sage Focaccia

MAKES 2 8-INCH (20-CM) ROUNDS
PREPARATION: 20 MINUTES
TOTAL RISING: 2 HOURS
BAKING: 15 MINUTES

This popular Italian snack bread was made originally from leftover pizza dough. The toppings can include everything from sautéed onion, cheese, herbs and tomatoes to anchovies. Use whatever ingredients appeal to you.

2¹/₂ tsp	12 mL	dry yeast (1 pkg)
1¹/₄ cups	300 mL	warm water
3 cups	750 mL	unbleached all-purpose flour or bread flour
2 tsp	10 mL	salt
2 tbsp	25 mL	olive oil plus 1 tbsp (15 mL)
		cornmeal for sprinkling on baking sheet
1¹/₂ tbsp	20 mL	chopped fresh rosemary or 2 tsp (10 mL) dried
or 1¹/₂ tbsp	20 mL	chopped fresh sage or 2 tsp (10 mL) dried
1 tsp	5 mL	coarse sea salt for sprinkling

By hand: In a mixing bowl, beat together the yeast, water and 1¹/₂ cups (375 mL) flour for several minutes with a wooden spoon. Cover and leave the yeast to bubble for ¹/₂ hour; this is the sponge method for a tastier dough. Stir 1¹/₄ cups (300 mL) flour, salt and 2 tbsp (25 mL) of oil into the dough and beat until well blended. Place the last ¹/₄ cup (50 mL) flour on a work surface and turn out the dough. Knead for 6 minutes until the dough is smooth and soft. Enclose the bowl with a plastic bag and leave it to rise for about 1 hour.

By food processor: Place the water, yeast and 1¹/₂ cups (375 mL) flour in the processor and process for 30 seconds. Leave the dough to sit for 30 minutes until bubbly. Add remaining flour, salt and 2 tbsp (25 mL) of the oil and process for 1 minute. Turn the dough onto a lightly floured surface and knead briefly until it's smooth. Enclose the bowl in a plastic bag and leave it to rise for about 1 hour.

Rising and baking: Cut the dough in half. Sprinkle cornmeal on a baking sheet or 2 cake pans. Pat and pull each portion into a 9-inch (22.5-cm) circle and place them on the baking sheet or in cake pans. Brush the loaves with the remaining oil and sprinkle herbs on the dough. Press the herbs into the dough in 5 or 6 places. Sprinkle the loaves with coarse salt. Allow the dough to rise for 20 minutes. Ten minutes before baking, preheat the oven to 450°F (230°C). Bake the focaccia on the lower shelf for 15 to 18 minutes. Cool on a rack to prevent sogginess.

White Bread

MAKES 2 7½- X 4¾-INCH (18.75- X 11-CM) LOAVES
PREPARATION: 30 MINUTES
TOTAL RISING: 3 TO 4 HOURS
BAKING: 40 MINUTES

Although bread-making takes a few hours, the feel of the dough, the aromas that rise during the baking and the joy in eating bread warm from the oven do wonders for the soul. These loaves are made in the smaller-sized loaf pan.

2½ tsp	12 mL	dry yeast (1 pkg)
¼ cup	50 mL	granulated sugar, honey or maple syrup
½ cup	125 mL	lukewarm water
2 cups	500 mL	lukewarm milk
2 tbsp	25 mL	soft butter or vegetable oil
1 tbsp	15 mL	granulated sugar, honey or maple syrup
2½ tsp	12 mL	salt
5½–6 cups	1375–1500 mL	unbleached all-purpose flour or bread flour

In a small bowl, dissolve the yeast with the first amount of sweetener in the water. Leave it to bubble for about 5 minutes.

The dough can be mixed by machine or by hand. Once the dough has been mixed, the method is the same.

By electric mixer: Using a dough hook on low speed, combine the milk, butter or oil, sweetener, salt and 3 cups (750 mL) flour. Add 2 cups (500 mL) flour and the yeast mixture. Continue beating for 6 minutes, adding a spoonful of the remaining flour at a time until the dough is no longer sticky, but soft, satiny and pliable — the last ½ cup (125 mL) may not be used.

By hand: In a mixing bowl, using a wooden spoon, combine the milk, butter or oil, sweetener, salt and 3 cups (750 mL) flour until well blended. Stir in 2 cups (500 mL) flour and the yeast mixture. When the mixture gets hard to stir, turn out onto a floured work surface with the remaining flour to the side. Begin to knead in the flour with the heel of your hand (page 62) for 6 to 8 minutes until the dough is no longer sticky, but soft, satiny and pliable. You may not need to use all of the flour. Clean out the mixing bowl with a little flour to remove bits of dough, lightly oil or butter it, and return the kneaded dough to the bowl.

Rising and baking: Place the bowl of dough in a large plastic bag. This creates a cozy atmosphere for rising. Leave the dough at room temperature until it rises 1½ times in volume, 1½ to 2 hours.

After the first rising, punch the dough down. Leave it to rise again, if you prefer a finer texture. Place the dough on a lightly floured surface. Cut the dough in half and knead it briefly. Cover the dough with the mixing bowl or a plastic bag and let it sit for 10 minutes to relax the gluten. Press each portion into a rectangle the length of the loaf pan and roll up into a tight cylinder. To seal the seam, press with the heel of your hand. Lightly butter the pans and add dough, seam side down, and leave it to rise for about 40 minutes or until the dough is 1 inch (2.5 cm) above the pan rim, then use a sharp knife to make 2 slashes on the diagonal across the top to let the steam out.

Ten minutes before the bread is ready to bake, preheat the oven to 375°F (190°C). Bake for 40 minutes. Remove the loaves from the oven and tip them onto a rack. The loaves should feel light if they're ready.

Whole Wheat Bread

MAKES 2 8¹/2- X 5-INCH (21- X 12.5-CM) LOAVES
PREPARATION: 30 MINUTES
TOTAL RISING: 3 TO 4 HOURS
BAKING: 40 TO 45 MINUTES

Whole wheat bread does not rise as high as white bread because the bran inhibits the yeast's rising ability. Keep the dough on the soft side and resist the temptation to add additional flour while kneading, as the bran in the flour will continue to absorb moisture.

2¹/2 tsp	12 mL	dry yeast (1 pkg)
¹/2 cup	125 mL	warm water
¹/4 tsp	1 mL	maple syrup, molasses or honey
2 cups	500 mL	lukewarm milk
2 tbsp	25 mL	vegetable oil or soft butter
2 tbsp	25 mL	maple syrup, molasses or honey
2¹/2 tsp	12 mL	salt
5 cups	1.25 L	whole wheat flour
¹/4–¹/2 cup	50–75 mL	unbleached all-purpose flour or bread flour

In a small bowl, dissolve the yeast in the water with the first amount of sweetener. Leave it to bubble for about 5 minutes.

Mix the dough by hand or by electric mixer.

By electric mixer: In a bowl, using a dough hook on low speed, combine the milk, oil or butter, sweetener, salt and 3 cups (750 mL) flour. Add 2 cups (500 mL) of flour and dissolved yeast. Let the machine do the kneading and add spoonfuls of the remaining flour just until the dough leaves the side of the bowl and is soft and pliable, about 6 minutes — you may not need all of the flour.

By hand: In a mixing bowl, use a wooden spoon to combine the milk, oil or butter, sweetener, salt and 3 cups (750 mL) of flour. Mix in 1 cup (250 mL) of flour and the yeast mixture. As the mixture becomes firm and hard to mix, turn it onto a work surface with the remaining flour to the side. Knead in the flour a little at a time, using the heel of your hand (page 62) to knead until the dough is no longer sticky, but is still soft and pliable, about 8 minutes. You may not use all the flour. Using a little flour, clean off any dough still attached to the bowl, lightly oil or butter the bowl and return the dough to the bowl.

Rising and baking: Place the bowl of dough in a large plastic bag. Leave the dough at room temperature until it rises 1¹/₂ times in volume, about 2 hours.

After the first rising, punch the dough down. Leave it to rise again, if you would prefer a finer texture. Place the dough on a lightly floured surface. Cut the dough in half and knead it briefly. Cover the dough with the mixing bowl or a plastic bag and leave it for 10 minutes to relax the gluten. Form each portion into a rectangle the length of the loaf pan and roll them up into tight cylinders. Seal the seam, pressing with the heel of your hand. Lightly butter the pans and add the dough, seam-side down. Leave the dough to rise until it is 1 inch (2.5 cm) above the rim of the pan, 45 to 60 minutes. Use a sharp knife to make 2 slashes on the diagonal across the top, to let the steam out.

Ten minutes before baking, preheat the oven to 375°F (190°C). Bake for 45 minutes. Remove the loaves from the oven and tip them onto a rack. The loaves should feel light if they are ready.

Country Grain Bread

MAKES 2 ROUND LOAVES OR 3 SMALLER LOAVES
PREPARATION: 20 MINUTES
TOTAL RISING: OVERNIGHT PLUS 2 HOURS
BAKING: 45 MINUTES

This rustic bread is a winner, with a crisp crust and airy interior dotted with whole, chewy grains. I like to buy whole grain cereal and mix it with extra flaxseed. The bread is based on the sponge method, which uses part of the water, flour, grains and yeast and lets the dough rise overnight. The dough "ripens" and allows the gluten extra time to develop, which produces a good-textured and fragrant loaf. It's most easily made in a machine, but you can make it by hand with a wooden spoon. Forming the loaves can be tricky but it's also fun and rewarding.

Sponge Dough

1 1/4 tsp	6 mL	dry yeast (1/2 pkg)
2 cups	500 mL	cool water
1 cup	250 mL	mixed grain cereal with flaxseed
2 cups	500 mL	unbleached all-purpose flour or bread flour

Bread Dough

1 1/4 tsp	6 mL	dry yeast (1/2 pkg)
1 cup	250 mL	lukewarm water
1 tbsp	15 mL	maple syrup or honey
		prepared sponge batter
3 cups	750 mL	unbleached all-purpose flour or bread flour
2 tbsp	25 mL	olive oil or melted butter
2 tsp	10 mL	salt
2 tbsp	25 mL	flour for work surface
1 tbsp	15 mL	cornmeal for sprinkling on baking sheet
1 tbsp	15 mL	mixed grains for garnish

To make the sponge dough in an electric mixer, using a dough hook, combine the first amounts of yeast, water, grains and flour and beat on low for 5 minutes. Alternatively, beat the mixture with a wooden spoon. This wet dough is called a "sponge." Leave it to rise overnight, but if the room is hot — over 70°F (20°C) — leave it in the refrigerator.

To make the bread the next day, combine the second amounts of yeast, water and maple syrup or honey in a small bowl. Leave the yeast to foam for 5 minutes. In an electric mixer, using the dough hook, mix the sponge batter with the yeast mixture, flour, oil or butter, and salt. The dough will be soft. Beat the dough for 10 minutes on low speed. The dough can also be mixed by hand with a wooden spoon. Place the bowl in a plastic bag and leave the dough at room temperature to double in volume, 1 1/2 to 2 hours.

Lightly sprinkle flour on the work surface and turn out the dough. Use a little bit of flour to clean any remaining dough in the bowl. The dough is soft, so it's best to use a floured pastry cutter to cut it in half or in 3 equal parts. Leave the divided dough to rest for 10 minutes. Grease and sprinkle cornmeal on a baking sheet (or you may need 2 sheets). With lightly floured hands, pick up a dough portion and toss it to form a round ball and place it on the baking sheet. Continue with the remaining dough.

Leave the loaves to rise until doubled in size, 40 to 50 minutes. Ten minutes before baking, use a sharp or serrated knife to make 3 slashes across the top of the loaves, about 1/2-inch (1-cm) deep on an angle. This allows the steam from the bread to escape.

Meanwhile, create steam in the oven by placing a baking pan half-filled with water on the lowest rack. Preheat the oven to 450°F (230°C).

Just before placing the bread in the oven, spray the loaves with hot water from an atomizer and sprinkle with the mixed cereal grains. Bake for 15 minutes. Reduce the heat to 375°F (190°C) and turn the baking sheet around to give the bread an even color. Bake 25 to 30 minutes until bread is crisp, golden brown and feels light. Cool on a rack.

Dinner Rolls — Knots or Rounds

MAKES 3 DOZEN SMALL ROLLS
PREPARATION: 40 MINUTES
TOTAL RISING: 2¹/₂ HOURS
BAKING: 10 TO 12 MINUTES

This dough recipe also makes cinnamon buns. It can be frozen for later use.

2¹/₂ tsp	12 mL	dry yeast (1 pkg)
		pinch sugar
¹/₄ cup	50 mL	warm water
1 cup	250 mL	warm milk
2	2	eggs, in warm water
3 tbsp	45 mL	soft butter
1¹/₂ tsp	7 mL	salt
1 tbsp	15 mL	sugar
4 cups	1 L	unbleached all-purpose flour or bread flour
1	1	egg, lightly beaten, or milk for glaze
2 tbsp	25 mL	sesame seeds or poppy seeds (optional)

In a small bowl, dissolve the yeast and sugar in the water. Let the yeast bubble for 5 minutes.

In an electric mixer with a dough hook or using a mixing bowl and wooden spoon, combine the milk, eggs, butter, salt, sugar and 2 cups (500 mL) of the flour. Mix in the yeast and 1³/₄ cups (425 mL) of the flour, reserving ¹/₄ cup (50 mL) for later use. Beat the dough until it is soft and smooth, 5 to 6 minutes. Place the bowl of dough loosely in a plastic bag and leave it to rise at room temperature until doubled in volume, about 1¹/₂ hours.

Punch the dough down and sprinkle the work surface with reserved flour. Cut the dough into 3 equal portions. Roll one portion into a 12-inch (30-cm) cylinder. Cover the remaining portions with a plastic bag or towel, or wrap and freeze. Cut the cylinder into 12 equal pieces.

Knot rolls: With lightly floured hands, roll each piece into a rope about 5 inches (12.5 cm) long and tie into a loose knot. Place the knots on a buttered baking sheet and slightly flatten rolls.

Round rolls: Roll each piece on the floured work surface with the palm of your hand until a smooth ball is formed and place the balls on a buttered baking sheet. Slightly flatten the balls.

Raising and baking: Leave the rolls at room temperature to rise until they have tripled in volume. For a shiny crust, brush the tops of the rolls with cream or beaten egg. If desired, sprinkle with sesame or poppy seeds.

Ten minutes before baking the rolls, preheat the oven to 400°F (200°C). Bake for 8 to 10 minutes or until lightly golden. To reheat for serving, enclose rolls in a brown paper bag and sprinkle lightly with water. Heat in a 350°F (180°C) oven for 10 minutes.

Cinnamon Buns

MAKES 24 BUNS
PREPARATION: 40 MINUTES
TOTAL RISING: 2¹/₂ HOURS
BAKING: 10 MINUTES

		1 recipe Dinner Rolls (page 74)
3/4 cup	175 mL	currants or dried cranberries
1/2 cup	125 mL	hot water
3/4 cup	175 mL	lightly packed brown sugar
1 tsp	5 mL	cinnamon
3/4 cup	175 mL	melted butter
3/4 cup	175 mL	icing sugar
1 tsp	5 mL	lemon juice or milk

Soften the currants or cranberries in hot water for 5 minutes, drain and reserve. Combine the brown sugar and cinnamon. Using 12-cup muffin pans, place 1 tsp (5 mL) melted butter and 1 tsp (5 mL) cinnamon/sugar mixture into each cup. On a floured surface, roll the dough into an approximate 12-x 18-inch (30- x 46-cm) rectangle. Brush with the remaining melted butter and sprinkle with the remaining cinnamon/sugar mixture, and the currants or dried cranberries.

Roll the dough into a cylinder from the long side and pinch the long edge to seal. Cut the cylinder into 24 slices, place each slice cut side down in the muffin cups and press down slightly so that the dough fits in the cups. Leave at room temperature to rise until doubled in volume, about 1 hour.

Ten minutes before baking, preheat the oven to 400°F (200°C). Bake for 8 to 10 minutes. Leave for 1 minute, then remove from the pan, spooning drippings over the buns. Leave them to cool for 5 minutes.

Frosting: Whisk icing sugar and lemon juice to a runny consistency and drizzle onto the buns from the end of a fork.

Popovers & Yorkshire Pudding

MAKES 12 POPOVERS OR 11-X 7-INCH (27.5- X 17.5-CM) PUDDING
PREPARATION AND STANDING: 45 MINUTES
BAKING: 25 TO 30 MINUTES

Popovers are a uniquely crisp hollow quick bread baked in a heated muffin pan in a hot oven. The popover recipe originated in England and can also be used to make Yorkshire pudding, the traditional accompaniment to roast beef. Years ago, when popovers were more popular, they were baked in heavy cast iron muffin pans that were heated in a blazing hot oven before the batter was added. Today, metal muffin pans work well, as they heat more quickly than cast iron.

3/4 cup	175 mL	unbleached all-purpose flour or bread flour
1/2 tsp	2 mL	salt
2	2	eggs
1 1/2 cup	375 mL	milk
2 tbsp	25 mL	soft butter or dripping from roast beef

In a mixing bowl, food processor or blender, combine the flour and salt, then add the eggs and milk and mix until well blended, about 30 seconds. Leave the mixture to rest for 30 minutes for the gluten to relax so the mixture will expand easily in the oven. Preheat the oven to 425°F (220°C).

Popovers: Add 1/2 tsp (2 mL) butter or beef dripping to each muffin cup and place the pan in the oven for 2 or 3 minutes. Meanwhile, stir up the batter and pour it into a pitcher. Carefully remove the heated pan from the oven, quickly pour in the mixture and bake for 25 to 30 minutes, until the popovers are puffed and golden brown with sides that are firm to the touch. For drier popovers, loosen them from the pan, prick several times, and return them to the oven for 5 minutes.

Yorkshire Pudding: Pour 2 tbsp (25 mL) beef dripping into a baking pan. Place the pan in the hot oven for 2 or 3 minutes. Carefully remove the heated pan from the oven, pour in batter and bake 30 to 35 minutes, until the pudding is puffed and golden brown. Cut into squares and serve immediately with roast beef.

Feather Dumplings

MAKES 4 TO 6 SERVINGS
PREPARATION: 10 MINUTES
COOKING: 10 TO 12 MINUTES

These are light dumplings, gently cooked on top of a stew in a covered saucepan — no peeking allowed!

1 cup	250 mL	unbleached all-purpose flour or bread flour
2 tsp	10 mL	baking powder
1/2 tsp	2 mL	salt
2 tbsp	25 mL	finely chopped fresh parsley or chives, or 1 tbsp (15 mL) dried
2 tbsp	25 mL	melted butter or chicken fat from stock
1	1	egg
1/3 cup	75 mL	milk

In a bowl, combine the flour, baking powder, salt and herbs. Rub the fat through the flour with your fingers until the mixture is crumbly. Mix the egg and milk together until blended and gently stir into the dry ingredients with a fork, just until the flour is moistened. If the batter is stiff, sprinkle in a little more milk. Drop a spoonful of the batter into the simmering stew, leaving a 1-inch (2.5-cm) space between each dumpling. Cover and simmer for 10 to 12 minutes. Remove lid and serve.

Cinnamon Pancakes or Waffles

MAKES 10 TO 12 4-INCH (10-CM) PANCAKES, OR 8 WAFFLES
PREPARATION: 10 MINUTES
COOKING: 4 OR 5 MINUTES

The secret for tender pancakes or waffles is to fold the dry ingredients with the liquids just until the flour is moistened. Don't be concerned if the batter is lumpy — the pancakes will be light. For crisp waffles, be sure the waffle iron is hot before baking them and wait an extra half minute after the light has gone on. Serve them as quickly as possible — waffles don't stay crisp very long. Adding bananas to the pancake or waffle batter makes them extra special.

1 cup	250 mL	unbleached all-purpose flour or bread flour
1 cup	250 mL	whole wheat flour
1 tbsp	15 mL	baking powder
1 tsp	5 mL	baking soda
1 tsp	5 mL	salt
1 tbsp	15 mL	sugar
1 tsp	5 mL	ground cinnamon
2	2	eggs
3 tbsp	45 mL	melted butter or vegetable oil
2 cups	500 mL	buttermilk
		maple syrup and softened butter

In a mixing bowl, combine the 2 flours, baking powder, baking soda, salt, sugar and cinnamon. In a separate bowl, whisk the eggs, butter or oil, and buttermilk together. Use a whisk to gently combine the liquids with the dry ingredients just until the flour is moistened — the mixture will be lumpy.

Pancakes: A flat cast iron griddle or large heavy skillet is best. Lightly brush the surface of the pan with a paper towel dipped in a little butter or oil. Heat the pan on medium-high heat until a drop of water sprinkled in the pan "jumps." Drop a heaping spoonful of batter onto the hot pan and spread it out to a 4-inch (10-cm) circle using the bottom of the spoon. Repeat with 2 or 3 more batter drops. Wait until the top surface of the pancake is covered with bubbles and the edges are slightly dry before turning to cook the second side, for half the time. Turn only once. Serve immediately or keep warm and spread with warm maple syrup and soft butter.

Waffles: Make the pancake batter and heat the waffle iron until the temperature indicator goes off. Lightly brush the surface of the iron with a paper towel dipped in a little butter. Pour and spread 1 ladle or 1/2 cup (125 mL) batter for each waffle or follow the manufacturer's directions. Close lid. Waffles takes from 4 to 5 minutes, depending on the iron, but wait 30 seconds after the light comes on for crisper waffles. Serve waffles while still hot and spread with butter and maple syrup — umm!

Variation: To make banana pancakes or waffles, add 1 medium banana, cut into small cubes, to the batter and cook the pancakes or waffles for an extra 30 seconds.

Blueberry Muffins

MAKES 12 LARGE OR 24 MINI MUFFINS
PREPARATION: 15 MINUTES
BAKING: 18 MINUTES FOR LARGE, 14 MINUTES FOR MINI

These muffins are made like a cake, by creaming the butter, sugar and egg together, then gently folding in the flour mixture alternately with the liquid. Nutmeg freshly grated on a rasp or nutmeg grater has a better flavor than a commercially grated product and you will use less. Whole nutmegs are found in the bulk food section of your market.

1/3 cup	75 mL	butter, softened to room temperature
3/4 cup	175 mL	granulated sugar
1	1	egg
2 1/4 cups	550 mL	unbleached all-purpose flour or bread flour
4 tsp	20 mL	baking powder
1/2 tsp	2 mL	salt
1/4 tsp	1 mL	freshly grated nutmeg
1 cup	250 mL	milk
1 1/2 cups	375 mL	fresh or frozen blueberries (do not defrost)

Preheat the oven to 400°F (200°C). Lightly brush a muffin pan with melted butter or use nonstick cooking spray. In an electric mixer, or mixing bowl using a wooden spoon, beat the butter, sugar and egg until creamy. In a separate bowl, stir together the flour, baking powder, salt and nutmeg, and with a rubber scraper gently fold dry ingredients into the egg mixture alternately with the milk and blueberries, just until the flour is moistened.

Fill the muffin cups to the top. Bake for 18 minutes for large muffins or 14 minutes for mini muffins, or until firm to a light touch. Cool for 5 minutes before removing muffins from the pan.

Corn Muffins

MAKES 12 LARGE OR 24 MINI MUFFINS OR 1 8-INCH (20-CM) PAN
PREPARATION: 15 MINUTES
BAKING: 16 TO 18 MINUTES FOR LARGE, 12 TO 14 MINUTES FOR MINI,
25 TO 30 MINUTES FOR CORNBREAD

These muffins are best when hot from the oven. The creamed corn provides the extra moisture often needed in cornmeal muffins or cornbread due to the drying effect of cornmeal.

1 cup	250 mL	yellow cornmeal
1 cup	250 mL	unbleached all-purpose flour or bread flour
1/2 tsp	2 mL	baking soda
2 tsp	10 mL	baking powder
2 tbsp	25 mL	granulated sugar
1 tsp	5 mL	salt
2	2	eggs
1/4 cup	50 mL	butter, melted, or vegetable oil
3/4 cup	175 mL	buttermilk or 1/2 cup (125 mL) plain yogurt mixed with 1/4 cup (50 mL) milk or sour milk
1	1	14-oz (398-mL) can cream-style corn

Preheat the oven to 375°F (190°C). Lightly brush a muffin or cake pan with melted butter or use nonstick cooking spray.

In a mixing bowl, combine the cornmeal, flour, baking soda, baking powder, sugar and salt. In a separate bowl, whisk together the eggs, butter, buttermilk or yogurt and creamed corn. Use a fork to gently blend the egg mixture into the flour mixture just until the flour is moistened. Fill the muffin cups or cake pan to the top. Bake for 16 to 18 minutes for large muffins, 12 to 14 minutes for mini muffins, 25 to 30 minutes for cornbread, or just until firm to a light touch. Cool for 5 minutes before removing muffins or bread from the pan.

> To sour milk, add 2 tsp (10 mL) lemon juice to 1 cup (250 mL) milk. Leave for 1 minute.

Orange & Raisin Muffins

MAKES 12 LARGE OR 24 MINI MUFFINS
PREPARATION: 15 MINUTES
BAKING: 18 MINUTES FOR LARGE, 14 MINUTES FOR MINI

In this recipe, a food processor works best for grinding the orange and raisins. Be sure to pulse on and off just until the flour is moistened. Raisins can be replaced with pitted dates.

1/2 cup	125 mL	raisins or chopped dates
1/2 cup	125 mL	orange juice (about 1 orange)
2	2	medium seedless oranges, cut into quarters
2	2	eggs
1/3 cup	75 mL	butter, melted, or vegetable oil
2 cups	500 mL	unbleached all-purpose flour or bread flour
2/3 cup	150 mL	granulated sugar
2 tsp	10 mL	baking powder
1 tsp	5 mL	baking soda
1/2 tsp	2 mL	salt

Preheat the oven to 400°F (200°C). Lightly brush a muffin pan with melted butter or use nonstick cooking spray.

Soak the raisins or dates in the orange juice for 5 or 6 minutes. In a food processor, finely grind the raisins or dates, juice and oranges. Add the eggs and butter or oil, until well blended. In a bowl, combine the flour, sugar, baking powder, baking soda and salt. Add this to the orange mixture and pulse the processor on and off just until the flour is moistened.

Fill the muffin cups to the top. Bake for 18 minutes for large or 14 minutes for mini muffins, or until firm to a light touch. Cool for 5 minutes before removing muffins from the pan.

Banana & Dried Cranberry Muffins

MAKES 12 LARGE OR 24 MINI MUFFINS
PREPARATION: 15 MINUTES
BAKING: 18 MINUTES FOR LARGE, 14 MINUTES FOR MINI

This is a great way to use up those bananas that are past their peak. Dried cranberries are a super product that may someday — when they become more affordable — replace raisins.

2 or 3	2 or 3	ripe bananas to make 1 cup (250 mL) mashed bananas
1/3 cup	75 mL	butter or shortening, softened to room temperature
2/3 cup	150 mL	granulated sugar
1	1	egg
2 cups	500 mL	unbleached all-purpose or bread flour
1 tsp	5 mL	baking powder
1/2 tsp	2 mL	baking soda
1/2 tsp	2 mL	salt
1/2 cup	125 mL	dried cranberries
1/4 cup	50 mL	sour milk (page 80), buttermilk or plain yogurt

Preheat the oven to 375°F (190°C). Lightly brush a muffin pan with melted butter or use nonstick cooking spray.

Mash the bananas with a fork and set aside. In an electric mixer or a food processor, beat the butter and sugar until creamy. Beat in the egg until fluffy and blend in the bananas.

In a separate bowl, combine the flour, baking powder, baking soda, salt and cranberries. With a rubber scraper, gently fold dry ingredients into the banana mixture, alternately with milk or yogurt, just until the flour is moistened.

Fill the muffin cups to the top. Bake for 18 minutes for large and 14 minutes for mini muffins, or until firm to a light touch. Cool for 5 minutes before removing the muffins from the pan.

From top : Rosemary or Sage
Focaccia (page 67), Country Grain Bread
(page 72), White Bread (page 68), and
Whole Wheat Bread (page 70)

Clockwise from bottom: Country Grain Bread (page 72), White Bread (page 68), Whole Wheat Bread (page 70), Cinnamon Buns (page 75) and Dinner Roll Knots (page 74)

Cheese Soufflé Roulade with
Spinach Filling (page 92)

Wild Rice Pilaf with Cranberries (page 114)

Eggs & Cheese

Eggs and cheese complement each other and both are powerful foods on their own.

Cheese contains more protein than meat and more calcium and vitamins than milk. Eggs have been described as "the most compact, versatile, convenient and most readily cooked little parcel of nutrition the world has ever known."

Eggs

Eggs have been much-maligned in recent years, but they are a great source of protein with only 75 calories, 5 grams of fat, 9 essential amino acids and vitamins B, D and E. Eggs do contain cholesterol, but research has found that dietary cholesterol has very little impact on the blood cholesterol levels of healthy people.

To test for freshness, immerse the egg in cool water. If the egg sinks, it's fresh, if it tilts a bit it is less fresh and if it floats, forget it. Old eggs lose flavor, the yolks break easily and the whites lose their shape and are runny in the pan. You can usually trust the "best before" date on the egg carton.

Always store eggs in the refrigerator in their carton, never at room temperature. This helps to prevent cross-contamination and absorption of other flavors. Never wash eggs; the shells have a light film to prevent the invasion of bacteria. Although one egg in a million is contaminated with salmonella bacteria, to be safe you should discard any eggs with cracked shells and avoid eating eggs raw.

Whenever I can, I buy omega-3 eggs because the hens are fed extra flax seeds to enrich their eggs with fatty acids. I also like to look for free-range eggs from small producers, for their great flavor.

How To Cook Eggs

Hard-cooked: Place the eggs in a saucepan and cover with warm water. Bring to a simmer over medium heat and time 12 minutes once a simmer is reached. The yolk will be firm and bright yellow. If the eggs are overcooked, there will be a greenish-black line between the white and the yolk. Another method is to remove the simmering pan from the heat and time the eggs for 18 minutes. Plunge the hard-cooked eggs into cold water and peel under cool running water. Fresh eggs will peel more easily because the membrane adheres to the shell.

Soft-cooked: Cook as for hard-cooked eggs, but simmer for only 4 minutes for soft yolks and firm whites.

Poached: Half-fill a medium skillet with water, salt lightly and add 1 tsp (5 mL) of vinegar to help set the egg white. Bring the water to a simmer, crack the eggshell on the side of the skillet and slip the egg gently into the water. After 2 minutes, loosen the egg from the bottom of the skillet with a slotted spoon. To cook the top of the yolk, either cover the skillet with a lid for 1 minute, or spoon simmering water over the yolk until it becomes opaque. Continue to cook until the whites are firm, but the yolks are still soft when touched.

Fried: A fried egg should have a firm (not hard) white and a golden (not brown) underside. For best results, use a heavy metal skillet and a small pat of butter per egg. Melt the butter over medium-high heat until it bubbles. Slip the eggs into the pan and cook until the whites are firm and the yolks are bright yellow. For "over-easy" eggs, gently flip the egg with a lifter and cook briefly, or cover with a lid until the yolks are opaque. Always gently touch the top of the yolk to be sure that the heat has penetrated the entire egg.

Scrambled: These eggs should be soft and creamy. The secret is to cook them on medium-high heat in a small heavy metal skillet and stir constantly with a fork. It will take less than a minute. It's not necessary to add milk or water to eggs, but butter is a must for texture and flavor. Allow 1 or 2 eggs per person. Break the eggs into a bowl and whisk with a fork to blend the yolks and whites — don't overmix or the eggs won't be as creamy. Season with salt and pepper. Heat a skillet over medium-high heat and add 1/2 tsp (2 mL) of butter per egg. When the butter bubbles, tilt the pan to distribute the butter and add the eggs. Whisk the eggs continuously with a fork until they are soft and shiny, then remove them quickly from the pan — they will continue to cook off the heat.

Cheese

Cheese can be made from the milk of cows, sheep, goats, camels, reindeer and even yak. To make cheese, the natural enzymes and lactic acids are allowed to coagulate and form solid curds and whey. Sometimes, the milk is heated with added cultures, such as rennet, that enable the aging process.

To complement cheese, serve it with fresh bread or plain crackers. Avoid highly flavored and salty crackers that compete with the flavor of the cheese. Nuts and fruit make perfect accompaniments, but stay away from citrus fruits that are too sharp, and tropical fruits that are too sweet.

The best wines for cheese are sparkling dry whites or fruity young reds and, of course, the best way to enjoy Stilton is with a glass of port.

Find a knowledgeable cheese merchant who will guide your experimentation, and only buy quantities of cheese that you will use within a few days. Store your purchases in the refrigerator, tightly wrapped in waxed or plastic wrap. If mold forms, just cut it off with a sharp knife; it's a perfectly natural phenomenon.

Types of Cheese

Fresh: These cheeses are made mostly from cow's milk and are not aged. They include: ricotta, cottage cheese, mascarpone, chèvre, cream cheese, quark, Panir (an Indian cheese) and Mozzarella.

Soft: Cheese that is not pressed or cooked, but has a soft, velvety rind. Includes: Brie, Camembert and Brillat-Savarin, a triple-cream cheese with a superb taste and aroma and a high fat content.

Semi-soft: Mild and supple cheeses, these include: Muenster, Havarti, Saint Paulin, Caciotta, Bocconcini and Monterey Jack. Also includes cheeses with more pronounced flavor such as: Feta, Limburger and Oka, which are kept cool while they age.

Firm: These cheeses range in flavor from mild to sharp, depending on the length of the aging process, from 4 months to 10 years! The ones I enjoy the most are: Cheddar, Edam, fontina, Gouda, Emmental, Gruyère, provolone and Raclette. I find Brick and Colby too mild.

Hard: These are the best cheeses for grating. Romano and Parmesan are the best known. And, of course, the king of cheeses, Parmigiano-Reggiano is produced only in Parma, Italy and is aged for at least 2 years to enrich its flavor.

Basic Omelet

MAKES 2 SERVINGS
PREPARATION: 3 MINUTES
COOKING: 2 TO 3 MINUTES

I had a fun experience a few years ago in France when I had the chance to spend time with one of the originators of Nouvelle Cuisine, Roger Vergé, at his restaurant in Provençe, making omelets at full speed. I quickly learned his trade secret; make light omelets quickly with a hot pan that are moist in the center, light golden on the outside and absolutely delicious. For best results, use a 7-inch (17.5-cm) cast iron or steel omelet pan.

3	3	eggs, lightly blended with a fork
		pinch salt
1 tsp	5 mL	butter
1 tsp	5 mL	chopped parsley for garnish

Break the eggs into a bowl. Blend the yolks and whites with a fork and add salt. Heat the skillet on medium-high heat — you should be able to feel the heat radiating from the pan when you hold your hand about 2 inches (5 cm) above it. Add the butter and, when it bubbles, tilt the pan to spread it around. Add the eggs. With the handle in one hand and a fork in the other, constantly move the eggs from the bottom of pan (as if you are making scrambled eggs). Stop as the eggs become firm on the bottom but soft and moist on top. Leave the pan on the heat for another 30 seconds so the bottom becomes lightly golden (gently lift up one corner of the omelet to peek at the underside). Remove from the heat. If using a filling, spread it over top. Loosen the edges of the omelet with a metal spatula. Tilt the pan to help you fold the omelet. Loosen the bottom again and carefully flip the omelet onto a warm plate and garnish with parsley.

Variations: You can make a herb omelet by adding 2 tsp (10 mL) of fresh chopped herbs or 1 tsp (5 mL) of dried herbs to the beaten eggs before cooking.

Another delicious option is a smoked salmon omelet, which is made by stirring 1 oz (30 g) of finely chopped smoked salmon into the beaten eggs before cooking. Cook as above, but omit the salt and add some fresh or dried dill just before folding the omelet.

Eggs Italiani

MAKES 6 SERVINGS
PREPARATION: 10 MINUTES
COOKING: 40 MINUTES TO MAKE TOMATO SAUCE,
5 MINUTES TO POACH EGGS

This is a zesty variation of Eggs Benedict. It is particularly elegant when garnished with sliced truffle (a rare aromatic fungus found in the ground around oak trees). This recipe uses prosciutto (salt-cured Italian ham) on toasted Italian bread, topped with poached egg, smothered with tomato sauce and garnished with capers. A homemade tomato sauce has so much flavor and once you have made one you will realize how easy—and satisfying—it can be.

6	6	slices Italian bread, 3/4 inch (2 cm) thick
2 tbsp	25 mL	melted butter
3 tbsp	45 mL	grated Parmesan cheese
6	6	thin slices prosciutto or smoked ham
6	6	eggs, poached (page 84)
2 1/2 cups	625 mL	Tomato Sauce, heated (page 103)
3 tbsp	45 mL	capers, drained, for garnish

Lightly brush both sides of the bread with butter and toast both sides under the broiler. Sprinkle with cheese and broil again just until the cheese has melted. Place the cheese toasts on a serving platter and top with the meat slices. Keep the platter warm. Place the poached eggs on top of the meat. Coat the eggs with the hot tomato sauce and garnish with capers.

Asparagus or Snow Pea Frittata

MAKES 4 TO 6 SERVINGS
PREPARATION: 20 MINUTES
COOKING: 25 MINUTES

A frittata is an open-face, pie-shaped Italian omelet — filled with blanched spring vegetables. While frittatas are usually cooked on the stove and finished under the broiler, I prefer to use the oven for most of the process.

6	6	eggs
1 tsp	5 mL	chopped fresh rosemary or 1/2 tsp (2 mL) dried
6 tbsp	75 mL	grated Parmesan cheese or Cheddar
1 tsp	5 mL	salt, or to taste
		freshly ground black pepper
1 lb	500 g	fresh asparagus or 1/2 lb (250 g) snow peas
1/2	1/2	red bell pepper, seeded and quartered
2 tbsp	25 mL	olive oil
1	1	onion, finely chopped
1 or 2	1 or 2	garlic cloves, finely chopped
1 cup	250 mL	grated Mozzarella cheese

Preheat the oven to 325°F (160°C). In a mixing bowl, whisk the eggs until blended and frothy.

Stir in the rosemary, cheese, salt and pepper. Set aside.

To prepare the asparagus, bend the stem to break off the tough end and discard or freeze to use in soup. Cut each stem diagonally into 1/4-inch (.5-cm) thick slices. Set aside. If using snow peas, pull off the stem and string from the straight side. Cut diagonally into thirds. Cut the red pepper into small cubes.

In a 10-inch (25-cm) skillet, heat the oil over medium heat. Stir in the onion, cover and cook for about 5 minutes until soft, stirring once. Stir in the garlic, asparagus or snow peas and red pepper. Raise heat to high, add 2 tbsp (25 mL) water, cover and steam for 2 minutes or until tender-crisp, giving the pan several shakes to loosen the vegetables. Remove from the heat.

Stir the egg mixture into the skillet until well combined. If the pan handle is not heatproof, protect it with foil. Place the pan in the oven and bake for 10 to 12 minutes or until the eggs are still a little runny on top. Remove from the oven. Sprinkle the cheese on top and place the pan about 4 inches (10 cm) under the preheated broiler until the frittata is golden, about 2 minutes. Remove from the heat and loosen the sides of the frittata from the pan. Cut into wedges and serve hot or warm.

Mushroom-Filled Crêpes

MAKES 20 CRÊPES
PREPARATION: 35 TO 40 MINUTES
COOKING: 20 MINUTES

Making crêpes can be fun once you master the technique. These delightful crêpes can be stuffed with a savory filling or, with 2 tsp (10 mL) sugar added to the batter, they are wonderful filled with ice cream or fruit. One of the nice things about crêpes is that they can be made ahead and frozen for future use. Use a cast iron or steel crêpe pan to evenly distribute the heat for a light texture.

2	2	eggs
3/4 cup	175 mL	milk
1/2 cup	125 mL	all-purpose flour
1/2 tsp	2 mL	salt
2 tsp	10 mL	granulated sugar (for dessert crêpes only)
1 tbsp	15 mL	butter, at room temperature
		1 recipe Mushroom Filling (page 90)

Place the eggs, milk, flour, salt, sugar (if using) and butter in a mixing bowl and use a whisk to mix for about 1 minute until well blended. Or, mix in a blender or food processor for about 20 seconds. Scrape down the sides with a rubber scraper and blend for several seconds more.

Chill the batter for 20 minutes, allowing the gluten or protein in the flour to relax, which makes tender crêpes.

Lightly oil a 6- or 7-inch (15- or 17.5-cm) crêpe pan with a paper towel dipped in vegetable oil. When the pan is smoking, on medium-high heat, remove from the heat. Quickly pour in 2 tbsp (25 mL) of the batter and tilt to spread it over the bottom. Return to the heat and cook until the crêpe is golden on the bottom and dry on top. Flip the crêpe over, cook another 30 seconds and remove to a plate.

Pile the crêpes on top of each other as they are cooked. Use immediately, or cool and freeze for later use.

Mushroom Filling

1 tbsp	15 mL	butter
1 tbsp	15 mL	vegetable oil
3/4 lb	375 g	fresh mushrooms, thinly sliced
2 or 3	2 or 3	garlic cloves, finely chopped
2 tsp	10 mL	fresh thyme or 1 tsp (5 mL) dried
1/2 cup	125 mL	light cream or white wine
2 tbsp	25 mL	fresh parsley, finely chopped
1/2 tsp	2 mL	salt, or to taste
1/4 tsp	1 mL	freshly ground black pepper
1/2 cup	125 mL	Cheddar or Swiss cheese, grated

Heat a medium-sized skillet on high heat. Add the butter and oil and stir-fry the mushrooms, garlic and thyme for about 1 minute. Stir in the cream or wine, reduce the heat to medium-high and cook until the liquid has reduced and the mixture has thickened, for about 2 minutes. Add the parsley, salt and pepper to taste.

To serve, spoon the mushroom mixture across the center of each crêpe and roll up. Place seam side down in a flat, heatproof dish. Any remaining filling can be spread down the center of the crêpes. Sprinkle the cheese over top. Broil just until the cheese is bubbly.

Cheese Soufflé

MAKES 4 TO 6 SERVINGS
PREPARATION: 25 MINUTES
BAKING: 30 MINUTES

Nutmeg and mustard are wonderful complements to cheese and either can be used to enhance the flavor of this soufflé. See page 93 for tips on making soufflés.

4 tbsp	50 mL	butter
6 tbsp	75 mL	unbleached all-purpose flour
1½ cups	375 mL	milk
2 tsp	10 mL	Dijon mustard, or freshly grated nutmeg
		salt and pepper to taste
1 cup	250 mL	Cheddar or Swiss cheese, grated, firmly packed
6	6	eggs, at room temperature, separated

In a medium-sized saucepan over medium heat, melt the butter and stir in the flour with a wooden spoon, creating a roux (see Glossary). Cook the roux for 1 minute. Add the milk, whisking until the mixture is smooth. Cook gently for 5 minutes, whisking several times to prevent burning; the sauce should be thick and smooth. Add the mustard or nutmeg and season with salt and pepper. Remove the sauce from the heat. Cool for 3 or 4 minutes.

Choose a pan large enough to comfortably hold a 6-cup (1.5-L) soufflé dish and half-fill the pan with water. Place on the middle rack of the oven. Preheat the oven to 375°F (190°C).

Stir the cheese into the white sauce until well blended, then add the yolks. In an electric mixer with whisk attachment, or by hand, beat the whites at medium speed until shiny and soft peaks form. Use a rubber spatula to gently fold the cheese mixture into the beaten whites. To fold the mixture, move the spatula around the side of the bowl, then dip it under the mixture and back up over the top. Continue to fold in the remaining cheese mixture. Turn the mixture into a buttered 6-cup (1.5-L) soufflé dish and smooth the surface. Using your finger, make a trench around the surface about 1 inch (2.5 cm) from the edge of the dish to help the soufflé rise evenly. Bake for 35 to 40 minutes until the surface is firm to the touch. Serve immediately.

Cheese Soufflé Roulade with Spinach Filling

MAKES 6 SERVINGS
PREPARATION: 30 MINUTES
BAKING: 13 TO 14 MINUTES

This is a melt-in-the-mouth soufflé that is baked in a flat pan, filled and rolled, then served in slices. It can be made two days ahead or frozen.

1¹/2 cups	375 mL	White Sauce (page 93)
1 cup	250 mL	grated Swiss or medium Cheddar cheese, lightly packed
5	5	eggs, at room temperature, separated
¹/8 tsp	.5 mL	cream of tartar
		pinch salt
3 tbsp	45 mL	freshly grated Parmesan cheese

Preheat the oven to 375°F (190°C). Line a 10- x 15- x ³/4-inch (25- x 38- x 2-cm) rimmed baking pan with parchment paper or buttered waxed paper.

Stir the cheese into the White Sauce and whisk in the yolks until smooth.

Beat the egg whites, cream of tartar and salt in an electric mixer with a whisk attachment, or by hand, until soft peaks form. Use a rubber scraper to fold the yolk mixture into the whites. Spread the mixture over the prepared pan and smooth. Sprinkle with Parmesan cheese.

Bake for 13 to 14 minutes, until the soufflé has puffed and is firm to the touch. Remove from the oven and leave to settle (it will fall) for several minutes. Gently invert the soufflé onto a dishtowel. Leave it to cook for several minutes before removing the liner by using the tip of a knife to gently separate the paper from the soufflé.

White Sauce for Soufflé & Filling

4 tbsp	50 mL	butter
6 tbsp	75 mL	all-purpose flour
2 cups	500 mL	milk
1 tsp	5 mL	salt

In a saucepan on medium heat, melt the butter and stir in the flour. Cook for 1 minute. Whisk in the milk until the sauce is thick and smooth. Simmer for 5 minutes. Season with salt. Remove from heat and reserve 1 1/4 cups (300 mL) of sauce for the filling. Leave the remaining sauce in the saucepan.

Although soufflés may seem intimidating, they are easy if you follow the simple tips outlined here.

- A soufflé cooked in a hot oven will rise quickly and fall quickly once it leaves the oven — don't worry about it.

- If baked in a bain-marie in a medium oven (see Glossary), the soufflé will take longer to cook and will not collapse as quickly.

- If you wish to slow the cooking time, reduce the oven heat to 250°F (120°C) and bake for an extra 20 minutes. To speed cooking, increase the heat to 450°F (230°C) and bake for 10 minutes less.

- To bring eggs to room temperature, warm them in a bowl of water for 5 minutes. This will give them more volume when beaten.

- Beat egg whites in a clean metal bowl (copper works especially well) with a balloon whisk or an electric beater, just until shiny peaks begin to form. Don't overbeat or the soufflé will not rise to its full height.

- An ovenproof soufflé dish that is circular, straight-sided and glazed will produce the best results.

Filling

1 tbsp	15 mL	butter
3 or 4	3 or 4	green onions, thinly sliced
1	1	10-oz (300-g) package frozen chopped spinach, thawed
1 cup	250 mL	reserved white sauce
1/2 tsp	2 mL	freshly grated nutmeg
		sprinkling of freshly ground black pepper

In a saucepan, melt the butter on medium-low heat, add the onions, cover and cook until soft, about 5 minutes. Squeeze excess water from the spinach and stir into the onions to cook for 1 minute. Stir in the reserved white sauce. Season with nutmeg and pepper.

To assemble, spread spinach filling over the soufflé to 1/2 inch (1 cm) from the edge. Beginning at one end, roll the soufflé into a cylinder, using a towel to guide the rolling. Loosely cover with foil and keep warm in a 250°F (120°C) oven. If not using the roulade immediately, cover and refrigerate or wrap well and freeze.

To serve, cut the roulade into 3/4-inch (2-cm) slices and arrange, partially overlapping, on a heated platter.

To reheat a cold roulade, cover it loosely with foil and warm it in a 350°F (180°C) oven for 20 to 30 minutes.

Baked Cheese Casserole

MAKES 6 GENEROUS SERVINGS
PREPARATION: 20 MINUTES
BAKING: 35 TO 40 MINUTES

This is a delicious and inexpensive dish, easily assembled the night before and popped into the oven for breakfast or for any meal. Grilled, sliced sausages or chopped ham can be sprinkled on the bread before baking.

8	8	bread slices, crusts removed
1/4 cup	50 mL	melted butter
2 tbsp	25 mL	chopped fresh chives or tarragon or 1 tbsp (15 mL) dried
3 cups	750 mL	medium Cheddar or Swiss cheese, grated, lightly packed
4	4	eggs
1/4 tsp	1 mL	cayenne, or to taste
1 tsp	5 mL	salt
2 1/2 cups	625 mL	milk or light cream

Preheat the oven to 375°F (190°C). Lightly butter a shallow 7- x 11-inch (17.5- x 27.5-cm) casserole. Line the bottom of the casserole with 4 bread slices, cutting the bread to fit the bottom. Brush the bread with half the butter, and sprinkle on half the herbs and half the cheese. Repeat with remaining bread, butter, herbs and cheese.

In a separate bowl, whisk the eggs, cayenne, salt and milk or cream until blended and pour over the bread and cheese. If not baking immediately, cover and chill.

Bake for 35 to 40 minutes until puffed and golden. If the casserole has been chilled, bake for 5 extra minutes. Leave to rest for 5 minutes before serving.

Old-Fashioned Macaroni & Cheese

MAKES 4 TO 6 SERVINGS
PREPARATION: 20 MINUTES
BAKING: 20 MINUTES

I will never forget the day my children informed me that my macaroni was "yucky" compared to the packaged one. It kind of hurt but now we have a great laugh about it. The key to this dish is not to overcook the macaroni— cook "al dente" or just until it still has a "bite."

Be sure to remove the sauce from the heat when adding the cheese to prevent it becoming rubbery and uneatable. Chopped ham or cooked vegetables are a great addition to this dish and beer is the perfect beverage for the adult who is enjoying this childhood favorite.

1¹/₂ qt	1.5 L	water
1 tbsp	15 mL	salt
2 cups	500 mL	macaroni, uncooked
2 tbsp	25 mL	butter
1	1	onion, finely chopped
2 tbsp	25 mL	all-purpose flour
2¹/₂ cups	625 mL	milk
¹/₂ cup	125 mL	Cheddar or Swiss cheese, grated
¹/₄ tsp	1 mL	hot pepper sauce
1 tsp	5 mL	salt, or to taste
1 cup	250 mL	fresh bread crumbs
1 tbsp	15 mL	melted butter

Preheat the oven to 375°F (190°C). Butter a 7- x 11-inch (17.5- x 27.5-cm) shallow casserole.

Bring the water and salt to a boil and stir in the macaroni. Cook for 8 minutes, or until al dente. Drain into a colander, shaking it to get all the water out of the macaroni "tunnels."

In a large saucepan, melt the butter on medium-low heat, stir in the onion, cover and cook for 5 minutes, without browning the onion. Stir in the flour and cook 1 minute. Raise heat to medium-high, whisk in the milk until smooth and simmer for 5 minutes, stirring often, until thickened. Remove the sauce from the heat and stir in the cheese, salt and pepper, then the macaroni. Pour the mixture into the casserole. Toss the crumbs with melted butter and sprinkle over top.

Bake for 20 minutes or until bubbly and golden. The casserole can be covered and refrigerated for up to a day before cooking, but add 10 extra minutes to the cooking time.

To make fresh bread crumbs, break up 2 bread slices in a food processor or blender and pulse on and off until crumbs form.

Pasta, Pizza, Grains & Legumes

The cooks of the Mediterranean and Asian realms have given us the gift of dishes featuring beans, lentils, rice, couscous and, of course, pasta.

Pasta

In Italy, I learned the importance of not rinsing cooked pasta, since its starchy coating helps the sauce to cling. I also learned that pasta should have just enough sauce to coat, not smother, it. In Italy, the pasta course is separate from the main course. You will never find a sauce-laden pile of pasta alongside your main dish, as is unfortunately too often the case in North America.

There are over 400 different shapes of pasta available in Italy. We have fewer available to us, but there is the choice of fresh or dried. It doesn't matter which you use, but fresh pasta cooks more quickly and has a lighter, more delicate taste.

Asian noodles are now more widely available to North American cooks.

We can enjoy the chewy, transparent cellophane noodles, made from mung beans. Or try rice noodles, which only require soaking to soften them before eating. Thin, flat soba noodles, ramen noodles, and thick, filling udon noodles are just some of the choices we have.

Whatever the origins of your noodles or pasta, allow about 4 oz (120 g) per person for a main course and 2 oz (60 g) for a side dish.

Pasta should be "al dente" or firm "to the tooth." It shoud be drained in a colander but not rinsed and tossed rapidly with a sauce in the saucepan or in a warmed serving bowl. The sauce should be evenly distributed and not sit in a puddle on top.

Grains

There are many grains available to us today, but they are all highly nourishing, with complex carbohydrates, proteins and fiber. Each grain has three parts: the germ, endosperm and bran.

To determine if a grain is cooked properly, bite into it. A properly cooked grain will be slightly chewy, not gummy or hard.

Types of Grain

- Barley is best if it is toasted briefly before cooking to enhance its flavor. Pot barley has its hull removed by milling and pearl barley is milled until the germ and bran are also removed.

- Buckwheat is a nourishing relative of rhubarb with a perfect amino acid balance. The seeds are toasted to make kasha.

- Bulgur is a high-protein wheat with a nutty flavor. Bulgur should be soaked in equal parts of boiling water before serving.

- Cornmeal is from a native plant of North America, corn, milled into fine or coarse meal. It is called "maize" in some countries and is made into polenta in Italy.

- Couscous is made of dried semolina and is the main ingredient in a delicious North African dish made in a couscousière.

- Millet is a small yellow cereal that is high in protein and has a nutty, cornmeal-like flavor.

- Oats are kernels or groats, milled into oatmeal for porridge or bread. Oatmeal can also be steamed, dried and rolled into flakes, or partially cooked and dried to make instant oatmeal.

- Quinoa is grown on high mountain slopes in South America. It has highly nutritious seeds with a nutty flavor.

- Spelt and kamut are ancient varieties of wheat.

- Rice is a semi-aquatic plant that is available in long-, medium- or short-grain sizes that are suited to different dishes. Brown rice has had the outer hull removed, but, unlike white rice, the bran is retained for flavor and fiber. Wild rice is not a true rice, but is actually a grass that is harvested by hand, which is why it is so expensive.

Legumes

The legume family — beans, peas and lentils — are all wonderfully nutritious and oh, so good for us! If you are cutting back on meat, beans are a great source of complex carbohydrates, iron, fiber, zinc and protein. A half cup of beans has as much protein as 2 oz (60 g) of beef, but the protein in beans lacks certain amino acids that allow it to be utilized by the body. Whole grains, rice, wheat, some nuts and seeds can supply those missing amino acids, so it's a good idea to eat beans in combination with these foods.

The only dried beans I knew when I was growing up were "shanty-style" baked beans. They cooked all night at my family's bakery, after the bread ovens cooled down. They were called "shanty-style" because the recipe came from the lumber camp cook. These sought-after beans were made with generous amounts of salt pork, mustard, brown sugar and whole onions. In the summer, so the cook's "shanty" didn't become unbearably hot, the beans were cooked in iron pots buried in sand, with a fire laid on top. These beans are still made the same way in the Gatineau Hills, north of Ottawa.

Legumes are dried, the age-old way of keeping and storing for culinary uses. Keep them dry and cool in an airtight container. (Helps to keep weevils away!) Legumes keep indefinitely, but after a year or so their taste weakens and they will take longer to cook. It's always wise to sort through them to remove any pebbles or broken beans. Most beans and chickpeas need to be soaked overnight to prevent the skins from splitting and to draw out the indigestible sugars that can cause intestinal gas. The secret for tender beans is gentle cooking and adding salt only at the end to prevent toughness.

A faster method than soaking is to simmer the beans in water for 5 minutes, remove from the heat and steep for 1 hour, then drain and continue cooking. I find this method makes the beans less tasty and they lose some nutrients compared to overnight soaking.

Here are some readily available legumes:

- Black beans, also called Mexican or turtle beans, are small and black with white lines. Their rich taste makes great soups. They cook within 1 hour.

- Black-eyed peas are small and off-white in color, with a black spot. They are popular in southern cooking and in salads. They cook within 45 minutes.

- Chickpeas or garbanzo beans, are dried or canned and often used in Mediterranean cuisine. The dried ones take up to 2 hours to cook. The convenient canned ones are already cooked.

- Cranberry beans are light in color and dappled with brown. They have a rich, sweet flavor and are a good replacement for pinto beans. They cook in about an hour.

- Fava or broad beans are kidney-shaped, white or brown and starchy in taste. They can be cooked fresh or dried, but the dried ones must be peeled after soaking.

- White kidney or cannelini beans are large flat, kidney-shaped beans. Great in salads or cooked with meat, as in cassoulet. They cook in 1 hour.

- Great northern or navy beans are small white beans used for baked beans. They cook in 1 hour.

- Kidney beans are most popular when canned and used in chili or salads or baked beans. The dried type are the same as red beans and they cook in 1 to 1 1/2 hours.

- Pinto beans have a mottled beige color, a creamy texture and are traditionally used in Mexican dishes. They cook in 1 hour.

- Limas or baby limas are pale green and available fresh, frozen or dried. The dried limas take about 1 hour to cook.

- Mung beans are small, and may be green, yellow or black. They sprout in high humidity and are used fresh or made into bean-thread noodles. The dried beans cook in about 1 hour and are used in Indian cuisine.

- Yellow and green split peas are tasty and easily digestible and need about 1 hour to cook. They are mostly used in soups.

- Lentils come in red, yellow or greeny-brown and cook for 20 to 40 minutes, depending on the type. They are high in protein and energy and delicious in soups or vegetarian dishes.

Homemade Pasta

MAKES 4 SERVINGS
PREPARATION: 30 MINUTES
COOKING: 2 TO 3 MINUTES

This dough is light and fine-textured, made by hand or in a food processor, then rolled and cut into shapes using a hand-cranked pasta machine — a great time-saver. You can also roll the pasta by hand.

2 cups	500 mL	unbleached all-purpose flour
1/4 tsp	1 mL	salt
1 tsp	5 mL	olive oil
2	2	eggs

To make pasta dough in a food processor, process the flour, salt, oil and eggs just until dough is formed. Remove the dough and knead into a smooth ball.

To make pasta dough by hand, combine the flour and salt on the work surface and make a well in the middle. Break the eggs into the well, add the oil and gently blend with a fork. Gradually incorporate the flour surrounding the well into the eggs until they are no longer runny. When half the flour is incorporated, begin kneading and continue until a smooth ball of dough is formed.

Divide the dough in half and keep it covered for at least 30 minutes before rolling it in the pasta machine. Set the pasta machine's rollers at the widest setting and pass half the dough through the rollers. Fold this dough into thirds, press down, sprinkle with flour and repeat rolling and folding 7 times, sprinkling with a little flour and moving the rollers to the next notch each time. As the sheet of dough gets longer during the rolling, allow it to hang over your arm or the back of a chair.

Cut the dough into desired lengths or shapes, then dry the pasta on towels for 10 minutes. If the kitchen is drafty or very hot, cover the pasta with a towel. Do not overlap the dough at this stage, as it will stick together. If making pasta for stuffing, such as ravioli, run the dough through the machine 8 times.

To cook 1 lb (500 g) pasta: Bring 4 qts (4 L) water to a boil and add 4 tsp (20 mL) salt. Never add oil to the water as it prevents the sauce from clinging to the pasta. Add the pasta and stir briefly with a wooden spoon to separate the strands. Boil for 2 minutes for fresh pasta, or 8 to 10 minutes for dried pasta.

Drain in a colander but do not rinse. Toss the pasta rapidly with your favorite sauce in the saucepan or in a warmed serving bowl.

Tomato Sauce

MAKES 4 TO 6 SERVINGS OR 3 CUPS (750 ML) SAUCE
PREPARATION: 20 MINUTES
COOKING: 20 MINUTES

This sauce is best made when tomatoes are at their peak of flavor. It can be preserved in glass jars or frozen for use on pizza or pasta. It can also be made with canned diced tomatoes.

2 tbsp	25 mL	olive oil
2	2	garlic cloves, chopped
1	1	small onion, chopped
2 lbs	1 kg	fresh plum tomatoes, peeled and chopped, or 1 28-oz (796-mL) can diced plum tomatoes
1 tsp	5 mL	fresh rosemary or oregano, or 1/2 tsp (2 mL) dried
2 tsp	10 mL	salt, or to taste
1/2 tsp	2 mL	freshly ground black pepper, or to taste
		generous pinch of dried red pepper flakes
		pinch brown sugar

In a non-reactive saucepan, heat the oil over medium-low heat. Add the garlic and onion, cover and sweat until tender, about 5 minutes, stirring twice to prevent browning. Add the tomatoes and cook gently on medium heat for 12 to 14 minutes or until excess juices evaporate. Purée in a food processor or blender until smooth, or pass through a food mill or sieve to remove the seeds.

Return the tomatoes to the saucepan and season to taste with rosemary or oregano, salt, black pepper, red pepper flakes and sugar. Keep warm until ready to serve. This sauce can be stored in the refrigerator for up to 4 days or frozen for up to 6 months.

Mushroom & Broccoli Lasagna

MAKES 4 TO 6 SERVINGS
PREPARATION: 45 MINUTES
COOKING: 35 TO 40 MINUTES

This delicious lasagna makes a good vegetarian alternative to the familiar lasagna with meat sauce. The broccoli can be replaced with rapini, a popular Italian vegetable with a pungent bitter flavor and small yellow flowers.

4 qts	4 L	water with 4 tsp (50 mL) salt
1/2 lb	250 g	lasagna noodles (about 9 noodles)
1 lb	500 g	button, cremini or portobello mushrooms
3 tbsp	45 mL	extra-virgin olive oil
2 tsp	10 mL	fresh thyme, or 1 tsp (5 mL) dried, finely chopped
		freshly ground black pepper
1 lb	500 g	fresh broccoli
3	3	garlic cloves, finely chopped
2 cups	500 g	smooth ricotta cheese
1/2 cup	125 mL	whipping cream
		zest of 1 lemon
1/4 tsp	1 mL	freshly grated nutmeg
1 tsp	5 mL	salt, or to taste
1 cup	250 mL	grated fontina cheese, firmly packed
1/2 cup	125 mL	freshly grated Parmesan cheese

In a large saucepan, bring water and salt to a boil. Add the pasta, gradually immersing in the water as the noodles soften, and cook for 8 minutes or until barely tender (it will continue to cook in the oven). Drain. Lay the noodles side by side on a tea towel.

Toss the mushrooms quickly in warm water with a small handful of flour and drain. Cut off the tough stem tip. Thinly slice the mushrooms or, if using portobellos, quarter and thinly slice. Heat a large skillet on high heat with half the oil and stir-fry half the mushrooms just until they are tender, about 1 minute. Sprinkle with thyme and pepper. Reserve. Heat the remaining oil and repeat with remaining mushrooms.

To prepare broccoli, discard the tough end. Cut into small florets, and cut the stems into 1/4-inch (.5-cm) slices. In a skillet over high heat, bring to a boil 1/4 cup (50 mL) water, then add the broccoli and garlic. Cover and steam for 2 minutes or until tender-crisp. Drain. Reserve.

In a small saucepan over medium-low heat, gently heat the ricotta, cream, lemon zest and nutmeg. Season to taste with salt.

To assemble, spread 2 tbsp (25 mL) sauce on the bottom of a shallow 8- x 12-inch (20- x 30-cm) ovenproof dish and cover it with 3 lasagna noodles, arranged side by side. Cover the pasta with 1/3 of the ricotta sauce. Top with 1/2 the mushrooms, 1/2 the broccoli and 1/2 the fontina cheese. Repeat the layers and finish with a layer of pasta topped with sauce and sprinkled with Parmesan cheese.

Bake in a preheated 350°F (180°C) oven for 30 to 35 minutes until bubbly and golden. Let the lasagna rest for 10 minutes before cutting into portions and serving.

Summer Tomato, Basil & Mint Sauce

MAKES 4 TO 6 SERVINGS
PREPARATION: 6 MINUTES
COOKING: 5 MINUTES

Basil and mint are two flavorful herbs, each bringing a special taste to this quickly made fresh tomato sauce. It's great on grilled vegetables, fish or pasta.

4	4	medium plum tomatoes, cored, about 1 lb (500 g)
2 tbsp	25 mL	olive oil
2–3	2–3	garlic cloves, chopped
4	4	fresh basil and/or mint leaves, chopped
1/2 tsp	2 mL	salt
		Parmesan cheese (optional)

Blanch the tomatoes in boiling water for 25 seconds. Drain, peel and finely chop. In a saucepan, heat the oil on medium-high heat and add the garlic, stir and cook for 30 seconds. Add the tomatoes and cook only 4 or 5 minutes. You can leave the sauce chunky or purée in a food processor or blender. If you wish to remove the seeds, use a food mill or press through a sieve. Stir in the herbs and season. Serve with grated Parmesan cheese, if desired.

Thin-Crusted Pizzas

MAKES 4 6-INCH (15-CM) OR 2 12-INCH (30-CM) PIZZAS
PREPARATION AND RISING: 1 TO 1½ HOURS
BAKING: 15 TO 18 MINUTES

I learned to make and enjoy pizza in Italy, where the preparation is a pleasure. It's a favorite food around our house. We prepare the dough in the food processor or electric mixer with a variety of toppings so everyone can customize a pizza. A preheated pizza stone cooks the pizza quickly with a crisp, tender crust, but a flat baking sheet works almost as well. A flat paddle called a "peel" is useful when using a pizza stone so you can safely slide the pizza onto the hot stone.

2¼ tsp	11 mL	dry yeast
		pinch granulated sugar
¾ cup	175 mL	warm water
1 tsp	5 mL	salt
2 tbsp	25 mL	olive oil
2–2¼ cups	500–550 mL	unbleached bread flour or all-purpose flour

By hand: Combine the yeast, sugar and water in a bowl and leave to bubble for 6 minutes. Stir in the salt, oil and flour and beat with a wooden spoon for 6 minutes, until the dough is smooth, soft and slightly sticky. If the dough is firm, sprinkle with a little water and beat briefly.

By food processor: Place the yeast, sugar and water in the bowl. Pulse the machine on and off just to combine and leave the mixture to bubble for about 6 minutes. Add the salt, oil and flour and process until a dough forms. Continue to process for 30 seconds. The dough should be soft and slightly sticky. If the dough is firm, sprinkle in a little water and process for 10 seconds. Turn the dough out onto a lightly floured surface and knead briefly until the dough is smooth and forms a ball. Lightly grease a bowl, add the dough, enclose the bowl in a plastic bag and leave the dough to rise until doubled, about 1 to 1½ hours.

By electric mixer: With a dough hook, briefly combine the yeast, sugar and water and leave it to bubble for 5 or 6 minutes. Add the salt, oil and flour and beat for 5 minutes. The dough will be soft and slightly sticky. If the dough is firm, sprinkle in a little water and beat until the dough is soft. Leave the dough in the bowl, enclosed in a plastic bag, to rise until doubled, about 1 to 1½ hours.

Divide the dough into 2 or 4 equal portions. Work each piece into a smooth ball and loosely cover with a plastic bag for 10 minutes. At this point, portions can be wrapped in waxed paper and foil and chilled for a day or frozen for future use. If you're using frozen dough, allow it to come to room temperature and rise slightly.

Preheat the oven to 500°F (260°C). Lightly brush olive oil on one or more baking sheets, depending on how many pizzas you're making, or on 2 12-inch (30-cm) pizza pans. Press and stretch the balls into circles. When you have the shapes you like, place them on the pans. Let the pizzas rest for 10 minutes, then brush the dough lightly with oil. Add your choice of topping. Each of the topping recipes makes enough for a 6-inch (15-cm) pizza.

Place the baking sheet or pans in the oven or slide the pizzas onto a preheated pizza stone. Bake for 12 to 15 minutes in the center of the oven until the pizzas are golden and bubbly.

Onion, Sausage & Black Olive

2 tsp	10 mL	olive oil
1/2	1/2	medium onion, thinly sliced
1 1/2 oz	45 g	dried, cured pork sausage or pepperoni, thinly sliced
3–4	3–4	Italian or Greek black olives, pitted and halved
1/4 cup	50 mL	small cubes smoked cheese

Heat the oil in a small skillet and add the onions. Sweat the onions on medium-low heat, covered, for 10 minutes, turning twice. Remove the lid, raise the heat to medium and continue to fry for another 10 minutes, stirring often, until golden. Spread the onions over the pizza; sprinkle with sausages, black olives and cheese. Bake as above.

Pesto, Sun-Dried Tomatoes & Goat Cheese

1 tbsp	15 mL	Pesto (page 108) or Parsley Pesto (page 45)
3	3	sun-dried tomatoes, thinly sliced
1 oz	30 g	dry chèvre cheese, crumbled

Spread pesto over each pizza. Evenly distribute tomato slices and cheese. Bake as above.

Grilled Eggplant or Zucchini, Tomato & Mozzarella

1/4	1/4	medium eggplant or 1 small zucchini, cut lengthwise into 1/2-inch (1-cm) slices
		olive oil for brushing
		salt and pepper to taste
3 tbsp	45 mL	Tomato Sauce (page 103)
1/2 tsp	2 mL	chopped fresh oregano or 1/4 tsp (1 mL) dried
1/4 cup	50 mL	cubed Mozzarella or fontina cheese

Brush the eggplant or zucchini slices on both sides with olive oil and sprinkle with salt and pepper. Place them on a preheated grill pan or under a broiler on medium-high heat until soft and lightly browned, about 10 minutes. Spread the tomato sauce over the pizza. Place the eggplant or zucchini slices on top and sprinkle with oregano. Top with cheese. Bake as above.

Tapenade, Fresh Tomato & Asiago Cheese

2 tbsp	25 mL	Tapenade (page 12)
1	1	fresh tomato, sliced
1/2 tsp	2 mL	fresh thyme or 1/4 tsp (1 mL) dried
1/4 cup	50 mL	Asiago cheese, cut into small cubes

Spread tapenade on each pizza. Top with tomato slices and sprinkle with thyme and cheese. Bake as above.

Pesto

MAKES 1 1/2 CUPS (375 ML)
PREPARATION: 10 MINUTES

When fresh basil is available, classic pesto is simple to make and wonderful for tossing with pasta or spreading on pizza. Fresh parsley can replace basil.

2 cups	500 mL	fresh basil leaves, firmly packed
1	1	sprig parsley (optional)
1 or 2	1 or 2	garlic cloves
4 tbsp	50 mL	pine nuts, walnuts or blanched pistachios
1/4–1/3 cup	50–75 mL	olive oil
1/2 cup	125 mL	freshly grated Parmesan, or half-Parmesan, half-Romano cheese
		salt and freshly ground black pepper to taste

Chop the basil, parsley, if using, garlic and nuts in a blender or food proces- sor. While the machine is running, slowly pour in the oil. If using the pesto immediately, stir in the cheese and taste for salt and pepper. If you're using the pesto later, stir in the cheese just before serving and taste for salt and pepper. Cover the surface with a little oil and refrigerate or freeze.

Clam Sauce

MAKES 4 TO 6 SERVINGS
PREPARATION: 10 MINUTES
COOKING: 10 MINUTES

This clam sauce will be on the thin side, but it will thicken when tossed with unrinsed cooked pasta.

2 tbsp	25 mL	olive oil
2	2	garlic cloves, finely chopped
1	1	onion, finely chopped
2	2	5-oz (150-g) cans of clams
1/2 cup	125 mL	chopped parsley
		good pinch red pepper flakes
2/3 cup	150 mL	dry white wine and/or juice from clams
1 cup	250 mL	whipping cream or 18% cream
		salt to taste, depending on saltiness of clams
1 lb	500 g	spaghetti or linguini

In a skillet, heat the oil and cook the garlic and onion on medium-low heat, covered, for 5 minutes, stirring often. Drain the clams and reserve the juice. Stir in the parsley and red pepper, then add the wine or clam juice and cream and simmer for 5 minutes to reduce the liquid by a quarter. Add the clams. Season to taste with salt and keep warm until ready to serve.

Long-Grain White Rice

MAKES 4 TO 6 SERVINGS
PREPARATION: 2 MINUTES
COOKING: 20 MINUTES

To achieve that "perfect" rice, I learned a great lesson from an East Indian restaurateur. Rinse, then cook the rice for 15 minutes without peeking, lift the lid and let the steam out — in India they say "let the devil out"— fluff it, cover and leave for 5 minutes. Delicious!

1 1/2 cups	375 mL	hot water or stock
1/2 tsp	2 mL	salt
1 cup	250 mL	long-grain rice

To rinse the rice, place it in a sieve and run tap water over it briefly. Bring the water or stock and salt to a hard boil in a medium saucepan. Stir in the rice. Cover and reduce the heat to low. Cook for 15 minutes without lifting the lid. Turn off heat then lift the lid and fluff up the rice with a fork. Replace the lid for 5 or 6 minutes more before serving.

Asian Short-Grain White Rice

MAKES 4 SERVINGS
PREPARATION: 5 MINUTES
COOKING: 18 MINUTES

Salt is not added to this "sticky" rice since it's usually served with foods that have been flavored with salty tasting soy or fish sauce.

1 cup	250 mL	short-grain rice
1 cup	250 mL	cold water

Cover the rice with cold water in a saucepan. Gently rub the rice to release the starch. Drain in a sieve. Repeat this process several times until the water runs clear. Return the rice to the saucepan and add the water. Bring to a boil, cover and reduce the heat to low. Leave for 18 minutes without lifting the lid. Remove the pan from the heat and use a wooden paddle (the rice will not stick to it) to serve the rice.

Herbed Brown Rice

MAKES 4 TO 6 SERVINGS
PREPARATION: 3 MINUTES
COOKING: 40 MINUTES

Because this rice has the bran left on, it takes about 20 minutes longer than white rice to absorb the liquid and fully cook.

2 cups	500 mL	water or stock
1 tsp	5 mL	salt (if using water)
1 cup	250 mL	brown rice
2 tsp	10 mL	fresh chopped thyme, oregano, basil or rosemary or 1 tsp (5 mL) dried

In a medium saucepan, bring the water and salt or stock to a boil. Rinse the rice in a sieve and add it to the boiling liquid. When it returns to the boil, cover, reduce the heat to low and cook for 40 minutes. Turn off heat. Toss the rice to let the steam out. Cover and leave for 5 or 6 minutes. Toss in the herbs.

Risotto Milanese

MAKES 3 TO 4 SERVINGS
PREPARATION: 5 MINUTES
COOKING: 20 TO 25 MINUTES

The frequent stirring during cooking releases the starch in the rice and turns this into a rich and creamy dish. Serve as a separate course.

2 tbsp	25 mL	olive oil or butter
1/2	1/2	medium onion, finely chopped
1 cup	250 mL	short-grain rice (such as arborio), rinsed
1/3 cup	75 mL	dry white wine
3 cups	750 mL	hot Chicken Stock, or as needed (page 36)
3–4 tbsp	45–50 mL	freshly grated Parmesan cheese
1/2 tsp	2 mL	salt, or to taste

In a heavy saucepan, heat the oil or butter. Add the onions and sauté on medium heat for about 5 minutes. Add the rice and stir to coat well. Pour in the wine and cook, stirring often, until the liquid is absorbed. Ladle in 1/2 cup (125 mL) stock at a time, stirring often, until the rice absorbs all the liquid, is barely tender and the mixture is creamy, 15 to 20 minutes. Stir in the cheese. Taste and add salt if needed. Serve immediately.

Barley & Mushroom Pilaf

MAKES 4 TO 6 SERVINGS
PREPARATION: 10 MINUTES
COOKING: 50 MINUTES

Barley is a grain with great flavor and a delightful chewiness. Toasting it adds a delicious, nutty taste. It's wonderful in soups and makes a good substitute for rice in recipes.

1 cup	250 mL	pearl barley
2 tbsp	25 mL	olive oil or butter
3	3	garlic cloves, minced
1/2	1/2	medium onion, finely chopped
2 tsp	10 mL	chopped fresh thyme or 1 tsp (5 mL) dried
1	1	red bell pepper, diced
3 cups	750 mL	Chicken, Beef or Vegetable Stock (page 35 or 36)
1/2 tsp	2 mL	salt, or to taste
1/2 lb	250 g	button or shiitake mushrooms, washed, thinly sliced
1/3 cup	75 mL	chopped parsley or cilantro
1/4 tsp	1 mL	freshly ground black pepper

In a dry, medium-sized saucepan, toast the barley over medium heat, stirring often, until it's fragrant and slightly brown, about 4 minutes. Remove the barley and reserve. In the same pan, heat half the oil or butter and sauté the garlic and onion until softened, about 5 minutes. Stir in the barley, thyme and red pepper. Add the stock and bring to the boil. Season with salt, if needed. Cover, reduce the heat to medium-low and cook for about 40 minutes until the barley is tender and slightly chewy and the liquid is absorbed.

Meanwhile, in a medium skillet, heat the remaining oil or butter on high heat and stir-fry the mushrooms, for about 1 minute. Remove and reserve the mushrooms.

Fluff up the barley with a fork and stir in the black pepper, mushrooms, parsley or cilantro. Serve immediately.

Rosemary-Scented Millet & Quinoa Pilaf

MAKES 4 SERVINGS
PREPARATION: 10 MINUTES
COOKING: 20 MINUTES

These two high-protein grains in combination make a delightful vegetarian main dish, especially when the grains are toasted. Either grain can be used alone in the recipe.

1 cup	250 mL	millet
1/2 cup	125 mL	quinoa, rinsed, well drained
1 tbsp	15 mL	olive oil
1	1	small onion, finely chopped
1 1/2 tsp	7 mL	chopped fresh rosemary or 1/2 tsp (2 mL) dried
2 cups	500 mL	Chicken or Vegetable Stock (page 36)
1 cup	250 mL	fresh or frozen peas
1/2 tsp	2 mL	salt, or to taste
1/4 tsp	1 mL	freshly ground black pepper
1/4 cup	50 mL	chopped parsley or cilantro

In a medium saucepan, toast the millet and quinoa over medium heat, stirring often, until the grains turn golden brown and begin to "pop," after 6 or 7 minutes. Remove the grains and reserve.

In the same pan, heat the oil over medium-low heat and sauté the onion for about 6 minutes, without browning. Add the rosemary and sauté for another minute. Stir in the toasted grains and stock. Cover and cook on low heat for 15 minutes.

Add the peas and cook for 3 minutes or until all the liquid is absorbed. Fluff with a fork. The grains should be slightly crunchy and still keep their form. Season with salt, if needed, and pepper. Stir in parsley or cilantro and serve.

Golden Rice Pilaf with Cashews & Raisins

MAKES 4 TO 6 SERVINGS
PREPARATION: 8 MINUTES
COOKING: 20 MINUTES

This is a favorite rice to serve with Indian curries or roast chicken. In pilafs, the grains are sautéed in hot fat and then heated liquid is added.

2 tbsp	25 mL	butter or olive oil
1/2 cup	125 mL	unsalted cashews
1/2 cup	125 mL	raisins
1/2	1/2	onion, finely chopped
1 cup	250 mL	long-grain rice, rinsed
1 1/2 cups	375 mL	Chicken or Vegetable Stock, heated (page 36)
1/2 tsp	2 mL	salt, or to taste
1 tbsp	15 mL	finely chopped fresh parsley or dill

In a medium saucepan, heat the butter or oil over medium-high heat, stir in the cashews and stir until they turn golden. Stir in the raisins and continue to stir constantly for another minute until they puff up. Remove the raisins and cashews and reserve. Add the onion and rice to the pan and sauté, stirring, until they are golden brown, 5 or 6 minutes. Stir in the hot stock and salt, if needed, and bring to a boil. Reduce the heat to low, cover and cook for 15 minutes. Turn off the heat, lift the lid, fluff with a fork, stir in the raisins and nuts and cover for 5 or 6 minutes. To serve, garnish with herbs.

Wild Rice Pilaf with Cranberries

MAKES 4 TO 6 SERVINGS
PREPARATION: 10 MINUTES
COOKING: 50 TO 60 MINUTES

Wild rice goes well with game meats and salmon. In place of fresh or frozen cranberries, use dried cherries, blueberries or cranberries.

1 tbsp	15 mL	butter or vegetable oil
1	1	medium onion, diced
1 tbsp	15 mL	chopped fresh sage or 2 tsp (10 mL) dried, crumbled
1 cup	250 mL	wild rice, washed
2 cups	500 mL	water or Chicken Stock (page 36)
1 tsp	5 mL	salt, or to taste
1 cup	250 mL	fresh or frozen cranberries

In a medium saucepan, heat the butter or oil and sweat the onions on medium heat, covered, until tender, about 5 minutes. Be careful not to burn the onions. Stir in the sage and rice until combined. Add the stock or water and salt and bring to a simmer. Cover, and cook for 35 minutes on medium-low heat. Stir in the cranberries. Simmer for another 15 to 20 minutes, stirring twice, until the liquid is absorbed and the rice is tender but still has a "bite." Leave the rice to stand for 5 minutes before serving.

Polenta

MAKES 4 TO 6 SERVINGS
COOKING: 15 MINUTES

Polenta is a delicious Italian preparation, especially good with cheese and olive oil or pasta sauce. If left to cool, polenta becomes firm and can be grilled and served with meats or vegetables. The tastiest cornmeal is stone-ground, which should be stored in the freezer. Also available is "instant" polenta — quick but flavorless.

6 cups	1.5 L	cool water
2 tsp	10 mL	salt
1 1/2 cups	375 mL	medium-ground cornmeal
1/2 cup	125 mL	freshly grated Parmesan cheese
2–3 tbsp	25–45 mL	butter or olive oil

In a heavy saucepan, combine the water, salt and cornmeal. Bring to a boil, stirring the mixture with a wooden spoon as it thickens. Reduce the heat to low, cover and continue to gently cook for 15 to 20 minutes, stirring often so the polenta becomes soft and creamy. To serve, add the cheese and butter or oil, and more salt, if needed.

Grilled Polenta: Omit the butter and cheese in the recipe. Turn the cooked polenta onto a board, and shape it into a cake about 3/4 inch (2 cm) thick. Leave the polenta to cool until firm. Cut into squares, triangles or circles. Brush both sides with olive oil and grill for 3 minutes on each side until crisp and brown. Serve with grilled meat, chicken or vegetables.

Moroccan Vegetable Couscous

MAKES 4 TO 6 SERVINGS
PREPARATION: 15 MINUTES
COOKING: 35 TO 40 MINUTES

This is a North African all-in-one dish that my family loves to cook when friends get together. The traditional couscous dish is made in a cous-cousière, but I find it works well when it's cooked in a colander over a saucepan. Couscous grains can be soaked in water, but when they're steamed the flavor and texture is unmatched.

2	2	medium onions, sliced
2 tbsp	25 mL	olive oil
3 or 4	3 or 4	garlic cloves, chopped
2 tsp	10 mL	ground cumin
1 tsp	5 mL	ground cinnamon
1 tsp	5 mL	freshly grated ginger
1/2 tsp	2 mL	red pepper flakes, or to taste
2	2	tomatoes, peeled and chopped, or 1/2 cup (125 mL) canned, diced tomatoes
1	1	medium carrots, cut into large dice
1	1	medium sweet potato, cut into large dice
1	1	small white turnip, cut into large dice
1	1	19-oz (540-mL) can chickpeas, drained, rinsed
1/2 cup	125 mL	raisins or apricots cut into quarters
3 cups	750 mL	water
1/4 tsp	1 mL	saffron threads, lightly packed, or 1 tsp (5 mL) turmeric
2 tbsp	25 mL	lemon juice
2 tsp	10 mL	salt, or to taste
1/2 tsp	2 mL	freshly ground black pepper, or to taste
2 cups	500 mL	quick-cooking couscous
5 oz	150 g	fresh spinach, stems removed, chopped
1 tbsp	15 mL	chopped fresh cilantro
1 or 2 tbsp	15 or 25 mL	butter
1/3 cup	75 mL	blanched, sliced almonds, or pistachios

If you don't have a couscousière, you can create one by using a large saucepan for the stew and placing a colander or sieve on top. The bottom of the colander must be above the level of the simmering stew. The lid should cover the colander and pot, but if it doesn't, seal in the steam by twisting 1 or 2 wet towels and wrapping around the exposed area.

Heat the saucepan and sauté the onions in the olive oil for 3 minutes on medium-low heat until soft. Add the garlic, cumin, cinnamon, ginger and pepper flakes and continue to sauté for 2 minutes, stirring often. Stir in the tomatoes, carrots, sweet potato, turnip, chickpeas, raisins or apricots, water, saffron, lemon juice, salt and pepper. Bring to a gentle simmer, then remove the pan from the heat while you prepare the couscous.

Lightly brush the couscousière or colander with olive oil so the couscous doesn't stick to it. In a small bowl, wet the couscous grains with warm water and drain. Leave for 3 minutes so the grains begin to swell. This prevents the grains from falling through the holes in the colander. Return the stew to the heat and when it begins to simmer, set the colander with the couscous over it. Cover to allow the fragrant steam to cook the grains. Wrap any opening around the lid with wet towels, if needed, and gently cook for 8 minutes.

Carefully remove the towels, lid and colander from the pan. Stir the grains with a rubber spatula. When cool enough to handle, gently rub the couscous between your hands to break up the clumps. Return colander to the pan, cover, rewrap and cook for 10 minutes. Lift the colander and fluff the couscous again. Add the spinach and cilantro to the stew. Return the colander to the pot, cover and cook 5 minutes or until the vegetables are tender.

Remove the colander. Add the butter and fluff the couscous with a fork, then mound it onto a platter. Make a large well in the center and fill it with the stew. Sprinkle on almonds or pistachios and serve.

Chickpea Patties in Pita Bread

MAKES 4 TO 6 SERVINGS
PREPARATION: 10 MINUTES
COOKING: 6 TO 8 MINUTES

Even non-vegetarians will enjoy this Middle Eastern patty accompanied by a variety of spreads.

1	1	bread slice, crusts removed, cut into quarters
2 tbsp	25 mL	water or Vegetable Stock (page 36)
1 or 2	1 or 2	garlic cloves, depending on size, coarsely chopped
1/2	1/2	medium onion, finely chopped
1 tsp	5 mL	cumin
1/4 tsp	1 mL	cayenne pepper
1	1	19-oz (540-mL) can chickpeas, drained and rinsed
1	1	egg
2 tbsp	25 mL	olive oil
1/2 cup	125 mL	Guacamole (page 23)
1 or 2	1 or 2	fresh tomatoes, cut into slices (optional)
4	4	thin slices of onion (optional)
1 cup	250 mL	lettuce, washed and coarsely chopped (optional)
4	4	pita breads, warmed

Place the bread, water, garlic, onion, spices, chickpeas and egg in a food processor and pulse on and off just until finely chopped but not puréed. Form into 8 1/2-inch (1-cm) thick patties and chill for 20 minutes to firm.

Add the oil to a large skillet or grill pan on medium-high heat and fry the patties until golden brown on both sides, or barbecue on medium heat for about 4 minutes.

Meanwhile, cut the pitas in half and warm in a 300°F (150°C) oven for 5 minutes. Spread a layer of guacamole inside each pita half and slip in a patty with the tomato, onion slices and lettuce, if using. Serve warm.

Baked Beans with Aromatic Herbs

MAKES 4 TO 6 SERVINGS
PREPARATION AND SOAKING: 2 HOURS, OVERNIGHT SOAKING
BAKING: ABOUT 3 HOURS

The times for precooking beans can vary from 45 minutes to 2 hours depending on the age and dryness of the beans, so testing is important. Slow cooking in the oven allows the beans to absorb the flavors. Canned white beans can be used instead, but they still need all the oven time.

2 cups	500 mL	dried navy, great northern or pea beans
2 tbsp	25 mL	olive or vegetable oil
1	1	medium onion, peeled and finely chopped
3	3	garlic cloves, chopped
1	1	celery stalk, finely chopped
2	2	medium carrots, finely chopped
1	1	red or green bell pepper, seeded, chopped
1 tbsp	15 mL	chopped fresh oregano or 2 tsp (10 mL) dried
1 tbsp	15 mL	chopped fresh rosemary or 2 tsp (10 mL) dried
1 tbsp	15 mL	chopped fresh thyme leaves or 2 tsp (10 mL) dried
2	2	bay leaves
2 tbsp	25 mL	maple syrup
		generous dash of hot pepper sauce
1 tsp	5 mL	salt, or to taste

Rinse the beans to remove any grit or pebbles. Cover the beans with water, soak overnight, drain and discard water. Place the beans in a saucepan with enough fresh water to cover them. Bring to a gentle simmer (do not boil as the beans will toughen), cover and cook for 45 minutes or until the beans are tender and the skins have begun to burst. Older beans take longer to cook. Set aside.

Preheat the oven to 325°F (160°C). In a heavy saucepan or Dutch oven, on medium-low heat, stir together the oil, onion, garlic, celery and carrots. Cover and gently sweat for 5 minutes, stirring several times so the vegetables don't burn. Stir in the bell pepper, oregano, rosemary, thyme and bay leaves, cover and cook for another 5 minutes. Add beans with their cooking liquid, maple syrup and pepper sauce. If you are using a saucepan, transfer the mixture to an ovenproof casserole with a lid and bake the beans for 2 hours, checking often, to make sure the beans have not dried out. Add a little water, if the beans have dried. Season with salt near the end of cooking.

Fish & Seafood

When I was small and spent summers with my family at our cottage in Quebec, fishing for bass and pike was a serious occupation for Dad.

We three daughters weren't quite so avid, so we took along our books, but kept them well hidden. The best part of the day was the shore lunch, with the heavy iron pan over a hot fire. It sizzled with bacon fat for the freshly caught fish, fried sliced potatoes, onions and baked beans. Tea boiled in a tin can and raisin pie from Dad's bakery were the finishing touches. Ummm!

Fortunately, fresh fish is available year-round no matter how far you live from water. There are hundreds of varieties of fish and shellfish. Oily fish are particularly important to our diet since they contain vital omega-3 fatty acids, which provide complete proteins. Oily fish include: salmon, arctic char, trout, turbot, mackerel, king fish, sardines, sea bass and herring. Lean fish are: cod, haddock, sole, halibut, red snapper, swordfish, tuna, monkfish, grouper and marlin. Lean fish are

delicious, but be careful not to overcook or they will dry out.

The store where you buy your fish should be sweet-smelling with no "fishy" odor. If the store, or the fish, smell "off" the fish is past its prime. Look for fish that have shiny eyes and clean gills. If you're buying raw fish, or shellfish, the flesh will feel mushy.

Fish is best when cooked rare to medium so that it stays moist and tender. The average cooking time for frying, broiling or grilling fillets or steaks is 6 to 8 minutes per inch (2.5 cm) thickness of the fish when measured at its thickest part. When barbecuing, put the lid down to cook the fish quickly. You'll know the fish is ready when the flesh turns opaque and the juices turn white. The flesh should flake easily from the bones when touched. Remove fish from the heat as soon as it's ready, to avoid overcooking.

You needn't serve only white wine with fish, although that is the common recommendation. I also enjoy lighter reds such as Beaujolais, Pinot Noir or Italian Valpolicella. If you prefer white, a well-chilled Riesling or Sauvignon Blanc works well with simple dishes, and a New World Chardonnay or a Burgundy is lovely with more complex creations.

The rules for cooking fish also apply to shellfish; cook simply for the shortest time possible and be certain not to overcook.

Here are some of the most common available seafoods:

- Lobster are known for their delicious rich meat. Rock lobsters are the claw-less cousins of the lobster and are used primarily for their tails.

- Shrimp can be one of several species, from small prawns to large tiger shrimp. Normally, the shrimp we buy have been frozen, although you can sometimes order them fresh at extra expense.

- Oysters are a royal treat at their flavor-ful best (in months with an "R" in them). Oysters from cold waters are superior in taste to those from warm waters and some of the very best tasting come from New Brunswick and Prince Edward Island.

- Mussels are usually commercially bred in hanging ropes in ocean bays. Wild mussels are more flavorful, but harder to find and clean than cultivated ones.

- Squid is a variety of cephalopod with a slender, white body and 10 tentacles. Squid is available, fresh or frozen, year-round.

Sole in Creamy Tomato Sauce

MAKES 4 TO 6 SERVINGS
PREPARATION: 8 TO 10 MINUTES
COOKING: 12 TO 15 MINUTES

Sole is a saltwater flatfish (flounder and halibut are larger flatfish) with a sweet, pearly-white texture that is delicious in this sauce.

1 lb	500 g	sole fillets
		salt and pepper for sprinkling
1/2	1/2	medium onion, finely chopped
		pinch thyme
1/2	1/2	bay leaf
3 tbsp	45 mL	butter, cut in small pieces
1/3 cup	75 mL	dry white wine or water with 1 tbsp (15 mL) lemon juice
1	1	tomato, peeled, seeded and chopped, juice reserved
2 tbsp	25 mL	all-purpose flour
1/2 cup	125 mL	table or half-and-half cream
		salt and freshly ground pepper to taste
2 tbsp	25 mL	finely chopped parsley

Preheat the oven to 350°F (180°C). Place the fish in a shallow ovenproof dish. Sprinkle with salt and pepper. Cover the fish with the onion, thyme, bay leaf and half the butter. Pour on the wine or water and reserved tomato juice. Bake for 12 to 14 minutes or until the fish flakes. Brush away the onion mixture from the fish and reserve. Discard the bay leaf. Gently lift the fish onto a platter and keep it warm, reserving the pan juices.

In a small saucepan, melt the remaining butter, stir in the flour and cook for 1 minute. Whisk in the reserved onion mixture and cook for 2 minutes more. Stir in the cream and cook for another minute. Taste for salt and pepper and adjust. Pour the sauce over the fish and garnish with tomato cubes and parsley.

Trout Meunière

MAKES 4 TO 6 SERVINGS
PREPARATION: 5 MINUTES
COOKING: 6 TO 8 MINUTES

This classic French recipe name means "miller's wife," from the old days when the miller, waiting for the flour to be milled, would go fishing in the nearby river. If he was successful, his wife would dip the whole fish in flour and cook it. If you have the courage to cook the fish with the head and tail left on, it will be very moist and, I think, tastier. It's simple to pull out the fins and the head after the fish is cooked rather than before. Covering the trout while frying keeps it moist.

4 or 6	4 or 6	fresh trout, about 10 oz (300 g) each with head and tail, cleaned
1/2 cup	125 mL	all-purpose flour
1 tsp	5 mL	salt
1/4 tsp	1 mL	freshly ground black pepper
3 tbsp	45 mL	butter
1 tbsp	15 mL	vegetable oil
		juice of 1 lemon
2 tbsp	25 mL	butter, cut into pieces
1 tbsp	15 mL	drained capers
1	1	lemon, cut into 8 wedges for garnish
3 tbsp	45 mL	finely chopped parsley

Rinse the trout under cold tap water and dry with a paper towel. Combine the flour, salt and pepper on a pie plate and dredge each trout in the flour, shaking off the excess. In a large skillet, over medium heat, add half the first amount of butter and oil. Fry the trout, covered, until golden brown, for about 4 minutes, then turn the fish and cook for another 3 minutes or until the flesh flakes easily along the backbone. It may be necessary to cook the trout in 2 batches with the remaining butter and oil to avoid overcrowding the pan.

Transfer the trout to a heated serving platter. Pull out the fins and peel off the skin. Flip the fish over and remove the skin from the other side.

To make the sauce, use a lifter to scrape up and loosen any brown bits in the pan. Stir in the lemon juice, butter and capers, stirring the sauce briskly for a few seconds. Pour over the trout. For the garnish, dip one side of each lemon wedge into the parsley and place on the trout.

Grilled Fish Steaks

MAKES 4 TO 6 SERVINGS
PREPARATION: 10 TO 12 MINUTES
COOKING: 6 TO 10 MINUTES

Most fish are delicately flavored and best prepared with a simple marinade left on for a brief time. This recipe offers a choice of two marinades and two chutneys for extra flavor. A fillet will take half the time required to cook a bone-in steak.

6	6	5-oz (150-g) boneless salmon or halibut steaks, 3/4 inch (2 cm) thick
		salt and freshly ground pepper
		1 recipe Lemon & Oil Marinade or Balsamic Marinade
		1 recipe Tomato Coconut Chutney or Mango Ginger Chutney (page 125)

Marinate the fish steaks in your choice of marinade for 5 to 10 minutes.

Preheat a grill, barbecue or grill pan on medium heat. Lightly oil a barbecue rack. Sprinkle the fish with salt and pepper just before cooking.

Place the fish about 4 inches (10 cm) from the heat source and cook for 3 to 4 minutes on each side until golden brown. The fish is cooked when you see the juices turn white and the flesh flakes, but is firm and tender. There is a tiny window between underdone and overdone fish, so cook just until the desired degree of doneness is reached. Serve with the Tomato Coconut Chutney or Mango Ginger Chutney.

Lemon & Oil Marinade

4 tbsp	50 mL	fresh lemon juice
		olive oil for brushing

Brush both sides of the fish with lemon juice, then with olive oil. Leave for 5 or 10 minutes.

Balsamic Marinade

3 tbsp	45 mL	balsamic vinegar
2 tsp	10 mL	brown sugar
		olive oil for brushing

Combine the vinegar and sugar. Brush both sides of the fish with the marinade and the olive oil.

Tomato Coconut Chutney

MAKES 1¹/₂ CUPS (375 ML)
PREPARATION: 5 TO 8 MINUTES

2	2	ripe tomatoes or 1 cup (250 mL) diced tomatoes
¹/₃ cup	75 mL	grated coconut
1 tsp	5 mL	chopped jalapeno pepper, or to taste
¹/₄–¹/₂ tsp	1–2 mL	salt, or to taste

Place tomatoes, coconut and jalapeno in a food processor and pulse on and off until the tomatoes are chopped into small pieces. Season to taste. Serve at room temperature.

Mango Ginger Chutney

MAKES APPROXIMATELY 1¹/₄ CUPS (300 ML)
PREPARATION: 10 MINUTES

1	1	large fresh ripe mango or 1 19-oz (540-mL) can of mango, drained
1	1	¹/₂-inch (1-cm) piece of fresh ginger, peeled and chopped
1 tbsp	15 mL	fresh lemon juice
¹/₄ tsp	1 mL	salt, or to taste

If using fresh mango, peel and cut the flesh from the pit. Place the mango, ginger and lemon juice in a food processor or blender and pulse on and off just until the mango is cut into small pieces. Season to taste with salt.

Baked Butterflied Fish with Spinach Stuffing & Caper Sauce

MAKES 6 SERVINGS
PREPARATION: 20 MINUTES
COOKING: 12 TO 18 MINUTES, DEPENDING ON THICKNESS

At my cooking school, this was a favorite. I know the thought of cooking a large, whole fish such as salmon or white fish might be overwhelming, but any fishmonger will "butterfly" the fish for you. This means the backbone and rib cage are removed while still leaving the fish whole. It makes an attractive presentation and renders the fish much easier to serve. If you want to butterfly the fish yourself, the directions follow this recipe. A whole fish can be poached in a fish stock, but I find enclosing the fish in foil with a stuffing is the best method, developed by Canada's Department of Agriculture. If serving the fish chilled, bake as above but without stuffing. If possible, avoid overnight chilling as the fish becomes firm and the flavor is diminished.

4 oz	120 g	fresh spinach, thick stems removed, finely chopped
2 tbsp	25 mL	chopped fresh mint or 1 tbsp (15 mL) dried
2 tbsp	25 mL	chopped fresh tarragon or 1 tbsp (15 mL) dried
2	2	green onions, finely chopped
1/2 tsp	2 mL	salt, or to taste
		oil for brushing
2–3 lbs	1–1.5 kg	fresh, whole salmon or white fish, butterflied
		parsley or watercress for garnish
1	1	lemon, cut into slices or wedges for garnish
		1 recipe Caper Sauce (page 127)

To make the stuffing, mix the spinach, mint, tarragon and onions together and add salt to taste.

Prepare a length of heavy foil extending several inches beyond each end of the fish and brush the foil's entire surface with vegetable oil. This step is important, particularly where the head and tail touch, as they will stick to the foil. Lay the fish on the foil and press the prepared stuffing into the cavity. Bring up the sides and ends of the foil and tightly twist to enclose the fish. Measure the height of the thickest section of the foil "package" and calculate the baking time at 10 to 12 minutes per inch (2.5 cm). Place the fish package on a baking sheet and bake for the calculated time.

To test for doneness, carefully open the foil and gently press your finger along the backbone. If the fish flakes, it is cooked. Gently pull out the fins. Pull off the top skin, if desired. Crumple the foil around the fish as a lifting aid. Gently lift the foil with the fish and tilt it over a bowl to pour off the liquid for the caper sauce. Gently flip the fish onto a heated platter. Remove the skin from the exposed side, if desired. Decorate with parsley or watercress, and lemon. Serve with Caper Sauce.

Caper Sauce

MAKES 2 CUPS (500 ML)
PREPARATION: 10 TO 12 MINUTES
COOKING: 6 MINUTES

2 tbsp	25 mL	butter
2 tbsp	25 mL	flour
1/2 cup	125 mL	reserved fish liquid or water
1 cup	250 mL	milk or cream or Chicken Stock (page 36)
2 tbsp	25 mL	capers with juice (if large, coarsely chop)
2 tbsp	25 mL	lemon juice
1/2 tsp	2 mL	salt, or to taste

Melt the butter in a small saucepan and stir in the flour. Cook over medium-low heat for 1 minute. Whisk in the reserved fish liquid and milk, stock or cream until thick and smooth. Cook for 5 minutes, stirring several times. Stir in the capers with juice, and lemon juice, and cook for 1 minute. Season with salt. Serve hot.

To butterfly a cleaned fish, lay the fish flat, open side facing you, on the work surface. Use a sharp boning or utility knife to separate the meat from the backbone. Begin at the tail and insert the tip of the knife into the meat so it lies flat on the backbone without penetrating the skin at the back of the fish. Gently move the knife to cut the flesh off the backbone, going from the tail to the gut opening.

Flip the fish over and repeat as above. With scissors, snip the backbone from the tail. Using the loosened backbone as a "handle," begin to pull gently, separating the rib cage from the flesh, using the knife as an aid. Now, separate the backbone from the head with scissors. Leave the head and tail on if desired. Open the fish with the skin side on the work surface. Rub your fingers over the flesh to find any small bones still left in the fish and remove them with tweezers or pliers.

Chinese Lemon Sea Scallops with Broccoli Stir-Fry

MAKES 4 TO 6 SERVINGS
PREPARATION: 20 MINUTES
COOKING: 5 MINUTES

There are two scallop varieties, bay and sea scallops. The large white sea scallops grow in cold water while the tiny dark bay scallops come from warmer waters. The delicate flavor of scallops comes alive in this stir-fry and the scallops almost melt in the mouth if they're not overcooked. Have all the ingredients organized before cooking so your timing is just right.

1 lb	500 g	bay scallops or sea scallops, cut in half
4–6	4–6	green onions, cut into 1/2-inch (1-cm) pieces, or 1 leek
1	1	head broccoli
1 tbsp	15 mL	cornstarch
1/4 cup	50 mL	water or Chicken Stock (page 36)
2 tbsp	25 mL	vegetable oil
2 tsp	10 mL	finely grated fresh ginger
2 tsp	10 mL	lemon juice
1 tbsp	15 mL	light soy sauce
		salt to taste

Wash the scallops and dry them well. If using a leek, cut off the tough green part. Cut the leek in half lengthwise and wash well to remove grit. Cut the broccoli head into small florets. Cut the small broccoli stems into julienne (see Glossary). Discard the tough, thick stem. Reserve. Combine cornstarch with water or stock. Reserve.

Heat half the oil in a wok or medium skillet over high heat and sear the scallops in 2 batches so the pan is not overcrowded. Turn the scallops constantly until they turn opaque and lightly golden, about 1 minute. Remove and reserve.

Heat the remaining oil on medium heat and fry the onions or leeks with the ginger for 1 minute. Add the broccoli with 2 tbsp (25 mL) water, cover and stir-fry for 2 minutes until tender-crisp. Push the broccoli to one side of the pan and add the cornstarch mixture. Cook until thickened, about 1/2 minute. Combine with the broccoli and stir in the scallops, lemon juice and soy sauce. Stir for 1/2 minute longer, then taste and adjust for salt and serve.

Shrimp Creole

MAKES 4 TO 6 SERVINGS
PREPARATION: 5 MINUTES
COOKING: 18 MINUTES

During a trip to Florida many years ago, this recipe was given to me by a shrimp fisherman who taught me how to cook shrimp in seawater or well-salted water. I still remember the way the shrimp melted in my mouth. You will love this dish!

1 lb	500 g	uncooked medium-sized shrimp, with shells
2 tbsp	25 mL	olive oil
1 tbsp	15 mL	butter
4	4	green onions, finely sliced
1	1	garlic clove, minced
1¼ cups	300 mL	canned diced tomatoes or 4 ripe tomatoes, peeled and chopped
1 tsp	5 mL	granulated sugar
1 tbsp	15 mL	vinegar
½ tsp	2 mL	oregano
1–2 tsp	5–10 mL	ground red chili pepper
1 tsp	5 mL	salt

To a saucepan of cold water add 1 tsp (5 mL) salt per cup (250 mL) water and the shrimp. Bring to a boil, then drain immediately. Remove the shells, black veins and tails.

Heat the oil and butter in a skillet over medium heat and sauté the onion and garlic for 2 minutes, covered, just until soft but not brown. Add the tomatoes, sugar, vinegar, oregano and chili pepper. Cook for 15 minutes. Add the shrimp and salt to taste. Heat for 30 seconds and serve.

Lobster with Clarified Butter

MAKES 4 TO 6 SERVINGS
COOKING: 6 TO 8 MINUTES

Although most fresh lobsters weigh 1 to 1½ lbs (500 to 750 g) there is more meat and less waste in larger lobsters. Every part of the lobster holds succulent meat, from the tail to the claws. Seawater is best for cooking lobster but second best is well-salted water — 1 tsp (5 mL) salt to 1 cup (250 mL) cold water. The method described below puts the lobster gently to sleep.

3 qts	3 L	cold water
¼ cup	50 mL	salt
4 or 6	4 or 6	live lobsters, about 1 to 1½ lbs (500 to 750 g) each
2	2	lemons, cut into wedges
½ cup	125 mL	clarified butter

Fill a large stockpot with cold, salted water. To prevent overcrowding the lobsters in the pot, cook them in 2 lots. Add the live lobsters. Place the pot on the stove and bring to a high heat. As soon as the water comes to a rolling boil and the lobsters have turned bright pink, remove them with tongs and place them on a large platter with lemon wedges. Serve clarified butter in small individual bowls so all diners have their own.

To tackle the lobster, twist off the claws and use a nutcracker to crack and split them, then remove the meat with a fork. Twist the body to separate the tail. Turn the tail over on its back, then cut the thin shell through to the meat with a knife or scissors and lift out the meat. Cut through the upper part of the body and pick out any small bits of meat. Even the legs contain delicious morsels.

> To make clarified butter, heat it in a small saucepan on low heat until the oil has separated from the milk solids.

Beer-Steamed Mussels

MAKES 4 TO 6 SERVINGS
PREPARATION: 12 TO 15 MINUTES
COOKING: 5 MINUTES

Enjoying a bowl of steaming mussels, crusty bread and a glass of cold beer or dry white wine is an experience not to be missed. You can use cultivated or wild mussels. Wild mussels are harvested from rocks on the ocean bed and have more flavor. They need to soak for 1 hour in cold water with a handful of cornmeal added to help flush out any grit and sand. Then the shells should be scrubbed and the "beards" (their clinging mechanism) removed. Cultivated mussels are grown in a controlled environment, and thus need less washing.

3–4 lbs	1.5–2 kg	fresh cultivated mussels in the shell
1 tbsp	15 mL	butter
3 or 4	3 or 4	garlic cloves, minced
1/2 tsp	2 mL	thyme
1 1/2 cups	375 mL	beer or ale (not dark)
1/2 tsp	2 mL	salt
1/4 tsp	1 mL	freshly ground black pepper, or to taste
2 tbsp	25 mL	finely chopped parsley or chives

Scrub the mussels well under cold water, rinse with fresh cold water and discard any that float or have open shells. Remove the "beards." Drain. In a saucepan large enough to hold the mussels, heat the butter on low heat and sweat the garlic and thyme, covered, for 3 minutes. Add the beer or ale.

Bring to a boil, add the mussels, cover and cook 5 minutes on medium-high heat. Lift the mussels out of the juice and place them in a serving bowl or individual soup bowls, discarding any that have failed to open. Season the juice with salt and pepper and pour over the mussels. Garnish with parsley or chives.

Poultry

Luckily, we are able to get all kinds of fresh poultry in modern markets for our culinary pursuits.

Unluckily, not all of the available birds are flavorful. This is because most of the poultry we buy has been raised commercially on a diet that includes chemicals and antibiotics, which means it has less flavor than the more expensive organically raised poultry. If the poultry has been water-chilled (faster and cheaper) instead of air-chilled, the flavor is also compromised.

Fortunately, we can do something to maximize the flavor of our poultry: cook it with the skin left on and the bones left in. Recently, there has been much discussion about taking the skin off before cooking poultry, chicken in particular. It's true that the fatty part of the poultry is in the skin, but so is the flavor. If you grill, barbecue or roast the meat, the fat will drip away, leaving the skin crisp and the flavor magnificent!

Poultry requires careful handling. Here are a few easy-to-follow rules to help avoid cross-contamination and the accumulation of food-borne bacteria:

- Refrigerate poultry as soon as possible after purchase, especially during warm weather.
- Always wash your hands before and after handling raw poultry.
- When you've finished preparing raw poultry, wash all utensils and surfaces with soapy water.
- The safest way to defrost poultry is in the refrigerator, allowing 4 hours per lb (8 hours per kg).
- It isn't necessary to rinse poultry before preparing it, since all bacteria will be killed during cooking.

Cooking Tips
- The dark meat in legs and wings is muscle and gives more flavor but takes longer to cook than the white meat of the breast.
- Cook poultry until the juices run clear when the meat is pressed firmly on the underside.
- Avoid using a fork or knife to test doneness since it allows precious juices to escape.
- If using a meat thermometer insert into the thickest part of the poultry breast or leg avoiding the bone. It should read 170°F (77°C) for individual pieces and 180°F (83°C) for whole poultry stuffed or non-stuffed.

Tarragon Chicken Breasts

MAKES 4 SERVINGS
PREPARATION: 10 MINUTES
COOKING: 30 MINUTES

Most butchers will supply you with boned chicken breasts with the wing left on — it adds character to the dish. If that's not possible, use boneless chicken breasts and reduce the cooking time by 5 or 6 minutes.

4	4	boned chicken breasts with skin and wing
		salt and black pepper to taste
1 tbsp	15 mL	butter
1 tbsp	15 mL	vegetable oil
2 tbsp	25 mL	fresh tarragon or 1 tbsp (15 mL) dried
1 cup	250 mL	hot Chicken Stock (page 36)
1/4 cup	50 mL	heavy or light cream
		red or white pepper to taste

There are 3 parts to a chicken wing; with a sharp knife, cut off the first 2 sections. Sprinkle the chicken with salt and black pepper on both sides. In a large skillet, heat the butter and oil on medium-high heat and brown 2 of the chicken breasts at a time on both sides. When all of the chicken has been browned, drain off the fat.

Return the chicken to the skillet on medium-low heat and sprinkle on the tarragon. Add the stock and cover. Gently simmer for 15 minutes or until the meat separates from the wing bone when gently pressed. Remove the chicken with tongs to a warm platter and cover loosely. Using a spoon, skim the fat from the pan juices. Return the pan to medium-high heat and add the cream. Reduce the sauce by half, which takes about 5 minutes. Season with salt, if needed, and a pinch of red or white pepper. Pour the sauce over the chicken.

Barbecued or Broiled Chicken

MAKES 4 SERVINGS
PREPARATION: 5 MINUTES
MARINATING: 30 MINUTES OR LONGER
COOKING: 10 TO 12 MINUTES

I can't stress enough how much more flavor there is in chicken when it's cooked with the bone in and the skin left on, but please note that bone-in chicken takes longer to cook than boneless. Barbecuing or grilling on medium-low heat allows the chicken to cook without the fat hitting the heat source and causing a flare-up.

	4	4	single chicken breasts
or	4	4	whole legs cut at the joint into drumsticks and thighs
			1 recipe Ginger Soy Marinade, Mustard Marinade or 4-Spice Rub (page 135)

Choose either of the marinades that follow or the spice rub to prepare chicken before cooking. Chill the chicken with the marinade or rub for 30 minutes.

To barbecue or grill: Preheat the barbecue or grill to medium-low. Use a paper towel dipped in a little oil to rub on the rack to prevent sticking. Chicken cooks more quickly when the lid is closed during barbecuing.

Remove the chicken from the marinade and place, skin side down, on the grill until the skin is golden brown and crisp, reducing the heat if there is a flare-up. Cook for 8 to 10 minutes on each side for bone-in white meat, 10 to 12 minutes for bone-in dark meat, or 5 to 6 minutes for boneless. The bone-in chicken is done when it's firm at the thickest part and the juices are clear next to the bone. The boneless chicken is ready when it's firm at the thickest part.

To broil: Preheat the broiler. Use a paper towel dipped in a little oil to coat the rack. Remove the chicken from the marinade and place it on the rack over a pan, skin side up. Place the rack at least 10 inches (25 cm) from the heat source. Broil until golden and crisp, about 12 minutes per side for bone-in or 6 minutes per side for boneless.

Ginger Soy Marinade

3 tbsp	45 mL	soy sauce
1 tbsp	15 mL	vegetable oil
1/2 tsp	2 mL	granulated sugar
2 tsp	10 mL	minced fresh ginger
2	2	garlic cloves, minced
1/4 tsp	1 mL	freshly ground black pepper

Combine the soy, oil, sugar, ginger, garlic and pepper and toss with the chicken.

Mustard Marinade

3 tbsp	45 mL	Dijon mustard
1 tbsp	15 mL	honey or maple syrup
1 tbsp	15 mL	vegetable oil or melted butter
1 tbsp	15 mL	lemon juice or white wine vinegar

Combine the mustard, honey, oil and lemon juice or vinegar and coat the chicken.

4-Spice Rub

1 tsp	5 mL	whole cumin
1 tsp	5 mL	whole coriander seeds
1 tsp	5 mL	whole black pepper
1 tsp	5 mL	whole cloves
1 tbsp	15 mL	olive oil

In a small skillet over medium-low heat, toast the spices in a dry pan, shaking the pan often, until the fragrance rises, about 3 minutes. Transfer to a coffee or spice grinder, blender, or mortar and pestle and finely grind. If you are unable to grind the spices, use powdered, but the flavor of the spices will be weaker.

The spices can be stored, covered, for future use or transferred to a bowl mixed with the oil for immediate use. Rub the mixture on the chicken.

Chicken Fricassee

MAKES 4 TO 6 SERVINGS
PREPARATION: 30 MINUTES
COOKING: 1¹/₂ HOURS

In this recipe, the chicken is cooked in a smaller amount of liquid, giving the chicken and stock great flavor. I suggest you tear the chicken into finger-sized pieces rather than cut it into cubes as it's more appealing to the eye. The fricassee is great on its own but the Feather Dumplings are a perfect accompaniment.

1	1	whole, 3¹/₂-lb (1.75-kg) roasting chicken
1	1	onion, stuck with 4 whole cloves
2	2	carrots, cut into 3 pieces
1	1	bouquet garni tied in cheesecloth (see Glossary)
2 tsp	10 mL	salt
1¹/₂ cups	375 mL	cubed potatoes (optional)
5 tbsp	65 mL	chicken fat from stock, or butter
¹/₂ lb	250 g	mushrooms, sliced, about 2 cups (500 mL)
6 tbsp	75 mL	all-purpose flour
3 cups	750 mL	Chicken Stock (page 36)
¹/₂ cup	125 mL	dry white wine or Chicken Stock (page 36)
1 cup	250 mL	whipping cream
1 cup	250 mL	cooked carrots from the stock, sliced
¹/₂ cup	125 mL	frozen green peas or corn
1–2 tsp	5–10 mL	lemon juice
		salt and pepper to taste
		1 recipe Feather Dumplings (page 77) (optional)

Remove the fat and giblets from the chicken. Use a lidded saucepan large enough to hold the chicken, breast side up. Pour in enough very hot water to cover the legs but not the breast. Add the onion, carrots, bouquet garni and salt. Add the neck, heart and gizzard, if available. Freeze the liver for a future pâté. Bring the pot to a simmer, cover and gently cook on the stove for 1 to 1 ¹/₄ hours or until the chicken legs move freely in the sockets. Lift the chicken out and place it on a tray to cool for 10 minutes. Use a slotted spoon or wire-mesh lifter to remove the carrots and onion and reserve for sauce. Add the potatoes, if using, and cook just until tender. Remove and reserve. Remove the skin and the meat from the bones. Tear the meat into finger-sized pieces and reserve in the refrigerator. For a richer stock, return the bones to the saucepan with the stock and cook for another 30 minutes. Strain the stock, spoon off the fat and reserve both for sauce.

In a large saucepan, heat half the reserved fat or butter, on high heat and sauté the mushrooms quickly for 1 minute. Remove and reserve. Reduce the heat to medium, add the remaining fat, stir in the flour and cook for 1 minute. Whisk in the stock until smooth and cook gently for 5 minutes, stirring often, to avoid burning the bottom. Whisk in the wine or additional stock and cream. Season to taste with lemon juice, salt and pepper. Stir in the chicken, potatoes if using, carrots, peas or corn and mushrooms. Heat to serve or cook the Feather Dumplings on top of the fricassee, if desired.

Thai Chicken & Coconut Curry

MAKES 4 TO 6 SERVINGS
PREPARATION: 15 MINUTES
COOKING: 20 MINUTES

The basic Thai ingredients include fish sauce, red or green curry paste, and canned coconut milk (see Glossary). These are readily available in most supermarkets or Asian specialty stores. Soy sauce can be substituted but do try fish sauce — you'll like its delicate pungency.

1 lb	500 g	chicken breasts, bone and skin removed
1	1	14-oz (398-mL) can coconut milk
1 tbsp	15 mL	Thai red curry paste, or to taste
1/2 cup	125 mL	water or Chicken Stock (page 36)
1 tbsp	15 mL	lime or lemon juice
1 tsp	5 mL	granulated sugar
2 tbsp	25 mL	fish sauce
4 oz	120 g	snow peas, cut diagonally into 3 pieces, or frozen peas
10	10	basil leaves, sliced

Partially freeze the chicken to make it easier to cut into small or bite-sized pieces. Keep the chicken pieces chilled. Heat a wok or large skillet on high heat, add half the coconut milk and bring to a boil. Reduce the heat to a simmer and whisk in the curry paste until dissolved. Add the remaining coconut milk and simmer for 10 minutes until it thickens. Stir in the chicken, water or stock, and lime or lemon juice. Cook for 5 minutes. Add the sugar, fish sauce and peas and cook for 1 minute. Arrange the chicken in a serving dish and garnish with basil leaves.

Southern Fried Chicken with Cream Gravy

MAKES 4 TO 6 SERVINGS
PREPARATION: 1 HOUR AND 20 MINUTES
COOKING: 10 TO 12 MINUTES

This recipe for one of the South's most famous dishes is one I learned from a wonderful Southern cook who was well known for her cuisine. Traditionally, it's made from a cut-up whole chicken. This is an opportunity, if you like, to cut the chicken yourself. Otherwise you can buy it in separate pieces.

1	1	2- to 2¹/₂-lb (1- to 1.3-kg) fryer chicken cut into 8 pieces
¹/₂ cup	125 mL	milk
¹/₂ cup	125 mL	all-purpose flour
1 tsp	5 mL	salt
¹/₂ tsp	2 mL	freshly ground black pepper
		vegetable oil (part butter, if desired)
		1 recipe Cream Gravy (page 139)

To prepare the chicken for frying, place it in a bowl with the milk and marinate for 1 hour. Combine the flour, salt and pepper and sprinkle over the chicken. Toss the chicken to coat in a flour and milk paste. Put the chicken on a tray to dry for 10 minutes.

Pour ¹/₂ inch (1 cm) of oil into a heavy deep frying pan with straight sides and a lid, such as a cast iron Dutch oven or a heavy aluminum pan. Heat the oil on medium-high until hot — to test, hold your hand 2 inches (5 cm) above the oil to feel the heat radiating from the pan. Using tongs, gently place the chicken pieces skin side down, not touching, in the pan. The fat should come halfway up the chicken. Cover and fry until the chicken is golden brown on one side, about 4 minutes. Turn the chicken over. When the chicken is golden on all sides, turn the heat down to medium, cover and cook for another 10 minutes.

Remove the breast pieces and place them on a rack over a tray in a warm oven to keep crisp until serving time. Continue cooking the thighs and drumsticks for another 5 minutes and add them to the rack. Serve with warm Cream Gravy.

Cream Gravy

3 tbsp	45 mL	oil from fried chicken
4 tbsp	50 mL	all-purpose flour
1½ cups	375 mL	milk
½ cup	125 mL	18% cream or 35% whipping cream
		salt and pepper to taste

Heat the oil in a saucepan on medium heat and stir in the flour. Cook just until the flour turns golden, then whisk in the milk and cream until the gravy is smooth. Cook for 3 or 4 minutes. Season to taste.

To cut up a whole chicken, use a sharp utility or boning knife. Place the chicken, breast side up, on a cutting surface. Grasp one leg, pull it outwards and cut the skin between the breast and leg. Hold the chicken with one hand and bend the leg with the other hand onto the cutting board, exposing the joint that separates the leg from the body. Cut through the joint and the skin, including the small "oyster" or piece of meat snuggled in the backbone. Cut through the joint between the thigh and drumstick.

Place the carcass on its side and cut away the backbone from both breasts. Place the breast, skin side down, press down slightly and cut through the cartilage and breast bone to separate the breasts. Cut the wings off at the joint, along with 1 inch (2.5 cm) of the breast meat. Cut off the wing tip. Use the backbone and wing tips for stock.

Herb Roast Chicken with Pan Juices

MAKES 4 TO 6 SERVINGS
PREPARATION: 8 MINUTES
COOKING: 1¼ HOURS, PLUS 20 MINUTES TO REST

Chicken roasted in a hot oven with herbs is moist and tender. Roasting vegetables in a separate pan or around the chicken is an efficient way to prepare the meal. I love a thin gravy made the way I learned in France, where it's called "jus," which means a reduced sauce made with the pan juices and not thickened with flour.

1	1	3- to 3½-lb (1.5- to 1.8-kg) roasting chicken with giblets
2 tsp	10 mL	salt
2 tbsp	25 mL	melted butter or rendered chicken fat
4 or 5	4 or 5	sprigs of fresh tarragon or thyme, or 2 tbsp (25 mL) dried
4 cups	1 L	assorted vegetables: potatoes, carrots, turnips, parsnips and/or beets, cut into cubes or quartered (optional)
		1 recipe Pan Juices (page 140)

Preheat the oven to 400°F (200°C). Remove the giblets, neck and liver from the cavity of the chicken and set aside for stock. Freeze the liver for a pâté. Remove the loose fat for rendering or discard. Rinse out the chicken's cavity and dry with paper towel. Tuck the wing tips under the breasts.

Rub salt over the cavity and the skin of the chicken. Brush or rub the outside with melted butter or rendered fat. Loosen the skin of the bird at the cavity opening, separating the breast meat from the skin. Insert half the tarragon or thyme and place the remainder in the cavity. Tie the legs loosely together with kitchen twine or string. Put the chicken, breast side up, in a roasting pan and place on the center rack of the oven, uncovered. Roast the chicken 1 to 1¼ hours. Baste the chicken twice by spooning the pan juices over it. If roasting vegetables, add them to the roasting pan 30 minutes after the chicken and turn them in the fat in the pan, or roast them on a separate baking sheet, tossing them in a little chicken fat.

To render chicken fat, place it in a bowl in the microwave oven and cook on high for 2 to 3 minutes until melted, or melt the fat in a small saucepan over medium-low heat for about 5 minutes.

To test for chicken's doneness, cut the string and move the legs up and down. If the leg moves easily in the socket and the juices in the cavity run clear, it's cooked. If the juice is pink, return the chicken to the oven and cook for another 5 to 10 minutes.

If you are using a meat thermometer, stick it into the breast meat between the breast and leg. When it reaches 180°F (83°C), the chicken is ready.

Lift the chicken out of the pan with a metal lifter and carefully tip any juice in the cavity into the pan. Place the bird on a warm platter, loosely cover with foil and rest for 20 minutes to allow the juices to settle. If there are vegetables, remove them from the pan and keep warm. Prepare the pan juices while the chicken rests.

To carve the chicken, use a sharp carving knife and cut through the skin between the leg and breast. Cut straight down through the socket (hip joint) and the skin on the underside to remove both legs. Cut between the thigh and drumstick at the middle joint. Cut the dark meat off the thigh and drumstick and place the meat on a warm platter. To carve the white breast meat, place the chicken upright and to support it, place a fork across the top without piercing the chicken. Cut the meat into 1/4-inch (.5-cm) slices, beginning on the outside and working into the breast bone. Place the meat on the platter and serve with the pan juices.

Pan Juices

1 1/2 cups   375 mL   strained chicken stock, white wine or water
salt to taste

Carefully tip the roasting pan and skim off the fat with a spoon. Place the pan over medium heat and add the stock, wine or water and allow it to simmer while using a metal lifter to scrape up the browned bits on the bottom of the pan. Carefully pour the liquid through a sieve into a small saucepan. Over medium heat, reduce the liquid to 1 1/4 cups (300 mL). Leave the juices for 10 minutes and skim off any fat that rises to the top. Reheat. Season if needed.

To make the stock, place the giblets and neck with a chopped onion in a small saucepan, cover with 2 cups (500 mL) cold water and gently cook while chicken is roasting. Strain and measure 1 1/2 cups (375 mL).

Grilled Duck Breast with Orange Wine Sauce & Skin Crisps

MAKES 4 TO 6 SERVINGS
PREPARATION: 10 MINUTES
COOKING: 8 TO 10 MINUTES, PLUS 4 MINUTES FOR THE SAUCE

This rich, tender duck breast grilled to medium-rare makes an elegant and uncomplicated dinner to prepare and cook. Frozen boneless duck breast is available in most butcher shops. Defrost in the refrigerator for 24 hours before cooking.

4	4	individual duck breasts, defrosted
		salt and freshly ground black pepper to taste
1/2 cup	125 mL	dry red wine
		zest and juice from 1 orange

Pull off the skin and fat from the duck breasts. Use a sharp knife to cut the skin into very thin slices.

Preheat a grill pan on medium-high heat. Add the skin slices and fry until they are crisp and brown. Pour off the fat as it accumulates. Reserve the crisps and keep warm.

Preheat the pan on medium-high heat. Salt and pepper each breast on both sides. Grill the breasts for 4 to 5 minutes on each side until medium-rare, with a slight give to the meat (touch-test, pages 147–148). Place the breasts on a warm platter to keep them warm for 10 minutes.

Pour the red wine and any juice from the duck platter into the pan and cook for several minutes to absorb any of the brown bits in the pan and reduce the liquid by half. Add the zest and juice.

Carve the duck into 1/2-inch (1-cm) slices on the diagonal and fan out onto the platter. Pour the sauce over the meat and sprinkle with the crisp skin.

Roast Boneless Turkey Breasts with Pecan-Orange Crust

MAKES 9 TO 10 SERVINGS
PREPARATION: 15 MINUTES
ROASTING: 45 TO 60 MINUTES, PLUS 20 MINUTES TO REST

Boneless turkey breasts are a super way to feed friends because the cooking and carving is so easy. The crust brings a subtle flavor to the mild taste of turkey. It's easiest if the breasts are boneless.

2–3 lbs	1–1.5 kg	boneless, joined turkey breasts, not tied
1 cup	250 mL	finely chopped pecans
2 tbsp	25 mL	maple syrup
		zest of 1 orange
1/4 cup	50 mL	orange juice
2 tbsp	25 mL	finely chopped parsley
3 tbsp	45 mL	melted butter or olive oil

Preheat the oven to 375°F (190°C). Lightly brush the underside of the breasts with melted butter or oil.

In a bowl, combine the pecans, syrup, zest and orange juice, parsley and remaining butter or oil. Pat the paste over the skin side of the breasts. Place them in a roasting pan and roast for 45 to 60 minutes or until the meat feels firm and the juices run clear when the underside of the turkey is pressed.

Remove the turkey and tent loosely with foil for 15 to 20 minutes. Place the breasts on a cutting board and, using a sharp carving knife, begin to slice at the front end into 1/4-inch (.5-cm) slices on the diagonal. The crust will crumble during the carving, so gather the crumbs and sprinkle them over the sliced turkey.

Roast Turkey with Fruit Stuffing & Gravy

MAKES 8 TO 10 SERVINGS; ALLOW 1 LB (500 G)
UNCOOKED TURKEY PER PERSON
PREPARATION: 15 MINUTES FOR THE TURKEY PLUS 20 TO 25 MINUTES FOR THE STUFFING
ROASTING: 12 MINUTES PER LB OR 24 MINUTES PER KG, PLUS 45 MINUTES FOR RESTING

Christmas or Thanksgiving wouldn't be complete for our family without the aroma of the turkey roasting to fill the house. Traditionally, gravy is made with flour as shown in this recipe but, over time, habits change and the rich-tasting pan juice sauce as given in the roast chicken recipe is just as delicious over mashed potatoes.

Turkeys are available year-round, fresh or frozen, but fresh, farm-raised, grain-fed turkeys are superior as they are more flavorful and moist, with less fat.

1	1	14- to 16-lb (7- to 8-kg) turkey
		1 recipe Fruit Stuffing (page 146)
4 tbsp	50 mL	melted butter
		metal skewer
		cotton kitchen string
		1 recipe Gravy (page 145)

To prepare the turkey, wash out the cavity and dry it well with a paper towel. Lightly press the stuffing into the neck cavity. Pull the loose skin over the stuffing and secure it with a metal skewer. Lightly press the stuffing into the body cavity and close the opening with a metal skewer or sew with a large needle and kitchen string. Sprinkle the outside of the turkey with salt and lightly brush with melted butter. Tie the legs together with string or secure them by tucking them under the band of skin at the opening. Fold the wing tips under the breast. Place the turkey in the roasting pan breast side up. Use the neck and giblets (freeze the liver for another use) for the gravy's stock.

To roast: Preheat the oven to 325°F (160°C) and calculate the roasting time by the turkey's weight multiplied by 12 minutes per lb or 24 minutes per kg. Roast the turkey in the oven and baste it at least 3 times by spooning the pan juices over the turkey.

If the turkey is browning too much, tent it loosely with foil to prevent further browning. To test for doneness, cut the string tying the legs together; when the turkey is done, the legs will move easily in the socket and the juices will run clear when the meat is pressed on the underside. If you are using a meat thermometer, insert it in the stuffing, where it should read 170°F (77°C), then insert it in the inner thigh, avoiding the bone, where it should register 180°F (83°C).

When it has cooked, remove the turkey to a heated platter, loosely tent it with foil and allow it to rest for 45 minutes so the juices can settle.

You can use a spoon to remove the stuffing before you carve the turkey. Or you can carve the turkey and spoon out the stuffing for each person.

To carve: Remove the skewer. Using a sharp carving knife, cut the skin between the legs and breast and cut through the socket (hip joint) to separate the legs from the breasts. Cut the legs in half at the middle joint. Slice off the dark meat from the thighs and the drumsticks. Cut the wings off at the joint next to the breast. Carve the breast meat in slices about 1/4 inch (.5 cm) thick on the diagonal, starting on the outside and working in to the breast bone. Place the meat on a warm platter with the stuffing. Serve with the hot gravy.

Gravy

3 tbsp	45 mL	fat from the roasting pan
5 tbsp	65 mL	all-purpose flour
3 cups	750 mL	stock, red or white wine, or water from cooked vegetables

Place the roasting pan on the stove and lift the pan so the juices gather at the opposite end. Spoon off the fat, leaving about 3 tbsp (45 mL). Set the pan over medium heat. Use a metal lifter to scrape up the brown bits in the bottom of the pan. Stir in the flour until the flour is combined with the fat and allow the mixture to cook to a dark golden brown. Whisk in the stock, wine or vegetable water until blended and leave to cook 5 minutes to combine the flavors. Sieve the gravy into a saucepan. Skim off any fat. Season with salt. Serve warm.

To make stock, place the giblets and neck in a saucepan with a sliced onion. Cover with 4 cups (1 L) water and simmer gently for 2 hours. Drain. Reserve for the gravy.

Fruit Stuffing

MAKES 6 CUPS (1.5 L)
PREPARATION: 20 MINUTES
COOKING: 5 MINUTES

The stuffing is best made the day ahead and chilled before the turkey is roasted.

1/4 cup	50 mL	butter or rendered chicken fat (page 140)
2 cups	500 mL	finely chopped onion
1 1/2 cups	375 mL	finely chopped celery
6 or 8	6 or 8	sage, leaves minced, or 2 tbsp (25 mL) dried
6	6	slices whole wheat, white or rye bread, to make 3 cups (750 mL) soft bread crumbs or bread cubes
3	3	cored and chopped apples
2 cups	500 mL	coarsely chopped dried apricots or cranberries
2 tsp	10 mL	salt and generous sprinkling of pepper, or to taste
2 tsp	10 mL	brown sugar, or to taste

Melt the butter or fat in a large skillet and sauté the onions, celery and sage on medium-low heat, covered, until tender but not brown, about 5 or 6 minutes. Remove from the heat. Place the bread crumbs and fruit in a large mixing bowl and toss in the onion mixture. If the stuffing seems dry, add 1 or 2 tsp (5 or 10 mL) water until the consistency is moist but not soggy. Toss in the salt, pepper and sugar. Chill if not using immediately.

To make soft bread crumbs, partially freeze the bread slices, cut off the crusts, place the slices in a food processor and pulse on and off until coarse crumbs form. If you do not have a processor, remove crusts and cut the slices into 1/2-inch (1-cm) cubes.

Grilled Salmon Steak (page 124) with
Tomato Coconut Chutney (page 125),
Mango Ginger Chutney (page 125), and
Cucumber Herb Sauce (page 16)

Chicken Fricassee (page 136)

Barbecued Boneless Leg of Lamb
(page 160) with Grilled Baby Onions
and Tomatoes (page 168)

Grilled Steak (page 151) with Caramelized
Onions (page 182) and Herb Butter (page 156)

Beef, Veal, Lamb & Pork

Cooking meat is all about "the feel" and learning how to test for readiness with your fingers.

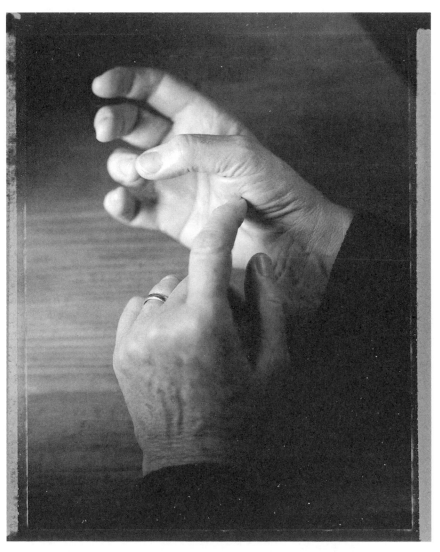

Touch-test method to determine meat doneness (page 148)

It allows you to judge doneness without having to probe the meat with a fork and allowing precious juices to escape. I would like the two-pronged fork banned from the barbecue and the kitchen! A meat thermometer is another accurate way to determine doneness of meat, but it's one thing I have never used because I prefer the touch-test method.

The trick in judging when meat is cooked rests right in your hand:

1. Loosely open your hand and lightly place your thumb on the tip of your first finger. Now take the index finger of the opposite hand and feel the fleshy bulge at the base of your thumb. That's how raw meat feels — flabby.

2. Now move your thumb to the tip of the second finger. That's the way meat cooked rare feels — a little firmer to the touch.

3. Next, move your thumb to the tip of the third finger — it's firm but gives when touched. That's medium-rare to medium.

4. Now, move your thumb to the tip of the little finger — that's well-done, when there is no give.

Simple, isn't it? And when you put this testing method into action, don't worry. Your fingertips are tough and won't easily burn unless you linger. If you prefer to use a meat thermometer, following is a chart to help you determine how long to roast.

Rare: 18 minutes per lb (500 g) or internal temperature 140°F (60°C)

Medium-rare: 20 minutes per lb (500 g) or internal temperature 150°F (65°C)

Medium: 22 minutes per lb (500 g) or internal temperature 155° to 160°F (68° to 70°C)

Well-done: 26 to 28 minutes per lb (500 g) or internal temperature 160° to 170°F (70° to 77°C)

When heat is applied to meat, the juices are pushed inwards, cooking it. That's one of the reasons meat should always rest before being cut or carved: so the heated juices can return to the outside, making the meat juicy throughout.

The measurement of meat quality by Canada's Beef Information Centre (CBIC) is based on the marbling of fat throughout the meat: AAA has the best overall eating quality with the most "marbling," adding tenderness, juiciness and flavor, AA has slightly less marbling and A has still less marbling.

Premium cuts are found where there is little or no muscle movement in the animal. The tenderloin, hidden under the animal's rib cage, is prized and gives us the fillet in roasts or steaks. The other tender section is the prime rib or loin. The meat comes from either side of the backbone in the central section where you find the standing rib or boneless rib-eye roasts. This section also provides the great steaks — ribeye, T-bone, or strip-loin steaks — perfect for grilling. Just beyond this, toward the tail end, are the sirloin steaks and roasts.

The process of roasting can be defined as food cooked, uncovered, with dry hot air. To roast prime cuts, place the meat fat side up in a roasting pan. Rub freshly ground black pepper over the roast if desired. If you wish to salt the meat, do it just before cooking because salting earlier draws out the moisture and makes the meat less juicy. Allow 4 oz (120 g) per person for boneless roast, or 6 oz (180 g) for bone-in roast.

Roast, uncovered, in an oven preheated to 375°F (190°C). Some like to roast at 325°F (160°C) to reduce shrinkage but I find the higher temperature gives the best flavor.

Less tender roasts, where there is a lot of muscle movement, are cheaper. This includes the front quarter or "chuck" with the cross rib, boneless blade, shoulder, brisket and short rib. These cuts have good flavor, but few uniform slices because of the bones. Other less tender cuts include the hip cuts, such as boneless roasts called inside and outside round, eye of round, sirloin tip or rump roasts and some steaks. "Pot roasting" is perfect for these less tender cuts, but they can also be dry roasted, as CBIC

suggests, by seasoning and placing them, fat side up, on a rack in the roasting pan with 1/2 inch (1 cm) water. Sear and brown the meat all over in a hot oven, then reduce the heat to lower than moderate and roast for 11/4 to 13/4 hours. If you're using a meat thermometer, insert it and roast the meat until the internal temperature reaches medium.

Stewing beef usually comes from a variety of less tender cuts and cube sizes which are tenderized when cooked in a liquid with a small amount of acidity, such as tomato or wine. It's usually cheaper — and much wiser — to buy a chuck or hip roast and cut it into uniform 1-inch (2.5-cm) cubes yourself or have the butcher cut to your specification.

It's worthwhile to establish a good relationship with a reliable, quality butcher and know that the meat has hung long enough to ensure it is tender. You'll find that he (or she) will guide you in your purchases, helping you to understand the different cuts.

To defrost meat, leave it to thaw in the refrigerator. Thawing at room temperature allows the meat to "bleed," losing precious juices and enabling bacteria to grow on the outside surface.

Mustard Pot Roast

MAKES 4 TO 6 SERVINGS
PREPARATION: 30 MINUTES
COOKING: 2¹/₂ TO 3 HOURS

Chuck or shoulder makes a juicy, flavorful pot roast. The drawback is that it will fall apart when carved because of the shoulder blade bone. Boneless cuts from the hip section will carve better for presentation but I prefer the bone-in cuts for their taste. Browning the meat and vegetables first adds a greater depth of flavor.

2 tsp	10 mL	salt
1 tsp	5 mL	freshly ground black pepper
3 lbs	1.5 kg	boneless or bone-in chuck, round or rump roast
3 tbsp	45 mL	dry mustard
1 tbsp	15 mL	all-purpose flour
1¹/₂ tbsp	20 mL	vegetable oil or 2 oz (60 g) salt pork, cut into small cubes
2	2	medium carrots, sliced
2	2	medium onions, sliced
2 cups	500 mL	dry red wine
¹/₄ cup	50 mL	water or stock
1	1	bay leaf
1 tsp	5 mL	dried thyme

Rub the salt and pepper over the roast. Combine the mustard and flour and rub the mixture over the meat. Heat the oil or melt the salt pork cubes in a Dutch oven or in a large, heavy saucepan with a lid, on medium-high heat. Sear the meat and turn the roast as it browns, which will take about 15 minutes. Remove the meat and set aside.

Add the vegetables to the same pot and let them brown for 6 to 8 minutes. Return the meat (fat side up) to the pot with the wine and water or stock. The liquid should come halfway up the meat. Add the bay leaf and thyme and cover. Very gently simmer over medium-low heat for 2¹/₂ to 3 hours, or braise in a 300°F (150°C) oven until tender. Remove the meat from the pan and keep it warm on a platter.

Boil the liquid for about 10 minutes until it reduces by half. Discard the bay leaf. To make the sauce, purée the stock and vegetables in a food processor or blender. Return the sauce to the pan, heat and taste to adjust for salt and pepper. With a sharp knife, carve the meat into slices and place them on a serving platter. Pour the sauce over the meat and serve.

Grilled or Pan-Fried Steaks with Caramelized Onions

MAKES 6 SERVINGS
PREPARATION: 10 MINUTES
COOKING: ONIONS 30 MINUTES, STEAKS 8 TO 10 MINUTES

To have a succulent, tender steak with grill lines, fry in a hot grill pan or over a hot grill or barbecue. The caramelized onions add great flavor to steak due to the natural sugars that are released during the long cooking.

| 6 | 6 | 1-inch (2.5-cm) thick ribeye, striploin or sirloin steaks |
| | | 1 recipe Caramelized Onions (page 182) |

Preheat the skillet or grill pan on medium-high heat. Cut any excess fat from the steaks, lightly brush them with the remaining oil and sprinkle with salt and pepper. When the skillet is hot, add the steaks, reduce the heat to medium-high and cook for 5 minutes or until droplets of juice appear on top of the steaks. Turn the steaks over and cook for another 5 minutes for medium-rare (use the touch-test on page 148). Let them rest for 5 minutes before serving to settle the juices.

Serve the steaks over Caramelized Onions.

Broiled Marinated Flank or Round Steak

MAKES 4 TO 6 SERVINGS
PREPARATION: 5 MINUTES PLUS 1 HOUR TO MARINATE
COOKING: APPROXIMATELY 10 MINUTES

Flank steak is a lean, flavorful meat found below the ribs. Round steak is from the hip section. Both can be barbecued, broiled or grilled.

1	1	beef flank steak, about 1½ lbs (750 g) or a 1-inch (2.5-cm) thick round steak

Choose one of the marinade recipes that follow to prepare the steak before cooking. Use a sharp knife to score 4 shallow slits across the top of the flank steak, or around the edge of the round steak to prevent it from curling. Marinate the meat for 1 hour, turning several times.

Ginger & Soy Marinade

2 tbsp	25 mL	olive or vegetable oil
3 tbsp	45 mL	light soy sauce
¼ tsp	1 mL	freshly ground black pepper
1 or 2	1 or 2	garlic cloves, minced
2 tsp	10 mL	freshly grated ginger
1 tsp	5 mL	brown sugar

Combine the ingredients in a large shallow dish or self-sealing bag.

Lemon & Mustard Marinade

⅓ cup	75 mL	lemon juice
2 tsp	10 mL	grated lemon rind
2 tbsp	25 mL	vegetable or olive oil
1 tsp	5 mL	dry mustard
1 tsp	5 mL	brown sugar
1 tsp	5 mL	Worcestershire sauce
2 or 3	2 or 3	green onions, sliced

Combine the ingredients in a large shallow dish or self-sealing bag.

Preheat the broiler. Place the steak on a rack over the broiler pan and broil about 4 inches (10 cm) from the heat for 6 minutes. Turn the meat over and broil for another 4 minutes for medium-rare. Brush the meat often with the marinade during cooking. Rest the meat for 10 minutes before thinly slicing, diagonally, against the grain.

Tender Pan-Fried Calf or Beef Liver

MAKES 4 TO 6 SERVINGS
PREPARATION: 30 MINUTES
COOKING: 5 MINUTES

Liver that is lightly cooked and still pink inside will melt in your mouth. Presoaking in milk removes any bitterness.

1 lb	500 g	calf or beef liver slices, 1/4 inch (.5 cm) thick
1/4 cup	50 mL	milk
1/4 cup	50 mL	all-purpose flour
1 tsp	2 mL	salt with 2 grindings of black pepper
1 tbsp	15 mL	butter
1 tbsp	15 mL	vegetable oil
2 tbsp	25 mL	balsamic vinegar or red wine

Soak the liver in the milk for at least 30 minutes. Combine the flour, salt and pepper on a pie plate. In a large skillet on medium-high, heat the butter and oil. Remove the liver from the milk and dredge it through the flour, shaking off excess. Carefully place the liver in the hot skillet. As soon as you see a few bubbles of juice on top of the slices, use tongs to flip them over and cook for 1 to 2 minutes more or until the meat is medium-rare. Remove to a warm platter. Add the vinegar or wine to the hot pan and scrape up any brown bits. Pour the sauce over the liver. Serve.

Cranberry Meatballs

MAKES 4 TO 6 SERVINGS
PREPARATION: 30 MINUTES
COOKING: 10 MINUTES

This is an inexpensive and tasty use for ground meat. The meatballs can also be made smaller and served as an appetizer. The cranberries add a special zest to the sauce.

1 cup	250 mL	soft bread crumbs or 2 bread slices
1/2 cup	125 mL	milk
1 tbsp	15 mL	butter
1/2	1/2	medium onion, finely chopped
1/2 lb	250 g	ground lean beef
1 lb	500 g	ground lean pork
1	1	egg
1/4 tsp	1 mL	ground allspice
1/8 tsp	.5 mL	freshly grated nutmeg
1 tsp	5 mL	salt
1/4 tsp	1 mL	black pepper
2 tbsp	25 mL	butter or the fat left in the pan
2 tbsp	25 mL	all-purpose flour
1 1/4 cups	300 mL	well-flavored Beef or Chicken Stock (page 35 or 36)
1 cup	250 mL	jellied or whole cranberry sauce
3 tbsp	45 mL	finely chopped parsley

To make the soft bread crumbs, tear the bread into several pieces and place them in a blender or food processor. Pulse the machine on and off several times until soft crumbs form. Soak the crumbs with the milk in a mixing bowl.

Preheat the broiler in your oven. In a small skillet, heat the butter on medium-low heat and sauté the onions until golden, about 5 minutes. Add the onions to the milk and crumbs with the beef, pork, egg, spices, salt and pepper. Use your hands or a spoon to mix just until blended. Shape into walnut-sized balls, dipping your hands into cold water to keep the meat from sticking. Arrange the meatballs on a baking pan with a rim. Place the pan about 3 inches (7.5 cm) from the preheated broiler for 3 minutes until lightly browned; turn the meatballs over and broil for another 3 minutes. Test by cutting into one meatball to make sure there is no pink meat showing.

Remove the meatballs from the pan and place them in a serving dish; keep warm. Pour off the excess fat, leaving about 1 tbsp (15 mL) in the pan. Using a rubber spatula, scrape the brown bits, fat and meat juices into a small saucepan. Stir in the flour and cook over medium heat for 2 to 3 minutes to brown the flour, giving the gravy color. Whisk in the stock until the sauce is smooth and simmer for 5 minutes. Whisk in half a can of cranberry sauce or more, if you like. Heat briefly. Taste for more seasoning if needed. Pour the sauce over the meatballs and garnish with parsley.

Juicy Beef Burgers

MAKES 4 PATTIES
PREPARATION: 10 MINUTES
COOKING: 7 TO 9 MINUTES

A little liquid added to ground meat will keep patties juicy. Resist adding other ingredients such as egg, bread or onions as patties do not need a binder nor extra flavors. Since there are so many condiments that are added later — from pickles to tomatoes — the true flavor of the meat is in danger of being lost. Unfortunately, there is a risk of bacteria occurring during the meat grinding process, so cook burgers until the juices run clear.

1 lb	500 g	medium-lean ground beef
1/3 cup	75 mL	water, milk or cream
1/2 tsp	2 mL	freshly ground black pepper, or to taste
1 tsp	5 mL	salt

Combine the meat, liquid and pepper just until blended. Divide the meat into 4 patties about 3/4 inch (2 cm) thick. It's important that they be of uniform thickness. Preheat a grill pan or barbecue on medium-high heat or, if using a skillet, heat and sprinkle lightly with salt to prevent patties from sticking. Cook the patties until several beads of juice appear on top (to indicate the heat has penetrated the patty), or for 5 minutes, then flip them over. Cook until the juices run clear when the center of the patty is gently pressed or until a meat thermometer reads 160°F (70°C). Let the patties rest for several minutes before serving.

Roast Fillet of Beef with Herb Butter

MAKES 4 TO 6 SERVINGS
PREPARATION: 22 MINUTES
COOKING: APPROXIMATELY 45 MINUTES

Tenderloin is a treat for a special occasion. There is little waste and no bone so it's a breeze to carve. Because it cooks quickly, it's best to brown it in a hot oven for color and taste first, then reduce the heat. A whole tenderloin or fillet weighs about 6 lbs (3 kg) so you may want to buy only a section; the butcher will cut it to order. The thickest end of the fillet is the most expensive — the other half has a thin tail that should be tucked under so it roasts evenly. To save money you can trim the fillet yourself by cutting away any fat and the thin, tough membrane found
along the surface.

3 tbsp	45 mL	Dijon mustard
2 tbsp	25 mL	bottled horseradish
3 lbs	1.5 kg	beef tenderloin, trimmed of fat and membrane
		freshly ground black pepper and salt for sprinkling
		parsley or watercress sprigs for garnish
		1 recipe Herb Butter

Preheat the oven to 475°F (240°C). Stir the mustard and horseradish together, rub them into all sides of the meat and generously sprinkle with pepper and salt. Place in a roasting pan or a heavy iron skillet.

Roast for about 15 minutes, turning several times just until the meat is brown on all sides, or brown under a broiler. Reduce the heat to 375°F (190°C) and roast for 20 to 25 minutes. Test for doneness using the touch-test (page 148) or roast until a meat thermometer registers 150°F (65°C) for medium-rare. Let the meat rest for 15 to 20 minutes in a warm place before slicing into 1/2-inch (1-cm) slices. Garnish with parsley or watercress "bouquets" and slices of Herb Butter.

Herb Butter

1/2 cup	125 mL	butter, softened to room temperature
2 tsp	10 mL	lemon juice
1/4 cup	50 mL	finely chopped chives, tarragon or sage
1/4 tsp	1 mL	salt, or to taste

Beat the butter until smooth. Stir in the lemon juice, herbs and salt to tatse. Chill just until barely firm. Roll into a sausage shape in waxed paper. Chill and slice diagonally.

Beef Stew with Roasted Vegetables

MAKES 4 TO 6 SERVINGS
PREPARATION: 25 MINUTES
COOKING: 2 1/2 TO 3 HOURS

In this classic beef stew, the acid in the tomato helps to break down the tough fibers in the meat. I find most vegetables added at the beginning of the cooking lose their characteristic flavors so I like to roast and add them at the end. If you like, keep the peel on the carrots, parsnips and potatoes for extra fiber.

2 tbsp	25 mL	beef fat or vegetable oil
2 lbs	1 kg	cubed beef, from bottom round or chuck
3 tbsp	45 mL	all-purpose flour
2	2	onions, finely sliced or chopped
2 cups	500 mL	hot Beef Stock (page 35), or hot water plus 2 beef bouillon cubes
1	1	bay leaf
1 tsp	5 mL	thyme
3 tbsp	45 mL	tomato paste
1 tbsp	15 mL	balsamic vinegar
3	3	carrots, cut in 1/2-inch (1-cm) cubes
3 or 4	3 or 4	potatoes, cut in 1-inch (2.5-cm) cubes
1 tbsp	15 mL	vegetable oil
1 cup	250 mL	frozen green peas thawed (optional)
		salt and freshly ground black pepper to taste
1/3 cup	75 mL	chopped parsley

In a Dutch oven or heavy pot, heat half the fat on high heat and sear the meat in batches. Sprinkle the flour on the meat during the searing. Stir often to brown all sides. Remove the meat and reserve. Add remaining fat and brown the onions, turning often for 5 minutes. Add the stock, all of the meat, bay leaf, thyme, tomato paste and vinegar. Bring to a very gentle simmer. Cover partially and cook for 2 to 2 1/2 hours until tender. If the liquid reduces to a level below the meat, add a little liquid.

To roast the vegetables, place the carrots and potatoes on a baking pan and toss with the oil. Roast for 30 minutes in a 375°F (190°C) oven until tender and add to the stew at the end of the cooking. Add the peas, if using, and simmer for 3 minutes. Taste for salt and pepper. Garnish with parsley and serve.

Chinese Beef & Green Bean Stir-Fry

MAKES 4 TO 6 SERVINGS
PREPARATION: 30 MINUTES
COOKING: 5 MINUTES

This is not an expensive meal because a little beef goes a long way. Take the time to assemble and prepare the ingredients for this dish in advance as it cooks so quickly.

1/2 lb	250 g	flank, round or chuck steak
2 tbsp	25 mL	soy sauce
1 tbsp	15 mL	rice wine or dry sherry
2 tsp	10 mL	cornstarch
2 tsp	10 mL	granulated sugar
2 tbsp	25 mL	vegetable oil
4 oz	120 g	Chinese long green beans or ordinary green beans
1 tbsp	15 mL	finely minced fresh ginger
2	2	garlic cloves, minced
1/2 tsp	2 mL	dried red chili flakes
1 cup	250 mL	Chicken Stock (page 36)
2 tsp	10 mL	cornstarch
2 tbsp	25 mL	water
2 tbsp	25 mL	balsamic vinegar
2	2	green onions, finely sliced

Remove the tough surface sinew from the meat. To make it easier to slice the meat, place it in the freezer for 20 minutes, then slice across the grain into diagonal wafer-thin slices.

In a bowl, toss the meat with the soy sauce, wine or sherry, cornstarch, sugar and half the oil. Leave to marinate for 20 minutes.

To prepare the beans, cut them into 1-inch (2.5-cm) pieces or, if they are thick, halve them lengthwise and cut them into pieces.

Heat a wok or skillet on high heat. Add the meat mixture and toss just until the meat browns and all the pink has gone. Remove and set aside. Add the remaining oil, ginger, garlic and chili flakes, tossing for 30 seconds. Add the stock and bring to a boil. Drop in the beans, cover and cook for 2 minutes or until tender-crisp. Combine the cornstarch with water and stir into the stock. When the stock thickens (after about 1 minute) add the vinegar, browned meat and green onions. Serve immediately.

Parmesan Veal Scallopini

MAKES 4 TO 6 SERVINGS
PREPARATION: 10 TO 15 MINUTES
COOKING: 3 TO 4 MINUTES

This is an elegant dish that cooks very quickly. Top-quality veal is pale pink and very tender, from calves 10 to 12 weeks old. Most of the veal sold in North America is baby beef, a deeper pink, and less tender.

1¹/₄ lb	625 g	veal scallops (10 to 12 pieces)
¹/₂ cup	125 mL	grated Parmesan cheese
2 tbsp	25 mL	melted butter
2 tbsp	25 mL	butter, for frying
¹/₂ cup	125 mL	Chicken Stock (page 36) or white wine
2 tbsp	25 mL	finely snipped fresh chives or chopped parsley

Ask the butcher to pound the veal scallops until they are wafer-thin. Or, if you wish to do it yourself, place the meat on a wooden board and use a mallet or rolling pin to gently pound the veal until it is very thin, without tearing the meat. Cut off any fat or tough membranes and cut the pieces in half if they are too large.

Put the cheese in a pie plate. Brush both sides of the veal with the melted butter, then coat the veal with the cheese. Heat the butter in a large skillet on medium-high heat until it's foaming, then fry the veal until it's golden brown, about 1 minute on each side. Remove the veal and keep it warm on a platter. Add the stock or wine to the pan, stirring to scrape up the brown bits and simmer to reduce the liquid by a quarter. The cheese will add saltiness to the sauce, so taste to check if more salt is needed. Pour the sauce over the meat and garnish with chives or parsley.

Barbecued Boneless Leg of Lamb

MAKES 6 TO 8 SERVINGS
PREPARATION: 5 TO 6 MINUTES
COOKING: 45 MINUTES TO 1 HOUR

When the bone is removed from a leg of lamb, it's called "butterflying," creating a roast ideal for grilling or barbecuing. The roast can be bought already boned, or you can ask the butcher to bone it, or bone it yourself! Barbecuing intensifies the great flavor of lamb, as does broiling. Lamb is best served medium-rare to retain maximum moisture and flavor.

1	1	boneless leg of lamb, about 4 lbs (2 kg)
1 tbsp	15 mL	olive oil
2 to 3	2 to 3	garlic cloves, minced
1 tbsp	15 mL	freshly ground black pepper
1 tbsp	15 mL	dried oregano
1 tbsp	15 mL	fresh rosemary or 2 tsp (10 mL) dried

Spread the meat open with the skin side down. To allow the meat to cook evenly, cut about 2 inches (5 cm) deep through the center of the thickest (the thigh) section of the roast and spread the 2 parts open. Combine the oil, garlic, pepper, oregano and rosemary in a bowl and rub the mixture over the meat.

Brush the barbecue rack lightly with oil and place it about 3 inches (7.5 cm) from the heat source. Preheat the barbecue on medium. Place the roast on the rack with the fat side next to the heat source. Close the lid of the barbecue and cook the lamb for 20 minutes. Turn the lamb and continue cooking for 20 to 25 minutes until the lamb is medium-rare. If you are using a meat thermometer, place it in the thickest part of the meat until it registers 150°F (65°C). To broil the lamb, place the meat in a pan, 6 inches (15 cm) from the heat and broil for 45 to 50 minutes, turning twice. Leave the meat to rest for 15 minutes before carving.

Minted Lamb Shish Kebabs

MAKES 4 TO 6 SERVINGS
PREPARATION: 20 MINUTES
MARINATING: 3 HOURS
COOKING: 12 TO 14 MINUTES

This is a perfect summer barbecue recipe featuring fresh herbs. Avoid using cherry tomatoes on a shish kebab as they cook quickly and become too soft.

2 tbsp	25 mL	chopped fresh mint leaves
1 tsp	5 mL	fresh thyme
1/4 cup	50 mL	olive oil
1	1	juice of lemon
1 lb	500 g	lamb leg or shoulder, cut into 1-inch (2.5 cm) cubes
1	1	large onion, cut into 1-inch (2.5 cm) squares
12	12	button mushrooms
1	1	green bell pepper, cut into 12 pieces
1	1	red bell pepper, cut into 12 pieces
10 or 12	10 or 12	metal skewers (if using wooden skewers soak in water first)
		salt and pepper to taste

Combine the mint, thyme, oil and lemon juice and marinate the meat for at least 3 hours, turning several times. Drain, reserving the marinade. Arrange the meat on skewers alternately with 4 or 5 vegetable pieces, and brush with the marinade. Sprinkle with salt and pepper.

Preheat the barbecue on medium and grill the shish kebabs for 6 or 7 minutes on each side, or until the meat is medium-rare. If using the broiler, preheat and place the skewers on a rack over the broiler pan about 6 inches (15 cm) from the heat. Broil for 6 or 7 minutes on each side.

Braised Lamb Shanks with Fennel

MAKES 4 TO 6 SERVINGS
PREPARATION: 20 MINUTES
COOKING: 2 HOURS

This delicious lamb dish is adapted from a classic Italian veal recipe. The long, slow cooking gives a deeply rich flavor and tender meat that falls off the bone. This recipe can be made up to two days ahead.

1/2 cup	125 mL	all-purpose flour
1 1/2 tsp	7 mL	salt
1/2 tsp	2 mL	freshly ground black pepper
6	6	lamb shanks, about 10 oz (300 g) each
3 tbsp	45 mL	olive oil
1	1	medium onion, diced
1	1	medium carrot, diced
1	1	medium fennel bulb, trimmed and diced
3 or 4	3 or 4	garlic cloves, finely minced
2	2	bay leaves
		juice and zest of 1 lemon
1 cup	250 mL	Beef or Chicken Stock (page 35 or 36)
1	1	28-oz (796-mL) can diced plum tomatoes
1 tsp	5 mL	fresh thyme, chopped
1 tsp	5 mL	fresh rosemary, chopped
1 tbsp	15 mL	fresh parsley, chopped
		salt and pepper to taste

In a dish, mix the flour with salt and pepper, dredge the shanks and shake off excess. Heat a large, heavy sauté pan (with lid), or Dutch oven on medium-high heat with half the oil. Brown the meat on all sides, for about 15 minutes. Remove and set aside.

Heat the remaining oil in the same pan on medium heat and sauté the onions, carrots and fennel for about 5 minutes, stirring often. Add the garlic and cook for 1 minute. Add the bay leaves, lemon juice, zest and stock, scraping up any brown bits in the pan. Cook for about 10 minutes, until the mixture reduces slightly. Add the tomatoes and herbs and season with salt and pepper, if needed.

Place the meat in the pan, making sure it's completely covered with sauce. Cover and place in a preheated 300°F (150°C) oven, or on top of the stove on low, for 2 hours. The meat must cook very gently so that it is tender and separates from the bone. Turn the shanks every half-hour. To serve, remove the shanks from the sauce and place them on a warm platter. Reduce the sauce on medium-high heat until it has thickened. Taste sauce and adjust seasonings.

Pour sauce over the meat and garnish with parsley. If the recipe is made ahead, reheat the lamb in a roasting pan, covered with foil, in a 350°F (180°C) oven for 30 minutes.

Pan-Fried Lamb Chops with Cucumber Herb Sauce

MAKES 4 TO 6 SERVINGS
PREPARATION: 5 MINUTES
COOKING: ABOUT 12 MINUTES

Lamb chops make a perfect springtime meal. Loin lamb chops have the tenderloin attached, while shoulder chops are less expensive but are not as tender. Mint is a delightful herb for the sauce.

6–8	6–8	lamb chops, 3/4-inch (2-cm) thick
2 tbsp	25 mL	olive oil
1 tsp	5 mL	salt
1/2 tsp	2 mL	freshly ground black pepper
		1 recipe Cucumber Herb Sauce (page 16)

Cut any excess fat from the chops and score three slits in the fatty edge to prevent curling. Brush oil over each chop. Allow the chops to stand for about 30 minutes at room temperature so the meat warms. Sprinkle both sides with salt and pepper. Heat a large skillet or grill pan on medium-high heat and cook the chops for 4 or 5 minutes on each side or until the meat is medium-rare. To test for doneness, gently press the meat near the bone until juices appear. If the juice is pink, the chops are perfect. If it's red, the chops need a little longer. Serve with Cucumber Herb Sauce.

Indian Lamb Curry

MAKES 4 TO 6 SERVINGS
PREPARATION: 20 MINUTES
COOKING: 1 1/2 HOURS

This dish offers just a few spices that create a taste explosion and it follows the traditional Indian method of gently frying the spices to bring out their flavors.

1	1	1-inch (2.5-cm) piece ginger root, peeled and coarsely chopped
6 or 7	6 or 7	garlic cloves, coarsely chopped
4 tbsp	50 mL	plain yogurt
2 tbsp	25 mL	butter
3	3	medium onions, finely sliced
1/2 tsp	2 mL	ground turmeric
1 tsp	5 mL	ground cumin
2 tbsp	25 mL	ground coriander
1/2 tsp	2 mL	ground nutmeg
1/2–1 tsp	2–5 mL	ground hot red pepper
2 lbs	1 kg	lamb shoulder or leg, cut into 1-inch (2.5-cm) cubes
1 cup	250 mL	hot water
1 1/2 tsp	7 mL	salt, or to taste
2/3 cup	150 mL	whipping cream or plain yogurt
1/2 tsp	2 mL	paprika

In a food processor or blender, blend the ginger, garlic and yogurt until smooth. Set aside.

Melt the butter in a large saucepan on medium heat. Fry the onions until lightly brown, about 6 minutes. Lower the heat and add the turmeric, cumin, coriander, nutmeg and red pepper and fry for 2 minutes. Raise the heat to high, add the meat and sear until browned on all sides, stirring constantly.

Reduce the heat to medium and slowly stir in the yogurt mixture. Continue to cook until oil begins to rise to the top, which indicates the spices have cooked properly. Add the water, bring to a gentle simmer, cover and cook for about 1 hour or until the meat is tender. Add the cream or yogurt and cook for another 5 minutes. To serve, sprinkle the top with paprika.

Lemony Pork Tenderloin Medallions

MAKES 4 TO 6 SERVINGS
PREPARATION: 10 MINUTES
COOKING: 3 OR 4 MINUTES

Pork tenderloin is a wonderfully tender meat that cooks quickly. This recipe calls for lemon grass, which adds a subtle flavor, but it can be replaced with lemon rind.

1 1/2 lb	750 g	pork tenderloin
1	1	lemon grass stalk or zest of 1 lemon
2	2	garlic cloves
2	2	canned jalapeno peppers
1/2 tsp	2 mL	freshly ground black pepper
2 tbsp	25 mL	light soy sauce
2 tbsp	25 mL	vegetable oil
1 tbsp	15 mL	cider or balsamic vinegar
2 tbsp	25 mL	honey or maple syrup

Remove any fat or white membrane from the meat and slice the meat into 1/2-inch-thick (1-cm) slices. If you're using lemon grass, finely slice or grate the cream-colored heart, discarding the tough outer green stems. To make the marinade, purée the lemon grass, garlic, peppers, soy, oil, vinegar and honey or syrup in a blender. Thoroughly coat the meat with the marinade and leave it for at least 1 hour in the refrigerator. Remove it from the refrigerator 45 minutes before cooking. Heat a wok or skillet on medium-high heat and sauté the meat just until brown, about 3 minutes, turning often. Remove and serve.

Pork Chops with Apple & Sauerkraut

MAKES 4 SERVINGS
PREPARATION: 15 MINUTES
COOKING: 20 TO 30 MINUTES

Pork today is raised to be much leaner so it's more of a challenge to keep it juicy during cooking. In the old days pork had higher fat content, but now it has the same as the white meat of chicken. Back then, it was always over-cooked for fear of trichinosis (a parasite), but that fear is gone today since pigs are raised in hygienic surroundings. Pork should be cooked until the juice is barely pink and it has an internal temperature of 155°F (68°C).

4	4	pork chops, about 1/2 inch (1 cm) thick
		salt and pepper
4 tbsp	50 mL	honey-style mustard
2 tbsp	25 mL	butter or vegetable oil
1	1	small onion, finely sliced
2 tsp	10 mL	caraway seeds
1	1	28-oz (796-mL) can sauerkraut
2	2	tart apples, peeled, cored, chopped
1/4 cup	50 mL	Beef, Chicken or Vegetable Stock (page 35 or 36)

Sprinkle salt and pepper on both sides of the chops and spread them with mustard. In a deep sauté pan, heat the butter or oil on medium-high heat and brown the chops on both sides. Remove and set aside. Add the onion and caraway seeds to the pan and sauté on medium heat until tender, about 5 minutes. Drain the sauerkraut in a colander and run warm tap water through it briefly to remove excess brine. Stir the sauerkraut into the onions. Add the apples and stock. Press the chops into the mixture. Cover and gently cook on low heat for 20 minutes. If chops are thicker, cook for 5 minutes longer.

Glazed Whole Ham

MAKES 12 TO 14 SERVINGS
PREPARATION: 10 MINUTES, 1 HOUR TO REST THE HAM
COOKING: 2 TO 2¹/₂ HOURS

Glazed baked ham is easy to prepare and the glaze complements the ham very well. Ham comes fresh, cured or smoked. It can be purchased whole or cut into the shank or butt end. Hams are sold with or without bone, and with or without rind. There is no doubt that ham has better flavor with the bone and rind, but it does mean you need more time to bake it.

A country-style ham has great flavor because it's usually salt-cured and, sometimes, smoked and aged, as with Black Forest ham. Less expensive smoked ham is dipped in liquid smoke. Years ago, when all hams were smoked, it dried them out so brine was added. Today, manufacturers add the brine by injection (10% of the ham's weight) to make them juicier. Boneless ham is pressed into a mold and packaged in a net bag, or in cans.

Even though most hams are sold cooked or "ready to serve," they need time in the oven to enhance flavor and cook out any brine. This recipe is for a bone-in ham, but any ham benefits from a glaze. Baked ham is best thinly sliced.

6 lbs	3 kg	bone-in cooked ham
1/2 cup	125 mL	brown sugar, lightly packed
1 tbsp	15 mL	Dijon mustard or 1 tsp (5 mL) dried mustard
1 tsp	5 mL	ground cloves
2 tsp	10 mL	apple cider or orange juice
1 cup	250 mL	water

Let the ham come to room temperature for 1 hour. Preheat the oven to 325°F (160°C). In a small bowl, combine the sugar, mustard and cloves. Add the cider or juice, just enough to make a thick paste. If the ham has a thick rind, pull it off and cut off most of the underlying fat with a sharp knife, leaving about ¹/₄ inch (.5 cm). Make diagonal cuts through the fat to form a diamond pattern and pat the sugar mixture over it. Place the ham on a rack set in a roasting pan and pour the water into the pan. Bake the ham for about 1¹/₂ hours or 15 minutes per lb (30 minutes per kg). If you are using a meat thermometer, it should read 140°F (60°C) at the thickest part of the ham — remember to avoid the bone. Raise the oven heat to 450°F (230°C) and continue to cook the ham just until the glaze is shiny and golden, for 5 or 6 minutes. Remove the ham from the oven and let it stand for about 20 minutes to settle the juices before carving.

168

Vegetables

Vegetable markets today offer a wonderful variety of colors and possibilities.

The greater selection is due, in part, to the many cultures of North America that have provided us with new ingredients and recipes. There are many ways to prepare versatile vegetables. Here are some of the most popular and successful methods:

Steaming: This quick and convenient method preserves vitamins and flavors and works best for up to three servings of vegetables. Place the vegetables in a metal or wooden perforated basket or on a heatproof plate, over simmering water. Cover and steam for 2 or 3 minutes, until the vegetables are tender-crisp.

Boiling: My favorite way to cook vegetables for more than three servings. For veggies that grow above the ground (e.g. asparagus, broccoli, corn, peas, green beans), plunge them directly into boiling salted water on high heat. Boil hard, uncovered, for 2 to 4 minutes, until the vegetables are tender-crisp. If the vegetables grow below the ground (e.g. potatoes, carrots, turnips, yams, beets), cover them with cold salted water, cover and cook gently until tender.

Stir-Frying: Another quick and tasty way to cook vegetables. Simply cut them into uniform size and heat a wok or skillet with 1 tbsp (15 mL) vegetable oil. Add the vegetables and about 2 tbsp (25 mL) stock and cook, stirring constantly, for 1 or 2 minutes.

Grilling: The best way to prepare vegetables for grilling is to toss them in a light coating of olive oil, then sprinkle with chopped fresh herbs such as sage, thyme, tarragon or oregano. Preheat the grill or barbecue to medium and put the vegetables in a metal basket so they don't fall onto the coals. Grill with the lid down, turning the vegetables often to avoid burning. Test for doneness by inserting the tip of a knife into the vegetables; they're ready when the knife slides in easily. Vegetables to try on the grill include: artichoke hearts, asparagus, beets, bell peppers, carrots, potatoes and squash.

Roasting: To roast, prepare vegetables as for grilling and distribute them in a single layer on a rimmed metal baking sheet. Roast in a preheated 400°F (200°C) oven until the vegetables are tender and golden.

Cutting onions (page 182)

Asparagus

MAKES 4 TO 6 SERVINGS
PREPARATION: 5 MINUTES
COOKING: ABOUT 4 MINUTES

Asparagus is the first green vegetable to appear in the spring. In Europe, white asparagus is very popular. White asparagus is protected from the sunlight to prevent the chlorophyll forming after it emerges from the earth. An asparagus etiquette note: It's quite OK to eat asparagus with your fingers, but using a fork is also acceptable.

| 2 lbs | 1 kg | fresh asparagus |
| 1 tsp | 5 mL | salt |

To prepare the asparagus, cut off only 1 to 2 inches (2.5 to 5 cm) of the stem end. Save the ends for soup. Wash in cool water and drain. If desired, peel the stems with a vegetable peeler.

To cook, lay the spears flat in a skillet. Place the skillet on high heat and add 1 qt (1 L) boiling water or just enough to cover the asparagus. Sprinkle in the salt. Return to the boil, uncovered, and cook for 3 to 4 minutes or until the asparagus is tender when pierced with the tip of a knife.

Drain and serve with lemon and butter.

String Beans with Browned Butter

MAKES 4 TO 6 SERVINGS
PREPARATION: 5 MINUTES
COOKING: 3 TO 4 MINUTES

Fresh bean varieties include green or yellow wax, Chinese long beans and the small tender French bean called haricot vert. To test for freshness, bend the bean — if it's fresh it will snap. Browned butter adds a superb nutty taste to cooked vegetables.

1 lb	500 g	fresh green or yellow beans, washed
2 tsp	10 mL	salt
		1 recipe Browned Butter (page 171)

To trim the beans, leave the tip but break off the flower or stem end and pull away any string from the seam side. Leave the beans whole or cut diagonally.

In a medium saucepan bring 2 qts (2 L) water with salt to a boil and drop in the beans. If they are cold, cover them with a lid briefly until the water returns to a boil, uncover and cook hard for 3 to 4 minutes until beans are tender and bright green. Drain and toss with browned butter.

Browned Butter

2–4 tbsp   25–50 mL   butter

Bring the butter to a boil on the stove and cook until the sediment turns golden brown, 3 to 5 minutes.

Beets & Beet Greens

PREPARATION: 5 MINUTES
COOKING: 30 TO 60 MINUTES, DEPENDING ON AGE OF BEETS; 5 MINUTES FOR GREENS

The beet is a root vegetable with a wonderful earthy, sweet taste. Beets come in deep red, gold or white varieties. When young, their leaves and stems are great steamed. The sugar beet is of the same family but has long white roots and is manufactured into sugar.

Young beets cook quickly while older ones take much longer. To boil, leave the beets whole without peeling, cut off the stem leaving 1 inch (2.5 cm) on, as beets "bleed" in water if cut or pricked. Place them in a saucepan, cover with cold water, bring to a simmer and cook until tender, from 30 minutes to 1 hour.

To test, remove one from the pan, cool slightly under cold water and rub the skin. If it slips off easily, the beet is cooked. Drain and cool.

If the beet greens are tender, wash them well and cut the leaves from the stems. Thinly slice the stems and leaves, keeping them separate. Steam or boil the stems first for 3 minutes, then add the leaves and cook for 2 or 3 minutes longer. Salt, if necessary, and serve with butter.

Broccoli—Plain or Puréed

MAKES 4 TO 6 SERVINGS
PREPARATION: 6 MINUTES
COOKING: 3 TO 4 MINUTES

Broccoli has been cultivated in Italy for centuries. When buying broccoli, avoid any with buds that have opened into yellow flowers — it shows it's passed its prime. Broccoli is high in calcium and vitamin C that is retained if the broccoli is cooked until tender-crisp. Broccoli and cauliflower are related and can be used interchangeably. Puréed broccoli adds color and texture to a meal.

2 tsp	10 mL	salt
1½ lbs	750 g	fresh broccoli
3 tbsp	45 mL	butter (optional)
		salt and pepper to taste

Cut off and discard the tough end of the main stem, leaving about 2 inches (5 cm). Cut off the florets, leaving 1 inch (2.5 cm) of stem on each. Split the florets with a knife. Peel the main stem and cut it into thin coins or matchsticks.

In a medium saucepan, bring 2 qts (2 L) water with the salt to a hard boil on high heat. Add the broccoli and return to a fast boil to cook for 2 to 3 minutes, or until tender-crisp. Drain. If you're serving the broccoli immediately, drizzle it with melted butter.

To purée broccoli: Cook the broccoli and chill it in ice water to set the color. Purée in a food processor or blender and taste for salt. To serve, reheat the purée in the microwave oven or in a saucepan and add butter before serving.

Brussels Sprouts with Pecans

MAKES 4 TO 6 SERVINGS
PREPARATION: 10 MINUTES
COOKING: 10 MINUTES

Brussels sprouts are tiny cabbage shapes that grow close together on a long tapered stalk. They come into season in the late autumn. The best ones are the small to medium size. The bigger ones have a strong taste and are best cut in half or into wedges to cook. Brussels sprouts should be cooked quickly as overcooking imparts a strong cabbage odor. To help them cook evenly, cut an X in the stem.

2 tsp	10 mL	salt
1 lb	500 g	brussels sprouts, trimmed, yellow leaves discarded
1 tbsp	15 mL	butter
1/3 cup	75 mL	toasted, chopped pecans

In a large saucepan, bring 2 qts (2 L) water to a boil with the salt. Add the sprouts, cover briefly until the water returns to a boil. Remove the lid and cook on high for 3 to 5 minutes or until the sprouts are tender when pierced with the tip of a knife. Drain. Toss the sprouts with butter and pecans.

To toast pecans, place them in a small skillet on medium-high heat until they become aromatic. Coarsely chop the nuts.

Red Cabbage Braised with Wine

MAKES 4 TO 6 SERVINGS
PREPARATION: 15 MINUTES
COOKING: 50 MINUTES

Cabbage varieties range from the round tightly packed leaves of the green or red heads to the elongated Napa and the lighter-colored Savoy cabbage with crinkly leaves. All are best cooked until tender-crisp. Braised red cabbage is especially good with roasted meat or game. It's coarser than green cabbage, so it needs longer cooking.

1	1	medium red cabbage about 1½ lbs (750 g)
4	4	bacon strips, thinly sliced
2	2	medium onions, peeled, thinly sliced
½ cup	125 mL	water or Chicken Stock (page 36)
2 tbsp	25 mL	red wine vinegar
1 tbsp	15 mL	brown sugar
1 tsp	5 mL	salt
½ cup	125 mL	dry red or white wine

Cut the cabbage into quarters. Cut out the white core and any thick white veins. Place the cabbage on a cutting board and thinly slice with a chef's knife.

In a large saucepan over medium-high heat, fry the bacon and onion until the bacon is crisp and the onion is tender, turning often. Add the cabbage a little at a time, mixing well. Stir in the water or stock, vinegar, sugar and salt.

Bring to a boil, cover and reduce the heat to medium-low for 30 minutes, stirring frequently. Pour in the wine and continue cooking for 20 minutes, or until the cabbage is tender.

Shredded Green Cabbage with Caraway Seeds

MAKES 4 TO 6 SERVINGS
PREPARATION: 6 MINUTES
COOKING: 2 TO 3 MINUTES

Cabbage is a winner whether it's for salads, preserved as sauerkraut, or shredded and lightly cooked. Cabbage doesn't have to emit a strong odor during cooking — that happens only if it's overcooked.

1 tsp	5 mL	salt
1/2	1/2	medium head of cabbage, Savoy or Napa
1 tsp	5 mL	caraway seeds
1 tbsp	15 mL	butter

Cut the cabbage into quarters lengthwise. Cut away the hard core. Place each quarter on a cutting board and thinly slice with a sharp chef's knife.

In a medium saucepan, bring 1 qt (1 L) water to a boil on high heat with the salt and add cabbage and caraway. Boil, uncovered, for 2 or 3 minutes until tender-crisp. Drain the cabbage and place it in a serving bowl. Toss the cabbage with butter.

Glazed Carrots

MAKES 4 TO 6 SERVINGS
PREPARATION: 3 MINUTES
COOKING: 12 TO 14 MINUTES

We've always known that carrots are good for you, but now there's even more good news. They contain beta-carotene that is not destroyed by cooking. Carrots are easily stored in the refrigerator in a plastic bag, but remember to twist off the green tops that drain away all of their moisture.

An easy way to bring a different texture to a meal is to purée cooked carrots, season with salt and pepper and use them as an accent to other vegetables. Carrots bring great color to a plate of food, especially when they are glazed.

1 1/2 lbs	750 g	carrots, sliced
1/2 tsp	2 mL	salt
1 tbsp	15 mL	butter
2 tsp	10 mL	corn syrup or maple syrup
2 tsp	10 mL	finely chopped fresh parsley, mint or dill

If the carrots are young, leave 1 inch (2.5 cm) of green stem; do not peel. Put the carrots in a saucepan with cold water and the salt. Bring to a boil, cover and cook for 8 to 10 minutes or until tender. Drain. To glaze, return the carrots to the pan on medium heat and toss them with the butter and syrup for 2 minutes. Garnish with the herbs.

Cauliflower & Broccoli Head

MAKES 6 SERVINGS
PREPARATION: 30 MINUTES
COOKING: 25 TO 30 MINUTES

Available in white, green or purple, cauliflower is best cooked when cut into florets. A whole head takes longer to cook and overcooks the florets.

1	1	head fresh cauliflower
1	1	head fresh broccoli

Cut a cauliflower head into florets, discarding the core. Drop the florets into boiling, salted water and boil hard for 3 minutes or until tender-crisp. Drain. Cut the broccoli head into florets, discarding the thick stem. Drop the florets into boiling salted water and boil hard for 3 minutes or until tender-crisp. Drain. Drop into ice water to set the color and chill them, then drain.

On a round, heatproof serving plate, create a round base, 6 inches (15 cm) across, using alternating broccoli and cauliflower florets. Continue to build the shape of a cauliflower head using alternating florets. Gently press the florets together to set the head firmly. Sprinkle the head with water, tightly cover with foil and place in preheated 300°F (150°C) oven for 20 minutes. Drizzle Browned Butter (page 171) on top. For extra color, surround the cauliflower and broccoli head with puréed carrots.

Cauliflower & Cashew Stir-Fry

MAKES 4 TO 6 SERVINGS
PREPARATION: 5 MINUTES
COOKING: 10 TO 12 MINUTES

You can easily substitute broccoli for the cauliflower in this tasty dish.

1	1	medium cauliflower, leaves removed
1/2 cup	125 mL	toasted cashew nuts
1 tbsp	15 mL	olive oil or vegetable oil
2	2	garlic cloves, minced
2 tbsp	25 mL	finely chopped fresh ginger
1 tsp	5 mL	salt, or to taste
1/2 cup	125 mL	water
1 tbsp	15 mL	cornstarch combined with 2 tbsp (25 mL) water
1 cup	250 mL	fresh or frozen green peas
		freshly grated black pepper

Cut out the cauliflower core. Cut into small bite-sized florets about 1¹/2 inches (3.5 cm) long. Remove and reserve. Coarsely chop the cashews. Reserve.

Heat the oil in the pan, add the garlic and ginger and stir-fry for 20 seconds. Add the cauliflower and salt and stir-fry for 1 minute. If the peas are fresh, add them now. Add the water, cover the pan and cook for 2 to 3 minutes until the cauliflower is tender-crisp. Stir in the cornstarch mixture with the frozen peas, if using, and cook for 2 minutes until the liquid has thickened and the peas are hot. Stir in the cashews. Grate pepper over the top.

To toast the cashews, place in a dry skillet or wok on medium-high heat, shaking the pan until the cashews turn light brown, about 3 minutes.

Corn on the Cob

For the full flavor of corn on the cob it's best to bring the cobs to room temperature before cooking. One can peel off the husk and cook the corn in water, but my favorite way is to leave the husk on the cob—the flavor is more intense and the silk clings to the husk, which makes it much easier peel.

Choose one of these cooking methods and serve with plain or Herb Butter (page 156):

Boiling: Drop the cobs with husks into boiling water. When the water returns to a boil, cook for 5 minutes. Use tongs to remove the cobs. Cool for 2 minutes and carefully pull off the husk and silk. Or, remove the husks and drop the cobs into boiling water. When the water returns to the boil, cook 4 minutes. Remove the cobs with tongs.

Grilling: Place the corn with husks on a hot grill or barbecue for 14 or 15 minutes, turning 3 or 4 times until the husk is lightly charred. Cool for 3 minutes, then carefully pull off the husk and silk.

To remove the kernels from a cooked cob, cut off the stem end for a firm base. Hold the cob upright on a plate to catch the kernels. Starting at the top, use a sharp knife to cut off kernels in sections, down to the stem end. Use the blunt side of the knife to scrape down the cob and remove the juicy pulp, which can be added to the kernels to make cream-style corn.

Roasted Ratatouille

MAKES 4 TO 6 SERVINGS
PREPARATION: 30 MINUTES
COOKING: 20 MINUTES

The critical ingredient in ratatouille is eggplant, which can range from a large egg-shape weighing about 1 lb (500 g) to an elongated finger-size. Their skin color varies from deep purple to mauve. Eggplants are bland-tasting, but they have the ability to absorb other flavors in cooking and they come alive with flavor when grilled. This classic dish from Provence can be served hot or cold, or puréed into a delicious soup. It uses summer vegetables that are roasted to retain their individual flavors.

1/4 cup	50 mL	olive oil
2	2	medium onions, thinly sliced
2–3	2–3	garlic cloves, minced
1 tbsp	15 mL	ground cinnamon
3 or 4	3 or 4	tomatoes, coarsely chopped in food processor
1	1	medium eggplant cut into 1/2-inch (1-cm) chunks
2	2	medium zucchini or yellow summer squash cut into 1/2-inch (1-cm) slices
1	1	medium bell pepper, red and/or green, seeded and cut into bite-sized pieces
1 tbsp	15 mL	brown sugar
1 tsp	5 mL	salt, or to taste
1/2 tsp	2 mL	pepper, or to taste

Preheat the oven to 400°F (200°C). In a saucepan on medium-low heat, heat half the oil and cook the onions, garlic and cinnamon, covered, for 5 minutes. Stir in the tomatoes and simmer for 10 minutes.

Place the eggplant, zucchini or squash and peppers on a rimmed baking pan. Drizzle on the remaining oil and roast in the oven for 15 to 20 minutes, turning several times until the vegetables are lightly browned and tender. Add the roasted vegetables to the tomato mixture and stir in the sugar, salt and pepper. Cook over medium heat for 3 minutes to combine the flavors.

Fiddleheads

MAKES 4 TO 6 SERVINGS
PREPARATION: 10 MINUTES
COOKING: 3 TO 4 MINUTES

This springtime treat has a delightful earthy taste. Fiddleheads are tightly coiled ferns with a loose brown skin that have just emerged from the earth. Fiddleheads are available year-round in the freezer section.

1 lb	500 g	fiddleheads, fresh or frozen
2 tsp	10 mL	salt
2 tbsp	25 mL	melted butter

If the fiddleheads are fresh, toss them in warm water and gently rub them between your hands to remove the brown skin. Leave any long tails as they are edible and tender. Rinse in fresh cold water. If frozen, defrost slightly under warm water. Bring to a rolling boil 2 qts (2 L) water with the salt. Plunge the fiddleheads into the boiling water, cover and return the water to a hard boil. Cook for 2 to 3 minutes, or until the fiddleheads are tender-crisp. Drain. Serve with the melted butter.

Roasted Garlic

A cousin of the onion, garlic forms a bulb consisting of many cloves. Garlic's potent taste is released when the clove is chopped raw, but if it is boiled or roasted, the potency disappears, leaving a slightly sweet nutlike taste and no aroma. Store garlic in a cool, dark place and remove green sprouts.

1	1	head garlic
		olive oil
		salt to taste

Cut off the top of the garlic bulb, exposing the cloves. Rub liberally with olive oil. Sprinkle with salt. Place in a small, ovenproof casserole with a tight lid or wrap in a double layer of foil. Roast in a 325°F (160°C) oven for 1 hour. A hotter oven does not bring out the sweet, rich flavor.

Cool and squeeze the soft garlic out of the skins. Purée until smooth and use for bread, salads, soups or sauces.

To remove the skin of a single clove, place it on a firm surface and press on it with the broadest part of a knife — the skin will lift off.

Jerusalem Artichokes with Chives

MAKES 4 TO 6 SERVINGS
PREPARATION: 10 MINUTES
COOKING: 25 TO 30 MINUTES

These knobby tubers of a tall, perennial sunflower are native to North America. Jerusalem artichokes have a mild, earthy taste that goes well with, or can substitute for, potatoes.

1 lb	500 g	Jerusalem artichokes, scrubbed and peeled
2 tbsp	25 mL	butter
1 tbsp	15 mL	finely chopped chives

Put the artichokes in cold salted water in a saucepan and bring to a simmer. Cover and cook for about 25 minutes, or until they are tender. Drain and slice. Place them in a serving dish, drizzle with butter and sprinkle with chives.

Mushrooms

Most mushrooms are cultivated on organic material, but edible wild mushrooms can be found in the woodlands. Wild mushrooms must be located with someone knowledgeable to avoid poisonous ones. I learned a useful trick to clean mushrooms a few years ago while cooking in Germany. Place them in a bowl, throw in a small handful of flour, cover with warm water, toss quickly and drain, shaking the colander to release excess water. This method cleans and draws out any particles on or under the cap and doesn't let the mushroom absorb the water. Store mushrooms in brown paper bags in the refrigerator.

Cultivated mushrooms are 90% water and contain vitamins, potassium and iron — don't let anyone say they are an "empty" food. Because of the water content, always stir-fry mushrooms quickly on high heat for 1 or 2 minutes before they release that delicious liquid.

Varieties

- White button are the most common cultivated mushrooms.
- Small brown cremini look similar to button mushrooms but are baby portobellos. They have less water and are more concentrated in flavor.

- Portobellos are large, dark cremini mushrooms with a concentrated flavor.
- Oyster mushrooms are a soft, peppery, shell-shaped mushroom with a gentle taste.
- Chanterelles are yellow, wild mushrooms with an aroma like ripe apricots.
- Shiitake are Japanese mushrooms similar to Chinese black mushrooms. Sold fresh or dry.
- Morels are dome-shaped with a honeycomb texture and an earthy flavor.
- Enoki mushrooms grow in clumps with long, thin stems and tiny caps. They have a crunchy texture and a mild flavor.
- Porcini (cepes) are available dried or fresh and have a rich, earthy flavor.

Rosemary Mushrooms in Croutons

MAKES 6 CROUTONS
PREPARATION: 15 MINUTES
COOKING: 10 MINUTES

These croutons are shaped, toasted bread slices, filled with mushrooms to make a delightful starter or side dish for any meal.

6	6	whole wheat or white bread slices, crusts removed
3 tbsp	45 mL	melted butter
1	1	small onion, peeled, finely chopped
1/2	1/2	green or red bell pepper, seeded and finely chopped
1/2 lb	250 g	mushrooms, washed, drained and finely sliced
1/2 cup	125 mL	dry white wine
1 tsp	5 mL	chopped fresh rosemary or 1/2 tsp (2 mL) dried
1/2 tsp	2 mL	salt, or to taste
1/8 tsp	.5 mL	freshly grated black pepper, or to taste
6	6	small fresh rosemary or parsley sprigs

Preheat the oven to 375°F (190°C). Use a rolling pin to flatten each bread slice to 1/4 inch (.5 cm) thickness. Cut out 3-inch (7.5-cm) circles with a cookie cutter or glass and lightly brush with half the butter. Press the rounds into muffin cups. Bake for 10 minutes or until lightly toasted and crisp. Set aside.

In a medium skillet, heat the remaining butter on medium heat. Add the onion and pepper and sauté for 5 minutes until tender, stirring often. Raise heat to high, add the mushrooms, and sauté about 1 minute, stirring often. Stir in the wine and rosemary and continue cooking until the wine has reduced by half. Season to taste. Spoon mixture into the croutons and garnish with rosemary sprigs. Serve warm.

Onions

Onions range in taste from mild to very strong. Store onions in a cool, dark place, never in the refrigerator.

To peel an onion, hold the onion firmly on its side and cut the onion in half from the root to the stem. Peel the brown skin from the tip to the root. Cut off the root, leaving the core to keep the layers intact for cutting.

To cut an onion into small cubes, place cut side down and hold the onion firmly with your fingers on the rounded side. Cut 3 horizontal, parallel slices starting at the tip end and go through the onion, stopping just short of the core. Make 5 vertical parallel cuts from the tip through the onion leaving the core uncut. Cut across in parallel slices beginning at the tip until you reach the core.

Varieties

- Yellow onions are all-purpose, strong and hot in flavor. Available year-round.
- White onions have a sharp, crisp flavor, and high in water content.
- Vidalia are large, sweet and highly perishable due to the sugar content.
- Red onions are mild, with less water than the yellow onion.
- Spanish or Bermuda are large, mild onions with a high water content.
- Pearl onions are small and sweet.
- Shallots are a cross between garlic and onion.
- Scallions are also called green onions.
- Leeks have a tall, white stem with green leaves, and mild flavor.
- Chives have slender green stems with a mild flavor; ideal for garnishes.

Caramelized Onions

MAKES 6 TO 8 SERVINGS
PREPARATION: 5 MINUTES
COOKING: 30 MINUTES

The long, slow cooking brings out a delicious sweetness in these onions.

4 tbsp	50 mL	olive oil
4	4	large onions, peeled, finely sliced
		salt and freshly ground black pepper to taste

Heat a large skillet over medium-high heat with the oil, add onions and sauté for 5 minutes, stirring often. Cover, reduce the heat to low and sweat the onions for 20 to 25 minutes. Uncover, raise the heat to high, stirring constantly for 5 minutes to allow the onions to brown and caramelize. Season with salt and pepper.

Buttered Peas with Mint

MAKES 4 TO 6 SERVINGS
PREPARATION: 20 MINUTES
COOKING: 3 TO 5 MINUTES

Peas are vine-grown edible seeds in a pod that are picked when mature. Although shelled peas are available frozen, fresh peas have a wonderful taste. Snow peas are immature peas with tender, edible pods that need the stem removed and the string along the pod's flat side pulled away. Snap peas are a cross between green peas and snow peas. They are tender enough to be eaten raw, or cooked in their pods.

1¹/₂ lbs	750 g	fresh unshelled peas
2 tsp	10 mL	salt
2	2	stems fresh mint
2 tbsp	25 mL	butter, melted
		pinch sugar
1 tbsp	15 mL	finely chopped mint leaves

Shell the peas. Bring 1¹/₂ qts (1.5 L) water to a boil with the salt on high heat. Add the mint stems and the shelled peas and cook for 3 to 4 minutes, depending on the tenderness of the peas. Drain and remove the mint stems.

Toss the peas with the butter, sugar and mint leaves and serve.

Broiled or Grilled Sweet Peppers

PREPARATION: 5 MINUTES, 10 MINUTES TO COOL
COOKING: 15 MINUTES

Sweet bell peppers are bell-like in shape, with thick, juicy flesh. Peppers range from green (unripened), yellow, orange and chocolate to dark purple. All peppers need to be seeded. To intensify their flavors, red or yellow peppers should be roasted and their skins removed.

1 or 2	1 or 2	red or yellow peppers, whole

Place peppers under a preheated broiler 2 inches (5 cm) from the heat source or place on a grill. Turn the peppers until all sides have blistered and browned, for about 15 minutes.

Place the peppers on a tray and cover with a towel for about 10 minutes to steam, making peeling easier. Resist removing the peel under water as you will lose some of the peppers' rich flavor.

Stuffed Baked Potatoes

MAKES 4 SERVINGS
PREPARATION: 20 TO 25 MINUTES
BAKING: ABOUT 1 HOUR

Potatoes are root vegetables that fall into one of two categories, mealy or waxy. Mealy potatoes have a high starch and low sugar content with a thick brown or purplish skin and are best for baking, mashing or frying. The waxy potato, including new potatoes, has a thin brown or red skin and is best for boiling, roasting or grilling because of its low starch. Waxy potatoes are not good for mashed potatoes — much too gluey. To tell the difference between mealy and waxy potatoes, put the raw potato in water. The mealy will sink and the waxy will float. Green potatoes have been grown too close to the surface or stored in light that makes them toxic — discard them.

This is a way to dress up baked potatoes that can even make a one-dish meal. During winter storage, baking potatoes lose some moisture, so they will absorb more liquid when made into mashed potatoes.

4	4	baking potatoes, scrubbed, pricked with a knife tip
1/3–1/2 cup	75–125 mL	heated milk, depending on the starch content of the potato
2 tbsp	25 mL	butter
1/2 tsp	2 mL	salt, or to taste
2 tsp	10 mL	chopped chives or 2 green onions, finely sliced
1/3 cup	75 mL	grated Cheddar or Parmesan cheese

Place the potatoes in a preheated 400°F (200°C) oven for 1 hour, or until tender. Hold the hot potato in a cloth and slice off the top, lengthwise. Use a small spoon to scoop the pulp into a bowl without breaking the skin of the shell or lid. Mash the pulp with a potato masher. Beat in the milk, a little at a time, with a wooden spoon until the mixture is light and fluffy. Beat in the butter and season to taste. Add the chives or onions. Pile the mixture into the potato shells. Top with the cheese. Reheat in the oven for 10 minutes until the cheese has melted. Replace the tops and serve.

New potatoes are best when they are small. Their skins are tender and they don't require peeling. They are delicious when simply boiled and served with butter and chopped fresh mint or chives.

Potatoes au Gratin

MAKES 4 TO 6 SERVINGS
PREPARATION: 10 MINUTES
COOKING: 1 HOUR

5 or 6	5 or 6	medium waxy potatoes, with or without peel, washed
1	1	onion, peeled, thinly sliced
1/2 tsp	2 mL	salt, or to taste
1 cup	250 mL	hot Chicken Stock or Vegetable Stock (page 36)
4 tbsp	50 mL	grated Parmesan, medium Cheddar or Swiss cheese

Preheat the oven to 375°F (190°C). Butter a shallow 2-qt (2-L) casserole. Cut the potatoes into 1/8-inch (.25-cm) thick slices. Place a layer of potatoes in the bottom of the casserole and sprinkle with onion, and salt. Continue, making 2 more layers. Pour in the stock and sprinkle with cheese. Bake for 1 hour until the potatoes are tender. Leave to settle for 10 minutes before serving.

Roesti Potatoes

MAKES 4 TO 6 SERVINGS
PREPARATION: 30 MINUTES, 2 HOURS TO COOL
COOKING: 35 MINUTES

A classic Swiss potato pancake that goes well with grilled chicken or meat.

6	6	mealy potatoes, with peel, about 2 lbs (1 kg)
1 tsp	5 mL	salt, or to taste
3 tbsp	45 mL	butter
1	1	onion, finely chopped

In a saucepan, cover the potatoes with cold water, cover and cook for about 20 minutes, or just until tender when pricked with a knife. Do not overcook. Drain. Cool for 2 hours or more, so they will not become gluey when grated. Peel and grate using the large holes of a grater. Sprinkle in the salt.

In a medium-sized skillet, melt the butter over medium heat and sauté the onion until tender, but not browned, about 5 minutes. Stir in the potato, pressing down to form a cake about 6 inches (15 cm) in diameter. Cover and continue to cook until a golden crust forms on the bottom, about 15 minutes. Loosen the roesti with a spatula and shake the pan several times. Remove the pan from the heat. Place a large plate over the pan and carefully invert the roesti onto it. Slide the roesti back into the pan. Cook for another 15 minutes until golden. Slide onto a serving plate.

Mashed Potatoes with Celeriac

MAKES 4 TO 6 SERVINGS
PREPARATION: 15 MINUTES
COOKING: 20 TO 25 MINUTES

Adding celeriac to mashed potatoes introduces a delicious new flavor. Of course, mashed potatoes are great on their own, too! Celeriac is the knobby root of the celery plant, with a brown skin that must be removed. Celeriac does not absorb milk as potatoes do, so add milk just until the mixture is light and fluffy.

2 lbs	1 kg	medium, mealy potatoes, peeled, quartered
1	1	celeriac root, peeled, sliced and cubed
2 tsp	10 mL	salt
1/4–1/2 cup	50–125 mL	milk, heated
2 tbsp	25 mL	butter
1 tsp	5 mL	salt, or to taste

Cook the potatoes and celeriac in 2 qts (2 L) cold water with the salt, covered, over medium heat until tender, for 20 to 25 minutes. Drain. Return to the pan on low heat. If you like the mashed potatoes slightly lumpy, use a masher, but if you like a smooth consistency, use a food mill or ricer. Gradually beat in the milk until the potatoes are smooth with a light and fluffy consistency. Beat in the butter and season with salt.

Cauliflower & Broccoli Head
with Puréed Carrots (page 176)

Spaghetti Squash with Tomato Sauce
& Parmesan Cheese (page 190)

Chocolate Pears with
Ginger Cream (page 201)

Chocolate Truffles (page 219) and
Fudge Peppermint Balls (page 218)

Baked Sweet Potatoes

MAKES 4 SERVINGS
PREPARATION: 5 MINUTES
COOKING: 45 TO 50 MINUTES

These elongated, tubular roots with orange skins and flesh are rich in carotene and vitamin E. Sweet potatoes are often mistakenly called yams. Yams are starchy non-sweet tubular roots with white flesh. Roasting helps intensify the flavor of sweet potatoes. They cook faster than white potatoes, so don't overcook or a sweet sap will ooze out into the oven.

4	4	sweet potatoes
2 tbsp	25 mL	butter

Preheat the oven to 375°F (190°). Prick each potato with the tip of a sharp knife. Bake for 40 to 45 minutes. To open the potatoes, cut a cross on the top. With the fingers of both hands, push against the cross to open it and place 1/2 tbsp (7 mL) butter in the opening.

Orange Sweet Potatoes Gratin

MAKES 4 TO 6 SERVINGS
PREPARATION: 10 MINUTES
BAKING: 40 TO 50 MINUTES

This sweet potato casserole is a winner with roast chicken or pork.

3 lbs	1.5 kg	Baked Sweet Potatoes (recipe above)
1/2 tsp	2 mL	grated nutmeg
1/2–1 tsp	2–5 mL	salt
2 tsp	10 mL	grated orange rind
1/4 cup	50 mL	orange juice
2 tbsp	25 mL	brown sugar
1	1	egg, whisked
2 tbsp	25 mL	finely chopped parsley

Cool baked potatoes for 20 minutes.

Peel and purée in a food processor or blender. Beat in the nutmeg, salt, rind, orange juice, sugar and egg until fluffy. Preheat the oven to 375°F (190°C). Place the mixture in a shallow casserole and bake for 20 minutes, until bubbly. Garnish with the parsley.

Spinach with Pine Nuts

MAKES 4 SERVINGS
PREPARATION: 5 MINUTES
COOKING: 1 MINUTE

Spinach leaves are potassium-rich, full of vitamins and best eaten when combined with calcium-rich food, such as butter or milk products, to neutralize the slightly astringent flavor. Spinach grows close to the ground, so it needs to be well washed to remove any grit. Although bags of fresh spinach say "washed," I like to briefly toss the spinach in water to be sure all the sand is removed, then drain well.

1	1	10-oz (300-g) package of fresh spinach
1/2 cup	125 mL	water with 1/4 tsp (1 mL) salt
1/2 cup	125 mL	sour cream or whipping cream
		several fresh gratings of nutmeg
		salt to taste
2 tbsp	25 mL	toasted pine nuts

Pull away the large stems from the leaves. In a medium saucepan, bring salted water to boil on high heat. Use a wooden spoon to carefully press the spinach into the water. Boil for 1 minute. Drain in a colander and press out excess water with a wooden spoon. Finely chop by hand or in a food processor, pulsing off and on. In a saucepan, heat the cream and stir in the spinach. Sprinkle in the nutmeg and salt, if desired. To serve, sprinkle with pine nuts.

> To toast pine nuts, add to a dry skillet over medium heat, shaking the pan often, until golden.

Summer Squash with Summer Herbs

MAKES 4 TO 6 SERVINGS
PREPARATION: 10 MINUTES
COOKING: 2 MINUTES

Squash are part of the edible gourd family. Summer squash are mild-tasting zucchini, yellow, crookneck and pattypan (disk-shaped) squash that need quick cooking to avoid becoming watery. Summer squash has a delicate flavor that is best accented with herbs.

1 lb	500 g	zucchini, yellow squash or pattypan, washed
2 tbsp	25 mL	butter or extra-virgin olive oil
2	2	garlic cloves, minced
2 tbsp	25 mL	chopped parsley, chives, tarragon, basil and/or dill
1/2 tsp	2 mL	salt, or to taste

Slice the squash into 1/4-inch (.5-cm) slices. In a wok or medium skillet, heat the butter or oil on high heat. Add the garlic with the squash and stir together. Cover and cook for 2 minutes, stirring once, until the squash is tender but slightly crisp. Toss in the herbs and season to taste.

Puréed Butternut Squash

MAKES 4 TO 6 SERVINGS
PREPARATION: 5 MINUTES
COOKING: 40 TO 45 MINUTES

Winter squash have hard shells and sweet concentrated flavors. Popular varieties include acorn, butternut, pumpkin, Hubbard, spaghetti and turban. Butternut squash is one of the sweetest tasting. It is beige with a long neck and a round bottom. It makes wonderful soups and delicious purées.

1	1	butternut squash, 1/2 to 1 lb (250 to 500 g)
2 tbsp	25 mL	butter
1 tbsp	15 mL	brown sugar, or to taste
1 tsp	5 mL	salt, or to taste
1/4 tsp	1 mL	pepper, or to taste

Preheat the oven to 375°F (190°C). Cut the squash in half lengthwise and place the halves, cut side down, on a buttered or parchment paper–lined, baking sheet. Bake for 40 to 45 minutes, or until tender when pierced with the tip of a knife. Cool for 10 minutes and remove the seeds using a spoon. Cut off the peel and purée the pulp in a food processor or blender. Stir in the butter and season with sugar, salt and pepper. Reheat to serve.

Spaghetti Squash with Tomato Sauce & Parmesan Cheese

MAKES 4 TO 6 SERVINGS
PREPARATION: 5 MINUTES
COOKING: 45 MINUTES TO 1 HOUR

This unique squash, when cooked, reveals a mass of spaghetti-like strands. It's a one-dish meal topped with pasta sauce, melted butter or extra-virgin olive oil and cheese.

1	1	small spaghetti squash, about 3 lbs (1.5 kg)
2 tbsp	25 mL	melted butter or extra-virgin olive oil
2 cups	500 mL	Tomato Sauce (page 103), heated
1/4 cup	50 mL	freshly grated Parmesan cheese

Preheat the oven to 375°F (190°C). Grease a rimmed baking sheet.

Use a chef's knife to cut the squash in half lengthwise and place each half, cut side down, on a buttered or parchment paper–lined baking sheet. Bake for 30 to 45 minutes, or until tender when pricked with the tip of a sharp knife. Invert the squash and cool for 10 minutes. Remove the seeds with a spoon. Use a fork to separate the pulp into strands and scoop the strands onto a platter. Toss the squash with the butter or olive oil, then cover with the Tomato Sauce and top with cheese.

Caramelized Baked Tomatoes

MAKES 4 TO 6 SERVINGS
PREPARATION: 15 MINUTES
BAKING: 30 MINUTES

There are many varieties of tomatoes, from tiny cherry to large and juicy beefsteak. The depth of flavor in tomatoes is amazing at the peak of their season. Unfortunately, between seasons tomatoes don't fare well in taste, but cluster tomatoes grown in greenhouses during the winter are second best. Avoid refrigerating tomatoes as it kills the flavor and texture. Keep them in a cool place, such as a windowsill not in direct sunlight, and always store stem end down.

These tomatoes go well with grilled steak or fish, especially in the summer and early autumn.

6	6	medium, ripe tomatoes
2 tbsp	25 mL	melted butter
3	3	slices bread, crusts removed, cut into small cubes
2 tbsp	25 mL	brown sugar, lightly packed
1 tbsp	15 mL	finely chopped fresh parsley or mint
1/4 tsp	1 mL	salt, or to taste
1/8 tsp	.5 mL	pepper, or to taste

Cut out the core of the tomatoes so the pulp can be scooped out. Chop the pulp to make 1/3 cup (75 mL). Cut a small slice off the bottom of the tomatoes so they sit evenly in the shallow baking dish.

In a bowl, combine the chopped pulp, butter, bread, sugar, parsley or mint, salt and pepper. Stuff the tomatoes and place them in a cake pan. Bake in a preheated 350°F (180°C) oven for 15 to 20 minutes, or until tender when tested with the tip of a knife.

Sweets, Cakes, Cookies, Pies & Tarts

When I was growing up, we had dessert at lunch and dinner in our home.

These days, many people are too busy for baked desserts and serve instead fruit and cheese, which are faster to prepare. If it's a special occasion and you choose to serve dessert, consider the rest of your menu before deciding on a rich creamy concoction, or a light refreshing one.

If you are serving a cream soup, don't present chocolate mousse for dessert; try a lime chiffon tart instead. Of course, the tastes and dietary requirements of your guests must also be considered. Does anyone have nut allergies? Is anyone trying to slim down? Have fun and be creative, but think carefully before you plunge in.

Cakes & Cookies

Because of our family bakery, I grew up with happy experiences of Saturday morning cake and cookie baking duties. I loved watching the icing being made in a large yellow mixing bowl but, even better, I loved licking the bowl! Following are some tips to help you to make light, buttery cakes that are alive with flavor.

Baking Tips

- Although it's more expensive, butter is worth every penny for its rich flavor. If you must, substitute shortening or lard, but never margarine because it contains water that will affect your baking.

- When a recipe calls for creaming butter and sugar together, have the butter at room temperature so that it incorporates easily. If necessary, warm the butter slightly in the microwave oven.

- Never beat the batter for cakes when the flour is added, or the result will be cavities in the finished product. Fold in gently with a rubber spatula.

- To test whether the flour you have is all-purpose or cake flour, squeeze a fistful tightly in your hand; if it clumps, it's cake flour.

Old-Fashioned Apple Pie (page 225)

- Never shake the cup as you are measuring flour or you could end up with more flour than the recipe requires, resulting in cracks in the top of your cakes.

- Use cookie sheets without rims for the best results; they allow the heat in the oven to circulate evenly.

- An ice cream scoop is a great way to measure cookie dough onto sheets.

- Bake cookies in the top half of the oven. If you are baking two sheets at once, they will take slightly longer. Switch the positions of the sheets halfway through baking.

- Bake cakes in the center of the oven.

- Remove cakes or muffins from the pan after they have been out of the oven for 5 minutes. This allows for some shrinkage and prevents sticking.

- Almost all cookies freeze well, but meringues and macaroons do not.

Pastry

I learned to make pastry that is tender, flaky and melts in your mouth when I was cooking in Europe. Once you have learned the tricks of the trade, perfect pastry is attainable every time. Personal preferences: use half-butter and half-lard for light, flaky crust; don't add sugar to pastry, even for dessert; leave the pastry neutral to complement the filling.

Pastry Tips

- Cut the cold fat into the flour by grating, or by pulsing in a food processor, rather than cutting in with knives or a pastry cutter, which is a slower process.

- To prevent shrinking during baking, pick up the pastry at least 4 or 5 times during the rolling and do not stretch the pastry into the pie plate — lay it gently in place.

- After rolling, chill pastry dough in the refrigerator or freeze it for 10 minutes to rest the dough and relax the gluten.

- Always bake pastry at a high temperature to melt the fat quickly, which creates flaky layers.

- There is no need to blind-bake single-crust pie shells (lining a pastry shell with foil and weighing the pastry down with dried beans during the baking). This process is supposed to stop the pastry from shrinking and losing its shape during baking. However, blind-baking is not necessary if you follow the steps for rolling, relaxing, chilling, pricking (if needed) and baking in a hot oven.

Grating fat into flour for pastry dough (see opposite)

Mixed Fresh Fruit Salad

MAKES 4 TO 6 SERVINGS
PREPARATION: 30 TO 40 MINUTES

A bowl of freshly cut fruit should be a rainbow of color gently tossed in a light juice or syrup. Cut the fruit with rounded edges; try to avoid the standard but unnatural cube shapes — nature hasn't yet produced a square fruit! Serve the fruit salad at room temperature for the best flavors.

4 cups	1 L	mixed, sliced fresh fruit
1/2 cup	125 mL	orange juice, apple cider, champagne or wine

Barely cover the fruit with fruit juice, champagne or wine and serve. The following suggestions depend on availability, ripeness and your preference:

- Apples and pears are best peeled if the skins are tough or blemished. Quarter, core, slice and put them into juice or wine to prevent discoloration. Bananas also discolor, so peel and cut them on an angle into 1/4-inch (.5-cm) thick slices.

- Nectarines are best sliced with their skin, but peaches should be peeled. To remove the skin, drop the peach into boiling water for 20 seconds; it will peel easily.

- Navel seedless oranges are best. To make orange segments, see page 60.

- Grapes should be cut in half and the pits removed with clean tweezers.

- Melon and papaya add sweetness. Cut crosswise in half, spoon out seeds, and cut in thin slices.

- Mangoes also add sweetness. Peel the skin with a small, sharp knife, cut the mangoes into 4 vertical sections around the large pit and slice.

- Ripe pineapples have a sweet aroma and feel heavy in the hand. To peel, twist off the stem and stand the pineapple upright. Cut the peel off in vertical strips. Cut the "eyes" out in V-wedges. Cut the pineapple lengthwise into quarters, cut off the woody core and slice thinly.

Chocolate Mint Fondue with Fresh Fruit

MAKES 6 TO 10 SERVINGS
PREPARATION: 30 MINUTES

This dish is the center of attention at any gathering. Use some, or all, of the following fruits: strawberries and sweet cherries with stems, mango, papaya, melon, nectarines, pear and apple wedges, and orange or mandarin segments.

1 cup	250 mL	semi-sweet chocolate
1/2 cup	125 mL	10% (half-and-half), 18% or 35% cream
1 tsp	5 mL	mint extract
2 qts	2 L	prepared fresh fruit

Melt the chocolate and cream in a heatproof bowl set over hot water on low heat. Don't let the water boil, as chocolate can't withstand high heat and burns easily. Stir the mixture until smooth. Add the mint extract. Transfer the mixture to a fondue pot over a warmer — a candle is best, as other heat sources are too powerful and cause the chocolate to burn. Dip the fruit into the warm chocolate-mint fondue with fingers or fondue forks.

Stewed Rhubarb or Rhubarb Sorbet

MAKES 4 TO 6 SERVINGS
PREPARATION: 10 MINUTES
COOKING: 10 TO 15 MINUTES

Stewed puréed rhubarb served over ice cream is special in the spring. It also makes a great sorbet — delightful if served with fresh strawberries.

2 cups	500 mL	sliced fresh rhubarb, 1/4 inch (1 cm) thick
1/4 cup	50 mL	orange juice
1/2 cup	125 mL	granulated sugar or maple syrup, or to taste

Stir the rhubarb and orange juice in a non-reactive saucepan, and cook over medium heat for 10 to 12 minutes, until the rhubarb is tender. Stir in the sugar or syrup. Chill and serve plain or over ice cream.

To make sorbet: Purée the stewed rhubarb in a processor or blender. It's easiest to use an ice cream maker, but if one is not available freeze the rhubarb in a shallow dish until mushy and almost firm. Stir the mixture until smooth or purée briefly in a processor or blender to prevent crystals from forming. Return the rhubarb to the freezer for at least 2 hours until firm. Remove about 20 minutes before serving.

Meringue Nests with Ice Cream & Fruit Coulis or Chocolate Sauce

MAKES 6 TO 8 SERVINGS
PREPARATION: 30 MINUTES
COOKING: 1½ HOURS, DRYING 4 HOURS OR OVERNIGHT

Delicate, elegant meringues may look difficult but they are fairly simple to make. You must, however, allow plenty of time to let them dry out after they're baked. This dessert uses "nests" filled with scoops of ice cream and topped with fruit or chocolate sauce. My family's favorite Easter dessert is the meringue nest made to look like a basket filled with colorful ice cream such as strawberry, mint and chocolate shaped like eggs.

3	3	egg whites, at room temperature
		pinch salt
1 tsp	5 mL	baking powder
1 tsp	5 mL	water
1 tsp	5 mL	white vinegar
3/4 cup	175 mL	granulated sugar
1 tsp	5 mL	vanilla
1–1½ pts	.5–.75 L	ice cream of your choice
		1 recipe Fruit Coulis (page 199) or Chocolate Sauce (page 200)

Preheat the oven to 225°F (110°C). Butter and flour 2 baking sheets, shaking off the excess, or line the sheets with parchment paper. Outline 8 3-inch (7.5-cm) circles with a knife tip on the floured surface or draw circles on the underside of the paper. (Invert the paper so the meringues are not directly on the outline.)

Using an electric beater on medium speed or a metal bowl and a balloon whisk, beat the egg whites until frothy. Sprinkle in salt, baking powder, water and vinegar (which acts as a drying agent) and continue whisking, until soft peaks form. Slowly sprinkle in the sugar, a spoonful at a time, until the meringue is stiff and glossy. Add the vanilla and continue beating for another 30 seconds. With 2 spoons, mound the meringue onto the circles and make wells in the centers to form nests. Bake for 1½ hours until crisp but still white. Turn off the oven and leave the meringues in it to cool overnight or for at least 4 hours.

Scoop out balls of ice cream ahead of time, place them on a tray and refreeze. To serve, place your choice of ice cream in the meringues and serve with fruit coulis or chocolate sauce.

Note: Beware — don't make meringues on a damp day — the sugar absorbs moisture and they lose their crispness. If the humidity is high, stir 1 tsp (5 mL) cornstarch into the sugar before adding it to beaten egg whites. If the whites are beaten too stiffly and have lost their sheen, whisk up another egg white until frothy, then gently fold it into the meringue until it's moist and shiny again.

Fruit Coulis or Sorbet

MAKES 4 TO 6 SERVINGS
PREPARATION: 15 MINUTES
FREEZING: 4 TO 5 HOURS

Coulis are puréed fruit sauces that add great color and contrasting flavors to the sweetness of a dessert. If they're frozen they become sorbets. Always taste the fruit before adding sugar. When serving a sorbet, accent it with a cookie, plain cake, other sliced fresh fruit, or even another fruit coulis in a contrasting color.

1 qt	1 L	fresh strawberries or raspberries or 10 oz (300 g) frozen, or 2 ripe mangoes, peeled and pitted
3 tbsp	45 mL	granulated sugar, or to taste
1–2 tsp	5–10 mL	lemon juice (optional)

Discard any deteriorated fruit. Place fresh or frozen fruit in a food processor and purée until smooth. Add sugar to taste and lemon juice, if desired. You can press the raspberries through a sieve to remove the seeds.

For Coulis: Chill for at least 1 hour to allow the flavors to develop.

For Sorbet: Place the fruit mixture in a metal bowl and set it over ice to chill quickly. Make the sorbet in an ice cream maker following the manufacturer's instructions. Or, freeze the mixture in a shallow dish until almost firm. Remove and purée briefly to prevent the formation of crystals. Refreeze for at least 2 hours. Remove the sorbet from the freezer 20 minutes before serving.

Chocolate Sauce

MAKES 2 CUPS (500 ML)
PREPARATION: 5 MINUTES
COOKING: 5 TO 6 MINUTES

This sauce will store well in the refrigerator. When served warm on cold ice cream, it sets firm — fabulous!

1 1/2 cups	375 mL	granulated sugar
2/3 cup	150 mL	cocoa
		pinch salt
2/3 cup	150 mL	boiling water
1/4 cup	50 mL	golden corn syrup
2 tbsp	25 mL	butter
1 tsp	5 mL	vanilla

In a saucepan, mix the sugar, cocoa and salt until well blended. Stir in the water and syrup. Bring the sauce to a boil, reduce the heat and boil gently for 5 minutes, stirring often. Remove the pan from the heat, add the butter, cool briefly, then add the vanilla. Store in the refrigerator in a closed glass or ceramic container. To reheat, stand the container in boiling-hot water for a few minutes.

Chocolate Pears with Ginger Cream

MAKES 4 TO 6 SERVINGS
PREPARATION: 25 MINUTES
COOKING: 30 MINUTES

This recipe may seem complicated, but the process involves three simple steps: poaching whole pears, chilling them and dipping them in melted chocolate. Baker's bittersweet chocolate, when melted with butter, keeps the best shine.

1 cup	250 mL	granulated sugar
2 cups	500 mL	water
1	1	cinnamon stick
2	2	whole cloves
6	6	firm, ripe pears — Bartlett or Bosc, with stems
		juice of 1 lemon
4 oz	120 g	bittersweet chocolate, chopped
3 tbsp	45 mL	butter
1 cup	250 mL	whipping cream for garnish
3 tbsp	45 mL	finely chopped candied ginger
4	4	fresh mint leaves for garnish

To make the syrup, use a saucepan small enough to firmly hold the pears upright and add the sugar, water, cinnamon and cloves. Simmer for 3 minutes.

Peel the pears, leaving the stem intact, and brush with lemon juice to prevent discoloration. Cut out the core from the blossom end using a melon baller or the tip of a vegetable peeler. Trim the bottom of each pear so they stand upright. Place the pears in the syrup and poach gently for 20 to 25 minutes, covered. Test for tenderness with the tip of a sharp knife inserted in the blossom end. Chill the pears in the syrup for 4 or 5 hours or overnight. Drain and dry well with a paper towel. Reserve the syrup for another use.

To melt the chocolate, place it in a small bowl over barely simmering water and stir until slightly lumpy. Remove the bowl from the heat and stir in the butter until the sauce is smooth and shiny. Dip the pears in the chocolate, coating the entire pear surface, using a spoon to coat any exposed areas. Set the pears upright on a rack to allow the chocolate to drip and set, about 1 hour. To keep the chocolate shiny, do not refrigerate the dipped pears.

For ginger cream, whip the cream to soft peaks and stir in the ginger. Place a dollop of cream on each serving plate. To garnish, use the tip of a sharp knife to make a small hole in the pears near the stems, and insert the mint leaves.

Baked Orange-Cinnamon Bananas

MAKES 4 TO 6 SERVINGS
PREPARATION: 10 MINUTES
COOKING: 15 TO 18 MINUTES

Use bananas that are still slightly green at the ends, as they will hold their shape in baking. This dessert is great with Fruit Coulis (page 199) or with ice cream.

6 or 7	6 or 7	medium bananas
1/2 tsp	2 mL	ground cinnamon
2 tbsp	25 mL	granulated sugar
		zest of 1 orange
1/2 cup	125 mL	orange juice
2 tbsp	25 mL	butter, cut into pieces (optional)

Preheat the oven to 375°F (190°C). Peel and cut the bananas diagonally in half or in thirds, depending on their size. Place the bananas in a shallow casserole. Combine the cinnamon and sugar and sprinkle over the bananas. Sprinkle the zest over the bananas and pour in the orange juice.

Dot the top with butter, if desired. Place the casserole in the oven and bake for 15 to 18 minutes or until the bananas are bubbling. Serve warm.

Maple Orange Mousse

MAKES 4 TO 6 SERVINGS
PREPARATION: 30 MINUTES
CHILLING: 1 OR MORE HOURS

When using gelatin, you can speed up the setting process by placing the mixture in a bowl, set over a bowl of ice and water. Setting gelatin in the refrigerator takes much longer.

1 pkg	1 pkg	unflavored gelatin
1/4 cup	50 mL	water
3/4 cup	175 mL	milk
1 cup	250 mL	maple syrup
1 cup	250 mL	whipping cream
2 tbsp	25 mL	orange zest, grated with a rasp (see Glossary)

Sprinkle the gelatin over the water in a small heatproof bowl and leave it to soak for 5 minutes. Sit the bowl over a saucepan with boiling water and stir until the gelatin has dissolved.

In a metal, glass or china bowl, combine the milk and maple syrup. Stir in the gelatin mixture. Set the bowl in a larger bowl containing ice cubes and water. Whisking often, chill the mixture until it becomes the consistency of thick molasses; it will take just a few minutes (a metal bowl works faster than china or glass). Remove immediately. If the gelatin mixture has set too firmly, heat briefly until it begins to melt and whisk until the right consistency.

Meanwhile, whip the cream until soft peaks form and add 1 tbsp (15 mL) of the orange zest. Use a rubber spatula to gently fold it into the setting gelatin mixture. Pour the mixture into a serving dish or individual dishes and chill for several hours before serving. Garnish with remaining orange zest.

Danish Baked Apple

MAKES 4 SERVINGS
PREPARATION: 15 MINUTES
COOKING: 30 MINUTES

This delicious baked apple recipe was one I made during my days working as a cook in Europe.

1/4 cup	50 mL	maple syrup or golden corn syrup
1/2 cup	125 mL	water
4	4	baking apples, peeled
4 tbsp	50 mL	marzipan (see Glossary), red currant or crabapple jelly
1/4 cup	50 mL	dry bread crumbs
3 tbsp	45 mL	brown sugar
2 tbsp	25 mL	orange or lemon juice
2 tbsp	25 mL	melted butter
1 cup	250 mL	sweetened, softly whipped cream (optional)

Preheat the oven to 400°F (200°C). Combine the syrup and water. Pour into an 8- x 8-inch (20- x 20-cm) baking pan. Core the apples but do not cut through the blossom end. Spoon the marzipan or jelly into the apple centers. Combine the crumbs and sugar in a bowl. Brush the apples with the orange juice, roll them in the butter, then in the crumb-sugar mixture. Place the apples in the baking pan. Bake for 30 minutes, basting often, until the apples are tender when pricked with the tip of a sharp knife. Spoon the remaining juice over the apples. Serve with sweetened whipped cream, if desired.

Apple Crisp

MAKES 4 TO 6 SERVINGS
PREPARATION: 20 MINUTES
COOKING: 35 TO 40 MINUTES

This is an old favorite with a crunchy topping. It works best with McIntosh, Spartan, Rome or Empire apples. You can also use pears, peaches, plums or rhubarb to replace the apples.

6 or 7	6 or 7	medium-sized ripe apples, peeled, quartered and cored
1/2 cup	125 mL	unbleached all-purpose flour
1/2 cup	125 mL	quick-cooking rolled oats
1/2 cup	125 mL	lightly packed brown or granulated sugar
		pinch salt
1/2 tsp	2 mL	ground cinnamon or lemon rind
1/4 cup	50 mL	chopped walnuts, pecans or almonds (optional)
1/3 cup	75 mL	butter, softened

Preheat the oven to 375°F (190°C). Butter a 2-qt (2-L) ovenproof, shallow casserole. Slice the apples and place them in the casserole. Combine the flour, rolled oats, sugar, salt, cinnamon or lemon rind, and nuts, if using. With your fingers, work the butter through the dry ingredients until the mixture is crumbly. Sprinkle the crumbs over the apples. Bake for 35 to 45 minutes, or until the apples are tender—test with the tip of a knife. Serve hot or at room temperature.

Pear & Dried Cranberry Strudel

MAKES 4 TO 6 SERVINGS
PREPARATION: 30 MINUTES
COOKING: 25 TO 30 MINUTES

Once you work with phyllo pastry, you'll appreciate its unique qualities. Phyllo (meaning "leaf" in Greek) is paper-thin pastry, sold in packages in most supermarkets. Always keep the pastry covered so it doesn't dry out. If you wish, you can substitute apples for the pears and raisins for the cranberries. To use phyllo, defrost it for at least 2 hours.

4 or 5	4 or 5	medium, ripe pears
1/2 cup	125 mL	granulated sugar
1/2 cup	125 mL	dried cranberries
1/2 cup	125 mL	coarsely chopped walnuts, pecans or almonds
6	6	sheets phyllo pastry
1/4 cup	50 mL	melted butter
2 tbsp	25 mL	icing sugar for dusting

Preheat the oven to 375°F (190°C). Butter a rimmed baking pan. Quarter the pears, core, peel, slice thinly and toss with the sugar and cranberries.

Remove 6 sheets of phyllo from the package and cover them with a slightly damp cloth. Repackage the remaining sheets and refrigerate or freeze. Lay one sheet on the work surface and cover the other sheets. Brush the sheet with melted butter. Lay another sheet on top and repeat the process until all 6 are used.

Spoon the fruit mixture 2 inches (5 cm) inside the narrow end. Firmly roll up as you would a jelly-roll, tucking in the ends as you roll. Brush with butter. Place the roll, seam side down, on the baking sheet. Bake for 25 to 30 minutes until the pastry is golden and the filling is tender and bubbling. Dust the top with sifted icing sugar. Cut into slices. Carefully transfer to a serving platter and serve at room temperature.

Baked Orange or Vanilla-Flavored Custard

MAKES 4 TO 6 SERVINGS
PREPARATION: 15 TO 20 MINUTES
COOKING: 45 TO 50 MINUTES

Baked custard is delicious, especially if it's made with cream but, if you are watching your fat intake, you can use milk instead of cream and whole eggs instead of only yolks.

1¹/2 cups	375 mL	milk
¹/2 cup	125 mL	whipping cream
3	3	eggs or 6 egg yolks
¹/3 cup	75 mL	granulated sugar or maple syrup
pinch	pinch	salt
1 tsp	5 mL	vanilla or grated zest of 1 orange

Custards require a bain-marie, or water bath, to prevent the custard from cooking too fast (see Glossary). To make the water bath, use a baking pan large enough to hold a 1-qt (1-L) shallow casserole or 6 custard cups. Line the baking pan with a tea towel to prevent the casserole from wobbling and half-fill the pan with water. Place the pan on the middle shelf of the oven and preheat to 325°F (160°C).

Butter a shallow casserole or custard cups. In a saucepan, heat the milk and cream on medium-low until it is "scalded," or small bubbles appear around the edge. Stir often to prevent the milk from scorching. Meanwhile, whisk the eggs in a heatproof bowl until well blended and stir in the sugar or syrup, salt, and vanilla or orange zest. Whisk the hot milk into the egg mixture. Pour the eggs and milk into the casserole or custard cups and gently place them in the bain-marie.

Bake for 45 minutes for a casserole, 30 minutes for cups, or just until the center is firm or a knife inserted in center emerges clean. Serve at room temperature or chilled.

Crème Caramel Flan

MAKES 4 TO 6 SERVINGS
BAKING: 40 MINUTES
CHILLING: AT LEAST 1 HOUR

This is a popular dish in many countries because of its smooth coolness on the palate after a spicy meal. The caramel turns into a liquid, so when the custard is inverted, it flows over the dessert. Scrumptious.

| 1/2 cup | 125 mL | granulated sugar |
| | | 1 recipe Orange or Vanilla-Flavored Custard (page 206) |

Preheat the oven to 325°F (160°C). Heat the sugar in a medium skillet over medium heat, shaking the pan often, until the sugar begins to turn to a golden brown syrup, 8 to 10 minutes. Be careful — the transition from golden to dark brown can occur very quickly; also, the liquefied sugar is very, very hot. Pour the syrup into an 8-inch (20-cm) shallow casserole or metal cake pan. Make the custard recipe and pour it into the caramel-lined dish. Bake the custard in a bain-marie (see directions on page 206).

Chill the custard for at least 1 hour. To invert the custard, carefully loosen the sides with a table knife. Place an inverted serving plate over the top of the custard dish and, holding firmly with both hands, invert. Lift the baking dish. Use a rubber spatula to remove any caramel left in the baking dish and spread it on the flan.

Basic Three-Egg Cake

MAKES 1 8-INCH (20-CM) 2-LAYER CAKE
PREPARATION: 15 TO 20 MINUTES
BAKING: 25 TO 30 MINUTES

I can't emphasize enough how important the thorough beating of the butter, sugar and eggs is in achieving a light cake. Remember to use a gentle hand to fold in the flour when the liquid is added to prevent overmixing. Here is a delicious cake to try.

3/4 cup	175 mL	butter and/or shortening, at room temperature
3/4 cup	175 mL	granulated sugar
1 tsp	5 mL	vanilla or finely grated rind of 1 lemon
3	3	eggs, at room temperature
2 cups	500 mL	unbleached all-purpose or sifted cake flour
2 tsp	10 mL	baking powder
1/2 tsp	2 mL	salt
3/4 cup	175 mL	milk

Preheat the oven to 350°F (180°C). Butter and flour 2 8-inch (20-cm) cake pans or line the pans with parchment paper.

In an electric mixer, or by hand using a wooden spoon, beat the butter until creamy. Beat in the sugar until fluffy. Add vanilla or lemon rind and blend in 1 egg at a time until well blended.

In a separate bowl, stir together the flour, baking powder and salt. Gently fold 1/3 of the flour into the creamed mixture with a rubber spatula, then add 1/3 of the milk, stirring from the bottom to the top. Continue folding in flour and milk by thirds until the mixture is combined and the flour is moistened. Spoon the batter evenly into prepared pans. Smooth the top, leaving a small well in the center that will fill in during baking, thus keeping the top of the cake level.

Bake for 25 to 30 minutes or until the center springs back to the touch, or a toothpick inserted in the middle comes out clean. Remove the cakes from the oven and allow them to rest for 5 minutes. To loosen the sides, run a table knife around the edges. Place a rack on top of the pan and invert, holding both firmly. Carefully remove the cake pan and leave the cake to cool. Ice with Butter Frosting, Lemon Frosting (page 210) or a frosting of your choice. You can use frosting between the layers or, if you prefer, berry or apricot jam or jelly, marmalade, or whipped, sweetened cream.

Gumdrop Cake: Add 2 cups (500 mL) gumdrops (no black ones, please). Cut the gumdrops into 4 pieces with scissors moistened with water. Follow the Three-Egg Cake recipe, but toss the gumdrops through the dry ingredients before folding into the creamed mixture. Add 5 minutes to the baking time. Ice with Butter or Lemon Frosting (page 210) and decorate with a few halved gumdrops.

Mocha Walnut Cake: Follow the Three-Egg Cake recipe, but toss 1 cup (250 mL) chopped walnuts through the dry ingredients before folding into the creamed mixture, and replace the vanilla and milk with 3/4 cup (175 mL) strong coffee. Ice with Coffee Frosting (page 210).

Chocolate Chip Cake: Follow the Three-Egg Cake recipe but toss 1 cup (250 mL) small chocolate chips or finely chopped semi-sweet chocolate into the dry ingredients to prevent the chocolate sinking to the bottom of the cake during the baking. Ice with Butter or Cocoa Frosting (page 210) and decorate with chocolate chips.

To ice a cake, place the bottom layer on a serving plate. Spread about 1/4 cup (50 mL) frosting evenly over the layer. Place the second layer on top.

I have found it easiest to pile the frosting on top of the cake and then, using a long pliable metal spatula or a rubber spatula, begin by pushing a little of the frosting down the side and continue to spread over a section at a time.

Continue until the cake sides are iced, then evenly spread any remaining frosting on the top. Clean the plate around the edge of the cake with a damp cloth.

Butter Frosting & Filling

MAKES ENOUGH FOR 8-INCH (20-CM) LAYER CAKE

1/2 cup	125 mL	butter, softened to room temperature
3 cups	750 mL	icing sugar
2 tbsp	25 mL	milk, plus more if needed
1 tsp	5 mL	vanilla

Whip the butter until creamy, then add the sugar, milk and vanilla, beating until smooth. Add extra milk, if needed, for a spreading consistency.

Cocoa Frosting: Replace 4 tbsp (50 mL) icing sugar with 5 tbsp (65 mL) cocoa in the Butter Frosting recipe.

Coffee Frosting: Substitute coffee for the milk in the Butter Frosting recipe.

Mocha Frosting: Replace the milk with strong coffee in the Cocoa Frosting recipe.

Lemon or Orange Frosting: Substitute 1 tbsp (15 mL) lemon or orange juice for 1 tbsp (15 mL) milk in the Butter Frosting recipe. Stir the milk and juice in separately with 1 tbsp (15 mL) of lemon or orange zest.

Chocolate Roll with Coffee Cream

MAKES 10 SERVINGS
PREPARATION: 20 MINUTES
BAKING: 15 MINUTES

This is a flourless cake that becomes an elegant dessert when the cake is rolled like a jelly-roll and filled with coffee whipped cream.

5 tbsp	65 mL	cocoa
3/4 cup	175 mL	granulated sugar
1/2 tsp	2 mL	salt
1 tsp	5 mL	baking powder
6	6	eggs, at room temperature, separated
		icing sugar for dusting
		1 recipe Coffee Cream Filling (page 211)
		1 recipe Chocolate Sauce (page 200) (optional)

Preheat the oven to 375°F (190°C). Butter and flour a rimmed 10$\frac{1}{2}$- x 15- x $\frac{1}{2}$-inch (26- x 37.5- x 1-cm) baking pan or line the pan with parchment paper.

Whisk the cocoa, sugar, salt and baking powder to combine.

In a separate bowl, whisk the yolks until pale yellow. Using an electric mixer or a balloon whisk, beat the egg whites until soft peaks form. Gently fold the yolks into the beaten whites, then sprinkle in the flour mixture, using a rubber spatula to move the mixture from the bottom to the top just until the mixture is blended. Pour into the prepared pan and spread evenly into the corners.

Bake for 18 minutes or until firm to the touch. Place a clean tea towel on a work surface, sprinkle it with icing sugar and gently invert the cake onto it. If using parchment paper, allow it to cool before gently pulling it away from the cake. Cool the cake for a few more minutes. Roll the cake up in the towel, from the narrow end, and cool completely.

To assemble, unroll the cake and spread Coffee Cream Filling to within $\frac{1}{2}$ inch (1 cm) of the edges. Roll up again, firmly and tightly. To even the ends, cut off $\frac{1}{2}$ inch (1 cm) of roll. Place the roll on a serving plate seam side down. Sprinkle the top with additional icing sugar through a fine sieve. Cut into 1-inch thick (2.5-cm) slices. Serve with Chocolate Sauce, if desired.

Coffee Cream Filling

1 tsp	5 mL	unflavored gelatin
4 tbsp	50 mL	cold strong coffee, preferably espresso
1 cup	250 mL	whipping cream
3 tbsp	45 mL	icing sugar

In a small saucepan, sprinkle the gelatin over the coffee and leave it for 5 minutes. Place the pan over low heat, stirring until the mixture dissolves. Cool for 10 minutes. In a chilled mixing bowl, whip the cream until soft peaks form. While still beating, sprinkle in the sugar and the warm gelatin-coffee mixture until blended.

Kugelhupf

MAKES 1 9-INCH (22.5-CM) TUBE OR BUNDT CAKE
PREPARATION: 25 MINUTES
BAKING: 1 HOUR

This is a rich, but light German cake, traditionally made in a turban-shaped Kugelhupf pan, which is similar to a bundt pan but shaped like a turban. Feel free to use a bundt pan. The cake is similar in texture to pound cake and doesn't need to be frosted.

1 cup	250 mL	butter, softened to room temperature
2 cups	500 mL	granulated sugar
6	6	eggs, separated
1 tsp	5 mL	pure vanilla or almond flavoring or 2 tsp (10 mL) freshly grated lemon zest
1¹/₂ cups	375 mL	unbleached all-purpose or sifted cake flour
2 tsp	10 mL	baking powder
¹/₂ tsp	2 mL	salt
6 tbsp	75 mL	milk
		icing sugar for sprinkling on cake

Preheat the oven to 350°F (180°C). Butter a kugelhupf pan or 9-inch (22.5-cm) tube or bundt pan.

In an electric mixer, or by hand using a wooden spoon, beat the butter until creamy. Add the sugar and beat until fluffy, 5 or 6 minutes. Beat in one egg yolk at a time until well blended. Add the flavoring or lemon zest.

In a separate bowl, combine flour, baking powder and salt. Fold the dry ingredients into the yolk mixture alternately with the milk. Beat the egg whites until soft peaks form. Gently fold the egg whites into the flour-egg mixture.

Spoon into the prepared tube pan, smoothing the top. Using a finger, make a trench around the surface 1 inch (2.5 cm) from the edge of the pan, to ensure a level surface. Bake for 1 hour or until a toothpick inserted comes out clean. Cool for 10 minutes. Loosen the cake around the rims, then invert it on a cake rack, but do not remove the cake from the pan until cool. Sprinkle icing sugar over the cake.

Orange Cranberry Torte

MAKES 1 10-INCH (25-CM) CAKE
PREPARATION: 20 MINUTES
BAKING: 55 MINUTES

This is a deliciously moist cake that will keep for 2 weeks in the refrigerator.

2¹/2 cups	625 mL	unbleached all-purpose flour or sifted cake flour
1 cup	250 mL	granulated sugar
¹/4 tsp	1 mL	salt
1 tsp	5 mL	baking powder
1 tsp	5 mL	baking soda
1 cup	250 mL	chopped walnuts or pecans
2 cups	500 mL	fresh, dried or frozen whole cranberries
1 tbsp	15 mL	finely grated orange zest
2	2	eggs
1 cup	250 mL	buttermilk, plain yogurt or sour milk (page 80)
³/4 cup	175 mL	vegetable oil
		1 recipe Orange Syrup

Preheat the oven to 350°F (180°C). Lightly brush a tube pan with removable sides and bottom with melted butter.

In a mixing bowl, combine the flour, sugar, salt, baking powder, baking soda, nuts, cranberries and zest. In another bowl, whisk together the eggs, buttermilk and oil until blended.

Use a rubber spatula to fold the egg mixture into the dry ingredients just until the flour is moistened. Spoon the batter into the prepared pan and smooth the surface. Make a trench around the surface, 1 inch (2.5 cm) from the edge of the pan, to ensure a level surface. Bake for 55 minutes until the cake is firm to a light finger pressure on top. Let it cool for 5 to 10 minutes. Prick holes in the top of the cake with a fork and drizzle the Orange Syrup over the surface, allowing it to seep through. Leave the cake to cool in the pan. Remove the pan sides and wrap the cake and pan bottom together in waxed paper and foil. Chill for 24 hours, then remove the pan bottom.

Orange Syrup

1 cup	250 mL	orange juice
¹/2 cup	125 mL	granulated sugar

Simmer the orange juice and sugar in a saucepan for 3 minutes.

Strawberry Shortcake

MAKES 1 9-INCH (22.5-CM) ROUND CAKE
PREPARATION: 15 MINUTES
BAKING: 30 MINUTES

There is a debate about whether shortcake should be made with biscuits or cake. I think the cake is scrumptious with the soaked-in juice and cream on top.

1 cup	250 mL	granulated sugar plus 2 tsp (10 mL)
1/4 tsp	1 mL	salt
		zest and juice of 1 lemon
4	4	eggs at room temperature, separated
3 tbsp	45 mL	warm water
1 cup	250 mL	unbleached bread or all-purpose flour
1 tsp	5 mL	baking powder
3 pts	1.5 L	fresh strawberries, stemmed and sliced, reserve 6 whole berries with stems for garnish
2 tbsp	25 mL	granulated sugar
2 cups	500 mL	whipping cream
1 tsp	5 mL	vanilla

Preheat the oven to 350°F (180°C). Butter 2 9-inch (22.5-cm) round cake pans and sprinkle each with 1 tsp (5 mL) sugar. With an electric beater or by hand, combine 1 cup (250 mL) sugar, salt, lemon zest and juice, and egg yolks and beat until lemon colored. Stir in the water.

Combine the flour and baking powder and set aside.

In an electric mixer with a whisk, or by hand with a balloon whisk, whisk the egg whites until soft peaks form. Fold the yolk mixture into the whites with a rubber spatula, alternately with the dry ingredients, just until blended.

Spoon the batter into the pans and smooth the surface. Bake for 30 minutes. Allow the cake to rest for 5 minutes, then loosen from the pans' edges with a table knife. Invert the cakes onto a rack to cool.

Combine the strawberries with 2 tbsp (25 mL) sugar and chill for several hours. Whip the cream until soft peaks form. Whisk in vanilla.

To assemble, spread half the berries on the bottom layer of the cake and top with half the whipped cream. Top with the second cake layer and spread the remaining berries on the cake. Cover with the remaining whipped cream and garnish with the whole berries. Chill for several hours before serving.

Chocolate Fudge Cake

MAKES 1 9-INCH (22.5-CM) 3-LAYER ROUND CAKE
PREPARATION: 20 TO 25 MINUTES
BAKING: 20 TO 25 MINUTES

Years ago, I was given this Waldorf Astoria recipe by a friend who lived in the Hotel in New York City. It's a heavenly cake, great for special occasions and just as good — or better — on the second day.

3/4 cup	175 mL	boiling-hot water
3 oz	90 g	bitter chocolate, coarsely chopped
3/4 cup	175 mL	butter and/or shortening at room temperature
2 cups	500 mL	lightly packed brown sugar
3	3	eggs
1 tsp	5 mL	vanilla
2 cups	500 mL	unbleached all-purpose flour or sifted cake flour
1 1/2 tsp	7 mL	baking soda
1 tsp	5 mL	baking powder
1/2 tsp	2 mL	salt
3/4 cup	175 mL	buttermilk or sour milk (page 80)
		1 recipe Chocolate Butter Frosting (page 216)

Preheat the oven to 350°F (180°C). Lightly brush with melted butter 3 9-inch (22.5-cm) cake pans. Pour the hot water over the chocolate and stir until smooth. Cool to room temperature.

In an electric mixer, or by hand using a wooden spoon, beat the butter until creamy, then beat in the sugar until fluffy. Beat in the eggs, one at a time, until well blended. Stir in the vanilla and chocolate.

In a separate bowl, stir together the flour, baking soda, baking powder and salt. Using a rubber spatula, gently fold the dry ingredients into the egg mixture, alternately with the buttermilk, just until the flour is moistened. Spoon into prepared pans. Smooth the top surface, leaving a shallow well in the center to ensure a level surface.

Bake for 20 minutes or until the cakes are firm when touched in the center. Remove the cakes from the oven and cool for 5 minutes before inverting pans onto a rack to cool. Ice cake when it is cooled (see page 209 for icing method).

Chocolate Butter Frosting

2 tbsp	25 mL	milk
4	4	squares semi-sweet chocolate, chopped
1/2 cup	125 mL	butter, softened to room temperature
4 cups	1 L	icing sugar
2 tsp	10 mL	vanilla

In a small saucepan, heat the milk and chocolate over medium-low heat until the chocolate begins to melt. Remove from the heat and stir until the mixture is smooth. Cool over ice cubes to room temperature. In a mixing bowl, beat the butter and sugar until well blended. Beat in the chocolate mixture and continue beating until light and fluffy. Stir in the vanilla.

Lemon Pecan Meringues

MAKES 3 TO 4 DOZEN
PREPARATION: 10 MINUTES
COOKING: 1 HOUR, PLUS 2 HOURS FOR OVEN-DRYING

These crisp meringues are useful for using up leftover egg whites. They are not difficult — the key is to follow the directions carefully to hold the trapped air in the beaten egg whites. If you would like to change the flavor, replace the nuts with chocolate chips and add several drops of peppermint essence.

2	2	egg whites, at room temperature
1/2 cup	125 mL	granulated sugar
1/2 cup	125 mL	coarsely chopped pecans
		grated rind of 1 lemon

Preheat the oven to 200°F (95°C). Butter and flour a baking sheet or line it with parchment paper. Beat the egg whites in an electric mixer with a whisk, or by hand using a balloon whisk, just until soft peaks form. Sprinkle in sugar while still whisking, until firm peaks form. Fold in the pecans and lemon rind. Drop a heaping teaspoon of batter onto the baking sheet (they will not spread) and bake for 1 hour. Turn off the oven and leave the meringues to dry in the oven for 2 hours or overnight, until crisp and hard.

Candied Ginger Gems

MAKES 4 TO 5 DOZEN
PREPARATION: 10 MINUTES
BAKING: 10 TO 12 MINUTES

These cookies have great flavor because of the candied ginger, available in the preserved fruit section of your market or in bulk food stores. Use a sifter to combine the spices and dry ingredients to be sure they are well distributed.

3/4 cup	175 mL	butter and/or shortening or lard, at room temperature
1 1/4 cups	300 mL	granulated sugar
1/4 cup	50 mL	molasses
1	1	egg
2 cups	500 mL	unbleached all-purpose flour
1/4 tsp	1 mL	salt
1 tsp	5 mL	baking soda
1/2 tsp	2 mL	ground cloves
1 tsp	5 mL	ground cinnamon
1 tbsp	15 mL	ground ginger
1/2 cup	125 mL	finely chopped candied ginger, lightly packed

Preheat the oven to 350°F (180°C). Lightly brush melted butter on a baking sheet. In the bowl of an electric mixer, food processor, or by hand, beat the fat until creamy. Beat in 1 cup (250 mL) sugar until fluffy. Beat in the molasses and egg until smooth.

In another bowl, sift together the flour, salt, baking soda, spices and candied ginger. Stir the dry ingredients into the egg mixture just until blended. Make 1-inch (2.5-cm) balls and roll them in the remaining sugar. Place the cookies 2 inches (5 cm) apart on the baking sheet and bake for 10 to 12 minutes. The cookies will puff up in the oven and fall as they cool. Cool for a minute before removing the cookies to a rack.

Fudge Peppermint Balls

MAKES 4 TO 5 DOZEN
PREPARATION: 10 MINUTES
BAKING: 9 TO 10 MINUTES

These are walnut-sized cookies topped with chocolate icing; they have great eye-appeal on a plate.

2 oz	60 g	unsweetened chocolate or 1/3 cup (75 mL) cocoa
2 cups	500 mL	unbleached all-purpose flour
1/4 tsp	1 mL	salt
3/4 cup	175 mL	butter and/or shortening, at room temperature
3/4 cup	175 mL	granulated sugar
2	2	eggs
2 tsp	10 mL	peppermint flavoring
1/2	1/2	recipe Cocoa Frosting (page 210)

Preheat the oven to 375°F (190°C). Lightly brush melted butter on a baking sheet. To melt the chocolate, cut it into quarters and place them in a small heatproof bowl set over a saucepan of barely simmering water. Stir until there are just a few small lumps. Remove the chocolate from the heat and stir hard until it's smooth. Cool for 5 minutes.

In a small bowl, combine the flour, salt and, if using, the cocoa. In the bowl of an electric mixer, a food processor, or by hand using a wooden spoon, beat the butter or shortening until creamy. Beat in the sugar until fluffy. Beat in the eggs and stir in the melted chocolate and peppermint. Stir in the flour mixture just until blended. Shape the dough into 3/4-inch (2-cm) balls and place them on a baking sheet 1/2 inch (1 cm) apart (they will not spread).

Bake the cookies for 8 to 9 minutes and cool on a rack. Swirl Cocoa Frosting on top of each cookie.

Chocolate Truffles

MAKES ABOUT 24 TRUFFLES
PREPARATION: 25 MINUTES

These superb chocolate sweets rolled in cocoa are called truffles because they resemble the treasured fungi of Europe. Truffles are sometimes rolled in nuts or dipped in melted chocolate or exotic flavors are added. They are decadently rich — the perfect ending to a wonderful meal with coffee or ice wine.

4 oz	120 g	bittersweet chocolate, chopped, or 3 oz (90 g) semi-sweet and 1 oz (30 g) bitter chocolate
1/2 cup	125 mL	unsalted butter, at room temperature
2 tbsp	25 mL	liqueur — whisky, brandy or vanilla
1/4 cup	50 mL	cocoa powder

Melt the chocolate in a heatproof bowl over a saucepan of barely simmering water until a few small lumps are left. Remove the bowl from the heat and stir the chocolate until smooth. Cool for 5 minutes, stirring often. Beat in cubes of butter until well blended. Add liqueur. Line a rimmed baking pan with waxed paper. Use 2 small spoons to scoop and form 24 rounded balls of chocolate on the baking pan. Chill the pan of truffles in the refrigerator for about 15 minutes. Roll each portion quickly between your fingers into a smooth ball — try to avoid the warm palm of the hand — so the chocolate doesn't melt. Place the cocoa in a small bowl and roll each ball in the cocoa. To store truffles, keep them chilled in a closed container. To serve, leave at room temperature for 30 minutes.

Variation: Place 1/4 cup (50 mL) finely chopped walnuts or almonds in a bowl and firmly roll each truffle in the nuts.

Chocolate Brownies

MAKES 1 8-INCH (20-CM) SQUARE PAN
PREPARATION: 10 MINUTES
BAKING: 20 TO 22 MINUTES

These are yummy moist brownies, since they are removed from the oven before being completely baked through. If cooked longer, they become somewhat crumbly.

1 cup	250 mL	sugar
2	2	eggs
1/2 cup	125 mL	butter
3 sq or 3 oz	3 sq 90 g	unsweetened chocolate
1/2 cup	125 mL	unbleached all-purpose or whole wheat flour
1/2 cup	125 mL	coarsely chopped nuts, pecans or walnuts (optional)
1/2 tsp	2 mL	vanilla

Preheat the oven to 350°F (180°C). Lightly butter an 8-inch (20-cm) square pan. Beat together the sugar and eggs until lemon-colored and thick, using an electric mixer or a wooden spoon.

On low heat, melt the butter and chocolate, stirring, just until chocolate is in small lumps. Remove from the heat, stir until smooth and cool slightly. Stir the chocolate mixture into the sugar mixture with the flour, nuts, if using, and vanilla.

Pour the batter into the prepared pan and bake for 20 to 22 minutes. The mixture should yield slightly when touched with the fingertips. Cut the brownies into the desired size while they're still warm.

Shortbread

MAKES 3 TO 4 DOZEN COOKIES OR 1 8-INCH (20-CM) CIRCLE
PREPARATION: 10 MINUTES
BAKING: 25 MINUTES FOR COOKIES, 50 MINUTES FOR CIRCLE

In Scotland years ago, I learned how to make traditional rich, tender, buttery shortbread by hand, baked in rounds and cut into wedges. On this side of the water we like convenience, so I succumb to using a mixer, which is great but not quite the real thing. The rice flour or cornstarch is added to short-bread for crispness. Shortbread is famous for its buttery taste, so never try to make it with margarine or try to dress it up with vanilla, eggs, nuts or choco-late chips. If you wish, you can replace half the flour with whole wheat flour.

1 cup	250 mL	unsalted butter, at room temperature
1/2 cup	125 mL	berry sugar (finer than granulated sugar)
1/2 cup	125 mL	cornstarch or rice flour
1 1/2 cups	375 mL	unbleached all-purpose flour or bread flour
		pinch salt

By electric mixer: Beat the butter and sugar until creamy. Blend the corn-starch, flour and salt and add to the butter mixture in thirds, beating briefly after each addition, just until the dough forms. Remove the dough, form into a disk, cover and chill for 30 minutes.

By hand: On a work surface, mound the flour and stir in the cornstarch or rice flour and salt. Make a well in the center, add the butter and sugar and begin to work them together, adding a little flour at a time until all the flour is used. Use the heel of your hand to knead briefly until the dough is pliable. Cover the dough and chill for 30 minutes.

Preheat oven to 325°F (160°C).

Cookies: Roll the dough to 1/2 inch (1 cm) thickness on a lightly floured surface. Cut into shapes, place the cookies on an ungreased baking sheet and prick the shapes twice with a fork. Bake for 20 to 25 minutes, or until light golden.

Rounds: Press dough into an 8-inch (20-cm) round 3/4-inch-thick (2-cm) circle on an ungreased baking sheet. Flute the edges by pressing your thumb between the thumb and first finger of the opposite hand. Use a knife to score the outline of 16 wedges in the surface of the shortbread. Prick the surface 8 to 10 times with a fork and bake for 45 to 50 minutes, or until light golden. Cool before removing from the baking sheet and then cut into wedges.

Flaky Pastry

MAKES ENOUGH PASTRY FOR THE TOP AND BOTTOM OF A 9-INCH (22.5-CM) PIE
PREPARATION: 20 TO 25 MINUTES
CHILLING: 20 MINUTES, OR FREEZE FOR 10 MINUTES
BAKING: 15 TO 16 MINUTES

The following is my favorite way to make pastry — it's quick and works very well if you follow my tips for making pastry on page 194.

2 1/2 cups	625 mL	unbleached all-purpose flour
1/2 tsp	2 mL	salt
1/2 cup	125 mL	cold butter
1/2 cup	125 mL	cold shortening or, if using lard, reduce by 2 tbsp (25 mL)
1/2 cup	125 mL	ice water

By hand: In a mixing bowl, combine 2 cups (500 mL) flour and salt and, using the largest holes in a grater, grate in the cold fat. Toss the flour lightly through the fat as you grate, to prevent clumps. Break up any fat clumps with your fingertips, or a table knife, to make coarse crumbs. Sprinkle in the ice water, while tossing the mixture with a knife, until a large mass forms. Gently knead with your fingers (the palms hold too much heat and will warm the dough) just until the dough forms a ball. Halve the dough and gently flatten each half into 2 3-inch (7.5-cm) disks. Chill for 20 minutes to rest the gluten.

By food processor: Combine 2 cups (500 mL) flour and salt in a bowl. Cut the fat into cubes and add to the machine. Pulse on and off just until the mixture is crumbly. Sprinkle in the ice water and pulse until the mixture begins to form a ball. Remove the dough and gently knead into a ball with your fingers. Halve the dough and flatten into 2 3-inch (7.5-cm) disks. Chill for 20 minutes.

Sprinkle the remaining flour on the work surface and the rolling pin. Sprinkle one disk with a little flour. Gently roll out to a 5-inch (12.5-cm) diameter. Pick the dough up and sprinkle more flour on and under it and on the rolling pin. Roll the dough into a slightly thinner and larger circle. Pick up the circle, sprinkle more flour under and over it and keep shaping the circle so the edges are unbroken. Clean off the rolling pin with flour and repeat this process at least 3 more times until you have a circle that is 1/8 inch (.25 cm) thick and 2 inches (5 cm) larger than the pie plate. Fold the pastry circle in half.

Place the folded pastry's straight edge across the middle of the pan. Unfold and gently press down into the pan sides and bottom without stretching the dough.

Fluting pastry dough (see Glossary)

Cut the overhanging pastry with scissors to 1/2 inch (1 cm) beyond the rim. Fold the overhang under the pastry edge. Prick the bottom and sides if prebaking the shell. Chill for 20 minutes or freeze for 10 minutes before baking.

For double crust pies, do not prick the bottom shell. Roll the second portion of dough for the top crust into a circle as above and fold in half. Add the filling to the bottom shell. Place the pastry over one half of the filling, allowing the pastry to overhang the edge, and unfold. Use scissors to trim the pastry to 1/2 inch (1 cm) from edge. Tuck the edge of the top pastry under the edge of the bottom pastry and flute (see photo above). Chill for 20 minutes, or freeze for 10 minutes.

Bake unfilled shells in a preheated 425°F (220°C) oven for 14 to 15 minutes until the fat no longer bubbles and the pastry is golden. For filled pies, follow recipe instructions.

Sweet Tart Pastry

MAKES 1 9-INCH (22.5-CM) TART OR 6 3¹/₂-INCH (8.75-CM) TARTLET SHELLS
PREPARATION: 8 MINUTES
CHILLING: 20 MINUTES
BAKING: 20 MINUTES

Sweet pastry, or pâte sucrée, is a kneaded pastry that melts in your mouth. It holds a filling firmly and can be removed from the pan it is baked in without collapsing. Pans with removable bottoms are especially handy.

1 cup	250 mL	unbleached all-purpose flour
		pinch salt
¹/₂ tsp	2 mL	grated lemon zest
3 tbsp	45 mL	granulated sugar
1	1	egg yolk
6 tbsp	75 mL	butter, cut in pieces, at room temperature

By hand: Combine the flour, salt, lemon zest and sugar on the work surface and make a well. Add the yolk and butter. Use a pastry cutter to gather flour into the well while cutting through the butter and yolk. Then use your fingers to combine the mixture. Use the heel of your hand to stretch the dough until it's pliable and smooth. Wrap and chill to rest the gluten for 20 to 30 minutes.

By food processor: Process the butter and sugar until creamy, then add the yolk. Add the flour, salt and lemon zest and process until the dough begins to clump. Remove and briefly knead with the heel of your hand until a smooth ball forms. Wrap and chill to rest the gluten for 20 to 30 minutes.

Press the dough into the pan, beginning at the center, and work the dough over the bottom and up the sides. Use your thumb to even off the top edge. Prick the bottom with a fork 5 times to prevent the expanding hot air from causing the pastry to bubble. Freeze for 10 to 15 minutes.

Bake in a preheated 375°F (190°C) oven for 18 to 20 minutes for the large tart or 14 to 15 minutes for tartlets, or until the pastry is golden and pulls away from the sides of the pan. Peek after 10 minutes to see if a bubble has formed; if so, just prick it with a fork and gently press it down again. Cool before lifting the tart (with pan bottom) away from the sides of the pan.

Chocolate Tart Pastry: Make the tart pastry as above, but add an extra 1 tbsp (15 mL) granulated sugar and reduce the flour to ³/₄ cup (175 mL), with 2 tbsp (25 mL) cocoa powder.

Old-Fashioned Apple Pie

MAKES 1 9-INCH (22.5-CM) PIE
PREPARATION: 35 MINUTES
BAKING: 45 TO 50 MINUTES

This pie is sensational in the autumn when apples are at their peak. After the first frost, they turn even sweeter. Using varieties such as McIntosh, Cortland or Empire allows you to reduce the amount of sugar required. Be sure to mound the apples high to make an appealing and delicious pie. When cooked, the apples should hold their shape and be tender to the bite.

		1 recipe Flaky Pastry recipe (page 222)
3 lbs	1.5 kg	firm, sweet apples
1/2 cup	125 mL	granulated sugar, more or less, depending on apple tartness
3/4 tsp	4 mL	ground cinnamon
2 tbsp	25 mL	butter, cut into cubes
		milk or cream for brushing

Preheat the oven to 425°F (220°C). Line a 9-inch (22.5-cm) pie plate with pastry.

I find the fastest way to prepare the apples is to first cut them into quarters, then peel and slice them 1/4 inch (.5 cm) thick.

In a bowl, combine the sugar and cinnamon and toss with the apples until coated. Place the apples in the pie shell and gently press into a mound. Dot the top with butter.

Drape and lightly press the top crust pastry over the apples. Use scissors to trim the pastry to 1/2 inch (1 cm) beyond the pan rim; tuck this edge under the bottom pastry and flute the edges (page 223). Cut 4 vents in the top pastry with scissors to allow the steam to escape. If desired, cut out decorative leaves with leftover pastry, pasting them on with milk or cream. For a shiny finish, brush the pastry with milk or cream. Chill for 10 minutes to rest the pastry.

Bake for 15 minutes, then turn the oven down to 350°F (180°C) for 30 minutes more, or until the apples are tender when pierced with a knife tip.

Pumpkin Pie

MAKES 1 9-INCH (22.5-CM) PIE
PREPARATION: 15 MINUTES
BAKING: 40 MINUTES

This recipe has been a favorite in our family for many years. Canned pumpkin is a great convenience, but if you're making fresh pumpkin purée be sure to use "pie" pumpkins, which are smaller and sweeter with more pulp than Hallowe'en pumpkins.

1	1	unbaked Flaky Pastry shell, not pricked (page 222)
1 1/2 cups	375 mL	puréed pumpkin, fresh cooked or canned
3/4 cup	175 mL	lightly packed brown sugar
3/4 tsp	4 mL	ground ginger
1/2 tsp	2 mL	cinnamon
1/4 tsp	1 mL	ground cloves
		pinch salt
2	2	eggs
1 cup	250 mL	milk, or part cream
1/2 cup	125 mL	whipping cream
2 tbsp	25 mL	icing sugar

Preheat the oven to 425°F (220°C). In a mixing bowl, combine the puréed pumpkin with sugar, spices and salt. Whisk the egg and 1 cup (250 mL) milk or cream together and stir into the pumpkin mixture. This mixture is thin, so either pour it into the unbaked pie shell and carefully place it in the oven, or place the shell in the oven and pour in the mixture. Bake for 15 minutes to cook the pastry, then reduce the heat to 350°F (180°C) and bake for 25 minutes, until the center is firm or a knife inserted in the center comes out clean. Cool the pie, but not overnight, as the filling shrinks from the pastry, which makes it less appetizing.

To serve, decorate with cream whipped to soft peaks and sweetened with icing sugar. Drop small dollops around the edge of the pie or place the whipped cream in a piping bag with rosette tip and pipe around the edge of the pie.

To cook fresh pumpkin, cut it in quarters and remove the seeds. Place it in a roasting pan, cover with tin foil and bake in a 350°F (180°C) oven until tender, about 45 minutes. Peel and purée.

Lemon Meringue Pie

MAKES 1 9-INCH (22.5-CM) PIE
PREPARATION: 30 MINUTES
BAKING: 5 MINUTES

This is a perennial favorite. This stovetop method makes a double boiler unnecessary and the egg yolks will not scramble if you follow the directions. Always grate a lemon before juicing.

1	1	9-inch (22.5-cm) pricked, baked Flaky Pastry shell (page 222)
2/3 cup	150 mL	granulated sugar
2 tbsp	25 mL	all-purpose flour
3 tbsp	45 mL	cornstarch
1/4 tsp	1 mL	salt
1 1/2 cups	375 mL	hot water
3	3	eggs, at room temperature, separated
2	2	lemons, grated rind and 6 tbsp (75 mL) juice
2 tsp	10 mL	butter
6 tbsp	75 mL	granulated sugar

In a saucepan, combine the 2/3 cup (150 mL) sugar, flour, cornstarch and salt, then stir in the hot water. Cook over medium heat, stirring constantly, until thick and transparent, about 5 minutes. Remove from the heat. In a bowl, blend the yolks, then whisk half the sugar mixture into the yolks and pour it back into the saucepan. Return it to the heat and whisk constantly until the mixture thickens, without boiling. Add the lemon juice, grated rind and butter. Set the hot saucepan in a bowl of cold water to cool the mixture, about 5 minutes. Pour the filling into the baked pastry shell.

To make the meringue, whisk egg whites on medium speed in an electric mixer, or by hand with a balloon whisk, until soft peaks form. Slowly sprinkle in 6 tbsp (75 mL) sugar, a spoonful at a time, while beating, until the meringue is stiff and shiny. Spread the meringue over the warm filling without leaving any lemon mixture exposed, mounding in the center. Use the back of a spoon to make small peaks in the meringue like a rough sea. Bake the pie in a preheated 375°F (190°C) oven until golden, for about 8 minutes. Watch the pie closely so the meringue doesn't overcook, causing unwanted beads of moisture to form. Cool pie for 15 minutes before serving.

Fresh Lime Chiffon Pie

MAKES 1 9-INCH (22.5-CM) PIE
PREPARATION: 25 MINUTES
CHILLING: 1 HOUR

Chiffon pies are light, airy and wonderful after a rich meal. The filling can be made with either lime or lemon. This recipe discusses how to chill a gelatin mixture quickly over ice, then fold it into a meringue — it's not difficult.

1	1	9-inch (22.5-cm) pricked, baked Flaky Pastry shell (page 222)
1 pkg	1 pkg	plain gelatin
4 tbsp	50 mL	cold water
1/2 cup	125 mL	freshly squeezed lime (about 4 limes)
1 tbsp	15 mL	finely grated lime zest
1 cup	250 mL	granulated sugar
4	4	eggs, at room temperature, separated
1/2 tsp	2 mL	salt
1/2 cup	125 mL	whipping cream for garnish (optional)
2 tbsp	25 mL	icing sugar

In a bowl, dissolve the gelatin in the cold water for 5 minutes. In a saucepan, combine the lime juice, zest, 1/2 cup (125 mL) sugar, yolks and salt. Cook on medium heat, stirring, until the mixture thickens without boiling, about 5 minutes. Remove from the heat and stir in the gelatin mixture until it melts.

Set the saucepan to cool in a bowl of water containing ice cubes. Stir often until the mixture thickens to the consistency of molasses, from 6 to 8 minutes, and remove from the ice bath. Continue to stir often to avoid setting. If the mixture does set too firmly, reheat and allow it to melt a little, stirring until it returns to molasses consistency.

Meanwhile, beat the egg whites in an electric mixer on medium speed, or by hand using a balloon whisk, just until soft peaks form; do not overbeat. Sprinkle in the remaining 1/2 cup (125 mL) sugar, a small spoonful at a time, until the whites are stiff and shiny. Beat for another minute. Gently fold in the gelatin mixture with a whisk or rubber scraper, until well combined. Mound into the baked pie shell, smoothing the top.

Chill for about 1 hour, until firm. Whip the cream until soft peaks form and sprinkle in the icing sugar. Spread over the top of the pie. If desired, garnish with grated lime zest.

Pear Ginger Almond Tart

MAKES 1 9-INCH (22.5-CM) TART
PREPARATION: 25 MINUTES
BAKING: 40 MINUTES

In this recipe, pears are snuggled in a frangipane mixture, a ground almond cream that has candied ginger added to make an outstanding tart. You will need to prepare the pastry shell in a tart pan with a removable base.

1	1	unbaked Sweet Tart Pastry shell (page 224)
4 or 5	4 or 5	ripe, firm, medium-sized Bartlett pears
1/2 cup	125 mL	water
		juice of 1/2 lemon
1 cup	250 mL	blanched almonds, toasted
1/4 cup	50 mL	butter, at room temperature
1/4 cup	50 mL	granulated sugar
1	1	egg
1 tbsp	15 mL	unbleached all-purpose flour
1/4 cup	50 mL	finely chopped candied ginger (about 10 to 12 slices)
3 tbsp	45 mL	red currant or crabapple jelly, melted

Preheat the oven to 375°F (190°C). Cut the pears into quarters, then core and peel. To prevent discoloration, place the pear quarters in the water with the lemon juice. Make lengthwise parallel slits on the rounded side of each pear quarter; these will fan open during baking.

To enhance the flavor of the almonds, place them on a rimmed baking pan and toast them in the oven for 10 minutes until they begin to crackle, without browning. Process the almonds in a food processor just to a coarse grind. Add the butter, sugar and egg and pulse on and off until creamy. Then add the flour and pulse just until the mixture is smooth. Add the candied ginger and pulse briefly.

Spread the mixture over the bottom of the tart shell. Starting around the edge, place the pear quarters in the mixture with rounded sides up and stem ends pointing to the center, then fill the center with the remaining pears.

Bake for 40 minutes or until the pears are tender when pierced with the tip of a knife. Brush with melted jelly. Serve pie at room temperature.

Glazed Fresh Berry Tart

MAKES 1 9-INCH (22.5-CM) OR 6 3½-INCH (8.5-CM) TARTLETS
PREPARATION: 30 MINUTES

Strawberries, raspberries or blueberries make a colorful tart that's always a winner. Custard is a traditional base, but in this recipe I use puréed fruit (coulis) or mascarpone (a triple cream cheese) with different flavors as the base, topped with fresh fruit. Picked when ripe, berries are fragile, so store them in the refrigerator and wash or spray just before using.

1	1	large Sweet Tart Pastry shell or 6 tartlet shells, baked (page 224)
		1 recipe Fruit Coulis or Mascarpone Cream (page 231)
1 qt	1 L	fresh, rinsed strawberries, raspberries or blueberries
¼ cup	50 mL	red currant or crabapple jelly, melted
		sweetened whipped cream (optional)

Spread Fruit Coulis or Mascarpone Cream over the bottom of the pastry shell or tartlet shells.

If using strawberries, trim the berries, cut in half lengthwise and place on the base very close together, in concentric circles, working from outside toward center. Brush on the melted jelly with a pastry brush.

If using raspberries, place the berries with the open end down in the filling in concentric circles, very close together. Brush on the melted jelly with a pastry brush.

If using blueberries, to hold the berries in place, toss them in the melted jelly. Spoon over the base into the tart, mounding in the center.

Chill the tart for about 1 hour until set. If desired, garnish with small mounds of sweetened whipped cream.

Fruit Coulis

2 cups	500 mL	fresh or frozen unsweetened strawberries or raspberries
2-3 tbsp	25-45 mL	icing sugar, or to taste

Purée the fruit until smooth. When using raspberries, you may wish to remove the seeds in a food mill or sieve. Add icing sugar.

Mascarpone Cream

1 cup	250 mL	mascarpone cheese
1/2 tsp	2 mL	vanilla or lemon zest
2 tbsp	25 mL	icing sugar

Remove mascarpone cheese from the refrigerator about 1 hour before needed. Stir in vanilla or lemon zest with icing sugar.

Chocolate Mascarpone Cream: Replace the vanilla or lemon zest with 2 squares (2 oz./60 g) of melted semi-sweet chocolate.

Mocha Fudge Tart

MAKES 1 9-INCH (22.5-CM) TART
PREPARATION: 30 TO 40 MINUTES
CHILLING: AT LEAST 1 HOUR OR FREEZE

This gorgeous, decadent pie is perfect for chocolate lovers and can be served in small portions. It freezes well and can be made up to 2 months ahead. Serving it with a fruit coulis cuts the richness of the tart.

1	1	9-inch (22.5-cm) pricked, baked Chocolate Tart Pastry shell (page 224)
1/4 cup	50 mL	strong brewed coffee
1 cup	250 mL	butter
3/4 cup	175 mL	granulated sugar
		pinch salt
9 oz	270 g	bittersweet or semi-sweet chocolate, chopped
6	6	egg yolks, at room temperature
3 tbsp	45 mL	brandy
3/4 cup	175 mL	whipping cream
1 1/2 cups	375 mL	Fruit Coulis (page 199)

In a saucepan, heat the coffee, butter, sugar and salt, until the butter has melted. Add the chocolate and stir until it has almost melted, then remove from the heat and stir until it is smooth. In a bowl, whisk the egg yolks until creamy, then slowly whisk in half the still-hot chocolate mixture. Pour the mixture back into the saucepan, stirring until smooth and thick. Add the brandy.

Measure 1 1/4 cup (300 mL) of the mixture and pour it into the baked shell and chill until set, about 30 minutes. Set aside 1/2 cup (125 mL) for garnish.

The rest of the mixture will be added to the whipping cream. Chill this until it's almost firm, about 40 minutes, then beat the cream until firm peaks form. With the beater set on low speed, add the chilled mixture in spoonfuls until it's well blended. Mound the mixture into the tart shell over the chocolate base. Chill for 3 hours, or freeze for 1 hour.

To garnish, place small dollops of the reserved chocolate around the edge of the tart, or pipe rosettes using a piping bag. Chill for 5 to 6 hours or freeze. To serve, cut the tart into 8 or 12 wedges. Serve the Fruit Coulis separately or spread the coulis on the dessert plate and place the tart on top.

Menus

When choosing a menu, keep in mind that each dish is meant to open up and not overpower the taste buds.

To help make your friends feel at home at a sit-down dinner, a brunch or a barbecue, take the time to preplan and organize it on paper. If you can, discreetly discover the likes and dislikes of your guests and family and plan the menu, being aware of the time of year, the weather, your budget and the availability of ingredients. Make a list of the food shopping to be done a few days ahead and a list of the fresh ingredients for the day of the event. Write down the timing needed for preparing, cooking and serving each dish and decide when and how to set the table.

Brunch or Luncheon:

Grapefruit and Orange Wedges
Baked Cheese Casserole (page 95)
Grilled Sausages or Bacon
Corn Muffins (page 80)

Artichokes with Lemon Butter
Mushroom-Filled Crêpes (page 89)
Green Salad
Baked Orange-Cinnamon Bananas
(page 202)
Wine: New World Pinot Noir

Shrimp with Cucumber
Herb Sauce (page 16)
Cheese Soufflé Roulade with
Spinach Filling (page 92)
Glazed Carrots (page 175)
Mixed Fresh Fruit Salad with Chocolate
Brownies (page 196 and 220)
Wine: Chilled dry sparkling wine

Casual Dinners:

Grated Carrot & Cumin Salad (page 53)
Tender Pan-Fried Calf or Beef Liver (page 153)
Stuffed Baked Potatoes (page 184)
Red Cabbage Braised with Wine (page 174)
Old-Fashioned Apple Pie (page 225)
Wine: Ontario Marechal Foch
or Chianti Classico

Fresh Pea Soup with Mint or Dill (page 40)
Beef Stew with Roasted Vegetables (page 157)
Popovers (page 76)
Pear & Dried Cranberry Strudel (page 205)
Wine: Pinot Noir or Corbières

Cream of Spinach Soup (page 42)
Pork Chops with Apple & Sauerkraut (page 166)
Mashed Potatoes (page 186)
Chocolate Chip Cake (page 209)
Beer or Wine: Chilled Lager or Spätlese

Minestrone Soup with Parsley Pesto (page 44)
Country Grain Bread (page 72)
Danish Baked Apple (page 203)
Wine: Chianti or Beaujolais

Chilled Minted Cucumber Soup (page 43)
Orzo Salad with Tuna & Vegetables (page 58)
Sliced Tomato Salad
Irish Soda Bread (page 65)
Kugelhupf (page 212)
Wine: Chilled Italian Orvieto or Valpolicella

Parties:

Chilled Minted Cucumber Soup (page 43)
Barbecued Boneless Leg of Lamb (page 160)
Warm New Potato Salad with Tarragon (page 53)
Roasted or Grilled Assorted Vegetables
(page 168)
Fresh Lime Chiffon Pie (page 228)
Wine: Australian Shiraz or French Gigondas or
Vacqueyras

Tomato or Gorgonzola Bruschetta (pages 18, 19)
Juicy Beef Burgers in Buns and/or Chickpeas in
Pita Bread (pages 155, 118)
Tomato and Onion Slices, Pickles and Relishes
Corn on the Cob with Herb Butter (page 177)
Bulgur, Feta & Mint Salad (page 59)
Ice Cream with Chocolate Sauce (page 200)
Wine: Bulgarian Cabernet
or chilled Beaujolais

Poached Pear with Roquefort Salad (page 55)
Lobster with Clarified Butter (page 130)
Black or Green Olives and Dill Pickles
Chocolate Mint Fondue with Fresh Fruit
(page 197)
Wine: Chilled Champagne or sparkling wine, or
Chablis or dry Riesling

Beer-Steamed Mussels with Crusty Bread
(page 131)
Vietnamese Salad Rolls with Peanut Sauce
(page 24)
Tender-crisp Asparagus, Green Beans or
Broccoli (pages 170, 172)
Apple or Peach Crisp (page 204)
Beer or Wine: Belgian-style beer
or Muscadet

Seasonal Dinners:

Spring

Fresh Asparagus with Lemon Butter (page 170)

Trout Meunière (page 123)

New Potatoes with Chives (page 184)

Snow Peas with Puréed Butternut Squash (page 189)

Strawberry Shortcake (page 214)

Wine: Chilled Sancerre or German Riesling Kabinett

Fresh Vegetable Tree with Roasted Red Pepper Dip (pages 20–21)

Broiled Marinated Flank or Round Steak (page 152)

Roesti Potatoes (page 185)

Coconut & Orange Couscous Salad (page 60)

Maple Orange Mousse (page 202)

Wine: Cabernet Sauvignon or fruity Merlot New World

Summer

Mushroom Pâté with Melba Toast (pages 12, 14)

Grilled or Pan-Fried Steaks with Caramelized Onions (page 151)

Roast Potatoes

Summer Squash with Summer Herbs (189)

Glazed Fresh Berry Tart (page 230)

Wine: California Merlot or Côtes-du-Rhône-Villages

Tomato Bruschetta (page 18)

Barbecued or Broiled Chicken (page 134)

Golden Rice Pilaf with Cashews & Raisins (page 114)

Summer Squash with Summer Herbs (page 189)

Rosemary or Sage Focaccia (page 67)

Maple Orange Mousse (page 202)

Wine: Chilled dry or off-dry Riesling or Pinot Gris

Autumn

Guacamole with Pita Wedges (pages 19, 23)

Shrimp Creole (page 129)

Long-Grain White Rice (page 110)

Shredded Green Cabbage with Caraway Seeds (page 174)

Strawberry Sorbet with Candied Ginger Gems (pages 199 and 217)

Beer or Wine: Chilled California or British Columbia unoaked Chenin Blanc or chilled Lager Beer

Tarragon Chicken Breasts (page 133)

Roesti Potatoes (page 185)

Beets (page 171)

Mixed Fresh Fruit Salad with Lemon Pecan Meringues (pages 196 and 216)

Wine: Chilled medium-bodied, lightly oaked Chardonnay or New World, fruity Sauvignon Blanc

Winter

Spicy Lentil Soup with Yogurt (page 38)

Baked Butterflied Fish with Spinach Stuffing & Caper Sauce (page 126)

Rice Pilaf (page 114)

Glazed Carrots with Green Beans (page 175)

Chocolate Pears with Ginger Cream (page 201)

Wine: Crisp Bourgogne Blanc or crisp Ontario or British Chardonnay

Poached Pear with Roquefort Salad (page 55)

Chicken Fricassee with Feather Dumplings (page 136)

Wilted Winter Salad (page 56)

Orange Cranberry Torte (page 213)

Wine: British Columbia or Ontario Chardonnay or Riesling

Themed Dinner Parties:

Italian Winter

Risotto Milanese (page 111)

Braised Lamb Shanks with Fennel (page 162)

Polenta with Crusty Bread (page 115)

Chocolate Roll with Coffee Cream (page 210)

Wine: Hearty red such as Valpolicella Ripasso

Indian Spring

Spicy Lentil Soup with Yogurt (page 38)

Indian Lamb Curry with Tomato Coconut Chutney (pages 164, 125)

Golden Rice Pilaf with Cashews & Raisins (page 114)

Grated Carrot & Cumin Salad (page 53)

Mixed Fresh Fruit Salad with Shortbread (pages 196 and 221)

Beer or Wine: Light cold beer or chilled Gewürztraminer or spicy Australian Shiraz

Asian

Chicken, Rice & Tofu Soup (page 45)

Chinese Lemon Sea Scallops with Broccoli Stir-Fry (page 128)

Cauliflower & Cashew Stir-Fry (page 176)

Asian Short-Grain White Rice (page 110)

Baked Orange-Cinnamon Bananas (page 202)

Beer or Wine: Asian beer, chilled Gewürztraminer or Gamay

Festive Dinner Parties:

Thanksgiving Dinner

Tomato Bruschetta (page 18)

Roast Boneless Turkey Breasts with Pecan-Orange Crust (page 143)

Golden Rice Pilaf with Cashews & Raisins (page 114)

Puréed Carrots with Buttered Peas and Sautéed Mushrooms

Pumpkin Pie or Old-Fashioned Apple Pie (pages 226 and 225)

Wine: Medium-bodied, fruity Merlot or chilled Alsace Pinot Gris

Christmas Dinner

Oysters on the Half Shell with Lemon Wedges (page 14)

Roast Turkey with Fruit Stuffing & Gravy (page 144)

Mashed Potatoes

Roasted Carrot, Sweet Potato and Turnip Sticks (page 168)

Stir-Fry Mushrooms and Green Peas (page 168)

Mocha Fudge Tart (page 232)

Wine: Sparkling wine, Pinot Noir or a rich Chardonnay

Easter Dinner

Ceviche with Corn or Avocado (page 25)

Glazed Whole Ham (page 167)

Orange Sweet Potatoes Gratin (page 187)

Cauliflower & Broccoli Head with Browned Butter (page 176)

Meringue Nests with Ice Cream & Fruit Coulis (page 198)

Wine: Chilled Beaujolais or Anjou (medium dry) or soft fruity New World Pinot Noir

Formal Dinner Parties:

Mushroom Pâté with Pita Wedges or Melba Toast (pages 12, 14)

Southern Fried Chicken with Cream Gravy (page 138)

Orange Sweet Potatoes Gratin (page 187)

Roasted Ratatouille (page 178)

Fresh Lime Chiffon Pie (page 228)

Wine: California Chardonnay or lighter-style Zinfandel

Poached Pear with Roquefort Salad (page 55)

Roast Fillet of Beef with Herb Butter (page 156)

Rosemary Mushrooms in Croutons (page 181)

Grilled Seasonal Vegetables (page 168)

Mocha Fudge Tart (page 232)

Wine: First course: Chilled French Sancerre or New Zealand Sauvignon Blanc; second course: wines based on Cabernet Sauvignon and/or California medium to full-bodied Zinfandel

Cream of Spinach Soup (page 42)

Grilled Duck Breast with Orange Wine Sauce & Skin Crisps (page 142)

Wild Rice Pilaf with Cranberries (page 114)

Fiddleheads with Mushrooms (pages 179, 180)

Pear Ginger Almond Tart (page 229)

Wine: Côtes-du-Rhône-Villages or Australian Shiraz

Three Sisters Bean Soup (page 39)

Herb Roast Chicken with Pan Juices (page 140)

Roasted Potatoes, Carrots or Parsnip (page 168)

Spinach with Pine Nuts (page 188)

Crème Caramel Flan (page 207)

Wine: Chilled medium-bodied, lightly oaked Chardonnay, Burgundy Red or New World Pinot Noir

Glossary

Al dente: Italian expression, "to the tooth," meaning the bite of perfectly cooked pasta.

Apples: Grow in cool or temperate climates and are harvested in the autumn. Store in the refrigerator crisper. Varieties include the following: *Cortland:* juicy, sweet, stay white when cut and hold their shape in cooking. *Empire:* a cross between Red Delicious and McIntosh, good eaten raw or used in cooking. Golden and Red Delicious: crisp and sweet but become mealy in storage. *Granny Smith:* bright green, tart and crisp for eating raw or cooking. *McIntosh:* sweet and crisp but lose their shape when cooked. *Paula Red* and *Jersymac:* both ripen early with a tart flavor. *Rome* and *Ida Red:* great flavor with a soft texture, and best for cooking. *Royal Gala:* sweet and crisp with yellowish-pink skins.

Apricots: Sweet with the highest carotene content of any fruit, strengthening our immune systems. They have a short midsummer season but provide superb dried fruit year-round.

Baguette: Long, thin loaf of French bread with a crackly crust.

Bain-marie: Water bath to gently cook food in a moderate oven or keep foods warm.

Baking powder: A compound of baking soda, an acidic ingredient such as cream of tartar, and cornstarch to keep the ingredients dry.

Baking soda: An alkaline of sodium bicarbonate; when mixed with an acid (eg; molasses, buttermilk) makes carbon dioxide, which makes baked goods rise.

Bananas: There are 400 varieties. Green bananas ripen fast as the starch develops into sugar.

Baste: To drizzle pan juices on meat, chicken or vegetables for flavor and moisture.

Blanch: To plunge fruit or vegetables into boiling water for 20 to 25 seconds to loosen skins for peeling or to partially boil vegetables prior to freezing, to set color and prevent deterioration.

Blend: To mix ingredients together.

Bouquet garni: Packet with 3 parsley stems, 1 bay leaf, 3 whole cloves and 1/2 tsp (2 mL) thyme tied in a piece of cheesecloth.

Braise: To gently cook meat or vegetables in a small amount of liquid, covered with a lid.

Butter: The fatty by-product of sweet cream. Salt is added to butter for flavor and as a preservative. Unsalted is called cultured or sweet butter, with a shelf life of 3 weeks, while salted butter can stay 6 weeks in the refrigerator — store extra in the freezer. Light butter is for table use, not for cooking. To prevent butter burning at high temperature, add a little oil to the pan.

Butterfly: Boning fish or meat and leaving it whole. When opened it resembles a butterfly.

Buttermilk: When butter is made from cream, the liquid left behind is called buttermilk. Today, buttermilk is made from low-fat milk with the addition of enzymes to thicken the mixture.

Capers: Pickled flower buds of a Mediterranean plant, which add flavor to savory dishes.

Caramelize: Granulated sugar melted until it caramelizes for desserts, pastries and candy.

Caviar: The fresh or salted roe (eggs) of the sturgeon fish. Lumpfish caviar is a lower quality.

Cheesecloth: A fine-meshed cotton cloth used to strain, or tie herbs or spices in cooking.

Cherries: Can be dark red or yellow for sweet cherries. Choose ones with stems or they go bad quickly. The red sour cherries are for cooking.

Chervil: A delicate, lacey looking herb with a parsley taste and a hint of anise.

Chèvre: The French name for goat's cheese made from non-homogenized milk.

Chilies: Seed pods of the *Capsicum* plant. Heat varies even in the same plant, depending on sunlight. Wear plastic gloves to handle chilies and do not touch eyes. *Habanero or Scotch bonnet* are hot, small, round, yellow, orange or pale green. *Thai* are slightly hotter than Habaneros, small, slender, red and green. *Cayenne* are hot, long, thin and red, larger than Thai. *Serrano* are hot, long, thin and green, shorter than cayenne. *Jalapeno* are hot, short, stubby and fat, dark green. *Chipotles* are very hot, smoke-dried jalapenos. *Poblano* are mellow, large, chubby, green and fleshy. *Cherry* are small, mild, round and red. *Banana* are sweet to slightly hot, long, tapered shape, yellow, orange or red.

Chocolate: Made from roasted, ground kernels of the cocoa tree. Unsweetened chocolate contains no sugar, semi-sweet chocolate contains more sugar than bittersweet, milk chocolate contains more fat and sugar. White chocolate contains cocoa butter, sugar and vanilla.

Cilantro (Chinese parsley): The fresh, minty leaves of the coriander plant. The seeds (coriander) are dried and ground for cooking.

Citrus fruit: *Valencia* and *Jaffas* are juice oranges. *Navels* are seedless, available December to March. *Blood oranges* are sweet, streaked with pink flesh. *Seville oranges* are sour, used for marmalade and liqueurs. *Mandarins, tangerines* and *clementines* are small, slightly flat to round, sweet with a loose skin, available from December through February. *Kumquats* are tiny, oval, tart orange-like fruits with edible rinds. *Grapefruit,* the largest of citrus fruits, are white or pink-fleshed and tart. *Lemons* and *limes* are valued for their juice and zest (rind), to accent flavors.

Clarified butter: Butter heated at a low temperature to separate the oil from the milk solids.

Cocoa: Cocoa butter is removed from chocolate and pulverized into cocoa. Dutch-processed cocoa is treated to neutralize its acidity, making it richer and darker. If using Dutch cocoa in baking, leave out any baking soda in the recipe.

Coconut: The white meat of the nut from a palm tree is used fresh, dried or grated. Canned coconut milk is chopped coconut meat combined with water and strained. Coconut cream is the rich fat that separates from the milk.

Combine: To mix ingredients together.

Concassé: To cube tomato by dropping in boiling water for 20 seconds, draining, peeling, cutting in half, squeezing over a sieve set in a bowl to catch the seeds and juice, and then cutting the pulp into cubes.

Cream: The fat component of milk. Whipping or heavy cream is 35% butterfat; light or table cream is 18%; "half and half" is 10%, and light is 6% butterfat.

Cream of tartar: A mild acid found in wine barrels. Added to baking soda to make baking powder.

Crème fraîche: Thick, slightly soured cream for enriching sauces. It's made by taking 2 tbsp (25 mL) buttermilk stirred into 1 cup (250 mL) heavy cream and warming it to 100°F (38°C) for 24 hours and then chilling.

Croutons: Fried, toasted or oven-dried bread slices or cubes for garnishes or soups.

Dash: Applies to a liquid ingredient measuring less than 1/8 tsp (.5 mL).

De-glaze: To clean off flavor-filled brown bits from a skillet or roast pan with a liquid to make a sauce.

Dredge: To coat food with seasoned flour, crumbs or cornmeal before cooking.

Fillet (filet): Boneless meat, chicken or fish.

Fish sauce: Pungent Thai sauce called nam pla and nuoc mam in Vietnam, made by fermenting layers of anchovies in salt and used as a way to salt dishes.

Flake: The way in which cooked fish separates into flakes when gently pressed.

Flute: A decorative pattern on the raised edge of a piecrust made by placing the thumb and first finger together on the edge and pressing the pastry into the groove with a finger of the other hand.

Fold: The method used to incorporate a heavy mixture into a light mixture, such as beaten egg white, by gently moving the mixture from the bottom up over the top in a circular motion.

Frangipani: Ground almonds in a creamy mixture for desserts or pastries.

Frittata: An Italian or Spanish omelet, usually with vegetables and cheese, browned under a broiler.

Fructose: Naturally occurring in fruits and vegetables. Manufactured from corn as a sweetener for commercial products.

Ghee: Clarified butter with the milk solids browned to produce a nutty taste. Used in Asia.

Ginger: A tuber or rhizome used fresh or dried and ground. Store fresh in a plastic bag in the refrigerator or freeze. When frozen, ginger is easy to grate on a rasp or fine grater.

Glace de viande: A dark, rich syrup made by reducing brown stock to flavor sauces.

Glaze: A glossy shine on meats or desserts, brushed or dripped on and set by heat or cooling.

Grapes: Floral aromatic green to deep black fruit that grows in clusters. Raisins are dried grapes.

Gratin: A baked dish with a cheese or crumb topping.

Green curry paste: Thai mixture made of herbs and green chilies for soups and sauces.

Julienne: To cut food into even matchstick-sized shapes.

Kiwis (Chinese gooseberries): Green fruit with tiny black seeds and fuzzy brown skin. Best eaten fresh, not cooked, as it falls apart and contains an enzyme that prevents jelling.

Knead: To use the hands or a mechanical device to stretch and fold yeast dough until smooth and elastic, to develop the gluten in flour.

Lemon grass: A tall stalk grown in southeast Asia that looks like a hard green onion, with a delicate lemon fragrance. To use, cut the white core from the green parts. Peel and discard the core's outer layers, releasing the flavor. Thinly slice the inner core, finely chop or grate on a rasp. Lemon zest can be substituted for lemon grass but it doesn't have the fragrance.

Liqueur: A strong, sweetened distilled spirit flavored with fruit or herbs, used as an after-dinner drink or in flavoring sweets or desserts.

Mangoes: Spicy-sweet in taste with a yellow to orange-red skin when ripe and a large flat pit inside. To slice, peel with a sharp knife, cut the fruit off the pit in four sections and slice them.

Margarine: Made of vegetable oil pressed from seeds, refined with color, water and preservatives then chemically processed to become a semi-solid stable fat. "Light" margarine has more water added. It is not advisable to bake or fry with margarine.

Marinate: To immerse food in a combination of oil, seasonings, and an acidic substance such as citrus, vinegar, wine or yogurt.

Marzipan: Sweetened almond paste.

Melons: Sweet cantaloupes, honeydew, casaba and watermelons. Their ripeness can be judged by the fragrance at the stem and the heaviness of the melon.

Molasses: The liquid left after refining sugar. Further processing produces blackstrap molasses.

Nap: To lightly coat food with a sauce.

Noodles: Ribbons of various widths, made from wheat flour, bean curd, buckwheat or rice. Thin, Asian rice noodles are called rice sticks.

Pancetta: An Italian-cured bacon that has been rolled, browned and steamed or braised, used to flavor traditional dishes.

Papayas: Pear-shaped fruit with a center cavity of black edible seeds. A yellow skin signifies a ripe fruit. Papaya contains an enzyme that prevents jelling.

Parboil: To partially cook food in a boiling liquid.

Parchment paper: A reusable treated paper to line baking pans or sheets to keep foods from sticking. Available in grocery stores.

Peaches: Golden, rosy or cream-colored when ripe, they also feel heavy in the hand. Big peaches are best, as they are picked ripe, while small peaches are picked when unripe for longer storage.

Pears: They ripen and sweeten after harvesting but soften in storage. *Anjou* are broad-bottomed with yellowish-russet skin. *Bartletts* are large, sweet with yellow or red, bell-shape. *Bosc* are juicy and sweet with a brownish skin and smaller bottom. *Asian or Chinese pears* are golden brown, large, round shape, moist and sweet.

Pinch: Measurement of dry ingredients less than 1/8 tsp (.5 mL).

Pineapples: A sweet, slightly tart tropical fruit. When ripe they have enzymes that prevent jelling.

Plantains: A non-sweet, cooking banana, used in tropical cuisine.

Plums: Fruit with green, red, yellow or purple skins. Will ripen after picking. Keep chilled after ripening.

Poach: To cook food barely submerged in a simmering liquid.

Prosciutto: Italian salt-cured and air-dried ham that is sliced paper-thin.

Purée: To finely mash food in a food mill, processor or blender, or press through a sieve.

Quark: Also called fromage frais, a soft, fresh, unpasteurized, tangy white cow's cheese, with less fat then cream cheese.

Ramekins: Individual 1/2-cup (125-mL) baking dishes made of ceramic or glass.

Rasp: A carpenter's tool ideally suited to grate garlic, citrus, nutmeg, ginger and lemon grass.

Reamer: An excellent cone-shaped citrus juicer with a ridged surface.

Reduce: To cook down a sauce or stock to thicken and strengthen flavor.

Render: To cook the raw fat of meat or chicken on medium-low heat until it liquefies.

Ricer: An instrument to press cooked food (such as potatoes) through tiny holes, making rice-sized shapes.

Ricotta: A fresh cheese similar to cottage cheese produced from the whey left after cheese is made.

Roulade: Rolled-up food around a filling that is cooked and sliced.

Roux: Mixture of fat and flour, cooked briefly before liquid is added, to avoid lumps.

Sauté: To fry food quickly in a skillet over high heat, stirring often.

Scald: To gently heat milk just below boiling until small bubbles form around the edge of the pan.

Sear: To brown meat quickly over intense heat to create flavor and color.

Shortening: A white, flavorless semi-solid vegetable fat.

Simmer: To gently cook just below the boiling point.

Soy sauce: Chinese soy sauce is dark and robust. The light sauce is thinner, pungent and less salty, made from fermented soybeans and roasted wheat. Japanese soy sauce, also called tamari, has a sweeter, more refined taste.

Star fruit (carambola): Sweet-tasting fruit with edible skin, shaped like a star. Best eaten raw.

Stir-fry: To cook small pieces of food quickly in a little fat over intense heat, stirring constantly.

Stock: A rich broth made by simmering meat, chicken, fish bones and/or vegetables and seasonings in water over a period of time to extract flavors for soups or sauces.

Sugar: White sugar is refined from sugar cane or beets; raw sugar is unrefined; icing sugar is white sugar processed with cornstarch; brown sugar is processed with molasses for color.

Sweat: To gently cook vegetables, covered, in a little fat to release flavor.

Tender-crisp: When steamed, boiled or stir-fried for a short time, vegetables are cooked but tender, and retain their vivid color.

Tofu: A bean curd made from soy milk, made firm or fresh (stored in water). High in protein, it is bland tasting with a custard-like consistency.

Vanilla: Comes from the pod of a vanilla tree. The seeds and pod are used for flavoring or extracted into an alcohol solution. Imitation vanilla is a poor substitute.

Worcestershire sauce: A spicy, pungent English condiment used to accent food and drinks.

Yogurt: A thick, tart mixture made from milk with bacteria cultures added.

Zest: The thin, colorful rind of a citrus fruit, removed by a grater, rasp, zester, peeler or knife.

Zester: A tool with five small holes with sharp edges, used to remove the zest of citrus fruits.

Index

Almond: Pear Ginger Almond Tart 229
Apéritifs, about 11
Appetizers, about 11
   Ceviche with Corn or Avocado 25
   Chèvre Cheese Dip 21
   Chicken Liver Pâté with Brandy 13
   Crostini 19
   Fresh Tomato Salsa 23
   Fresh Vegetable Tree (Crudités) 20
   Gorgonzola Bruschetta 19
   Guacamole 23
   Homemade Melba Toast or Pita Wedges 14
   Mexican Tortilla Chicken or Beef Wraps 22
   Mushroom Pâté 12
   Oysters on the Half Shell 14
   Roasted Red Pepper Dip 21
   Shrimp with Cucumber Herb Sauce 16
   Tapenade 12
   Tomato Bruschetta 18
   Vietnamese Salad Rolls with Peanut Sauce 24
   Whole Artichokes with Lemon Mayonnaise Sauce 17
Apples:
   Apple Crisp 204
   Danish Baked Apple 203
   Old-Fashioned Apple Pie 225
   Pork Chops with Apple & Sauerkraut 166
Artichokes, about 17, 180
   Jerusalem Artichokes with Chives 180
   Whole Artichokes with Lemon Mayonnaise Sauce 17
Asian Short-Grain White Rice 110
Asparagus, about 170
   Asparagus or Snow Pea Frittata 88
Avocados: Guacamole 23

Baked Beans with Aromatic Herbs 119
Baked Butterflied Fish with Spinach Stuffing & Caper Sauce 126
Baked Cheese Casserole 95
Baked Orange-Cinnamon Bananas 202
Baked Orange or Vanilla-Flavored Custard 206
Baked Potatoes: Stuffed Baked Potatoes 184
Baked Sweet Potatoes 187
Bakeware 8
Baking Powder Biscuits 64
   Cheese Biscuits 65
Balsamic Vinegar 48
   Vinaigrette 50

Bananas:
   Baked Orange-Cinnamon Bananas 202
   Banana Cinnamon Pancakes or Waffles 79
   Banana & Cocoa Smoothie 32
   Banana & Dried Cranberry Muffins 82
Barbecuing:
   Barbecued Boneless Leg of Lamb 160
   Barbecued or Broiled Chicken 134
   Broiled Marinated Flank or Round Steak 152
Barley, about 99
   Barley & Mushroom Pilaf 112
Basic Omelet 86
Basic Three-Egg Cake 208
Basic Vinaigrette 50
Beans, dried 99–101
   Baked Beans with Aromatic Herbs 119
   Three Sisters Bean Soup 39
Beans, fresh, about 170
   String Beans with Browned Butter 170
Beef, about 147–49
   Beef Stew with Roasted Vegetables 157
   Broiled Marinated Flank or Round Steak 152
   Chinese Beef & Green Bean Stir-Fry 158
   Cranberry Meatballs 154
   Grilled or Pan-Fried Steaks with Caramelized Onions 151
   Juicy Beef Burgers 155
   Mustard Pot Roast 150
   Roast Fillet of Beef with Herb Butter 156
   Roasting and grilling tips 148–49
   Tender Pan-Fried Calf or Beef Liver 153
   Testing doneness of meat 148
Beer, about 27
   Beer-Steamed Mussels 131
Beets & Beet Greens 171
Berries, about 230
   Fruit Coulis or Sorbet 199
   Glazed Fresh Berry Tart 230
Beverages:
   Banana & Cocoa Smoothie 32
   Beer 27
   Chocolate Coffee Cooler 32
   Eggnog 33
   Hot Chocolate 30
   Hot Mulled Cider 30
   Minted Fresh Lemonade 31
   Minted Ice Tea 31
   The Perfect Cup of Coffee 29
   The Perfect Pot of Tea 28
   Sangria Blanca 33
   Wine 26–27

Blueberry Muffins 79
Boiling vegetables 168
Braised Lamb Shanks with Fennel 162
Bread crumbs, to make 97
   Soft bread crumbs 146
Breads, Quick, about 61
   Baking Powder Biscuits 64
   Baking Tips 62
   Banana & Dried Cranberry Muffins 82
   Blueberry Muffins 79
   Cinnamon Pancakes or Waffles 78
   Corn Bread 80
   Corn Muffins 80
   Feather Dumplings 77
   Ginger Tea Bread 66
   Irish Soda Bread 65
   Orange & Raisin Muffins 81
   Popovers & Yorkshire Pudding 76
Breads, Yeast, about 62
   Cinnamon Buns 75
   Country Grain Bread 72
   Dinner Rolls – Knots or Rounds 74
   Rosemary or Sage Focaccia 67
   White Bread 68
   Whole Wheat Bread 70
Broccoli:
   Broccoli – Plain or Puréed 172
   Cauliflower & Broccoli Head 176
   Mushroom & Broccoli 104
Broiled or Barbecued Chicken 134
Broiled Marinated Flank or Round Steak 152
Brown Stock 35
Browned Butter 171
Brownies, Chocolate 220
Bruschetta:
   Gorgonzola Bruschetta 19
   Tomato Bruschetta 18
Brussels Sprouts with Pecans 173
Buffets, tips on preparing 11
Bulgur, about 99
   Bulgur, Feta & Mint Salad 59
Burgers: Juicy Beef Burgers 155
Butter:
   Browned Butter 171
   Herb Butter 156
Buttered Peas with Mint 183
Butterflying fish 127
Butterflying lamb 160
Butter Frosting & Filling 210
Butternut Squash: Puréed Butternut Squash 189

Cabbage
   Red Cabbage Braised with Wine 174
   Shredded Green Cabbage with Caraway Seeds 174
Cakes, about 192–94
   Baking Tips 192–94
   Basic Three-Egg Cake 208
   Chocolate Chip Cake 209
   Chocolate Fudge Cake 215
   Chocolate Roll with Coffee Cream 210
   Gumdrop Cake 209
   Kugelhupf 212
   Mocha Walnut Cake 209
   Orange Cranberry Torte 213
   Strawberry Shortcake 214
Calf Liver: Tender Pan-Fried Calf or Beef Liver 153
Candied Ginger Gems 217
Caper Sauce 127
Caramelized Baked Tomatoes 191
Caramelized Onions 182
Carrots, about 175
   Glazed Carrots 175
   Grated Carrot & Cumin Salad 53
Cashews, to toast 177
   Cauliflower & Cashew Stir-Fry 176
Cauliflower, about 176
   Cauliflower & Broccoli Head 176
   Cauliflower & Cashew Stir-Fry 176
Celeriac, about 186
   Mashed Potatoes with Celeriac 186
Ceviche with Corn or Avocado 25
Cheese, about 85
   Baked Cheese Casserole 95
   Cheese Biscuits 65
   Cheese Soufflé 91
   Cheese Soufflé Roulade with Spinach Filling 92
   Chèvre Cheese Dip 21
   Frisée Salad with Warm Chèvre 54
   Old-Fashioned Macaroni & Cheese 96
   Poached Pear with Roquefort Salad 55
Chicken:
   Barbecued or Broiled Chicken 134
   Chicken, Mango & Grape Salad 57
   Chicken, Rice & Tofu Soup 45
   Chicken Fricassee 136
   Chicken Liver Pâté with Brandy 13
   Chicken Stock 36
   Cooking Tips 132
   Cutting up a whole chicken 139
   Herb Roast Chicken with Pan Juices 140
   Making chicken stock for pan juices 141
   Rendering chicken fat 140

Chicken (cont.)
  Southern Fried Chicken with Cream Gravy 138
  Tarragon Chicken Breasts 133
  Thai Chicken & Coconut Curry 137
Chickpeas (garbanzo beans), about 100
  Chickpea Patties in Pita Bread 118
Chilled Minted Cucumber Soup 43
Chinese Beef & Green Bean Stir-Fry 158
Chinese Lemon Sea Scallops with Broccoli Stir-Fry 128
Chocolate:
  Chocolate Brownies 220
  Chocolate Butter Frosting 216
  Chocolate Coffee Cooler 32
  Chocolate Fudge Cake 215
  Chocolate Mascarpone Cream 231
  Chocolate Mint Fondue with Fresh Fruit 197
  Chocolate Pears with Ginger Cream 201
  Chocolate Roll with Coffee Cream 210
  Chocolate Sauce 200
  Chocolate Tart Pastry 224
  Chocolate Truffles 219
  Hot Chocolate 30
Chutneys:
  Mango Ginger Chutney 125
  Tomato Coconut Chutney 125
Cider: Hot Mulled Cider 30
Cinnamon Buns 75
Cinnamon Pancakes or Waffles 78
Clam Sauce 109
Cocoa:
  Cocoa Frosting 210
  Fudge Peppermint Balls 218
Coconut & Orange Couscous Salad 60
Coffee, about 29
  Chocolate Cooler Coffee 32
  Coffee Cream Filling 211
  Coffee Frosting 210
  The Perfect Cup of Coffee 29
Cookies and Squares:
  Baking Tips 192, 194
  Candied Ginger Gems 217
  Chocolate Brownies 220
  Chocolate Truffles 219
  Fudge Peppermint Balls 218
  Lemon Pecan Meringues 216
  Shortbread 221
Cornmeal, about 99
  Corn Muffins 80
  Polenta 115
Corn on the Cob, about 177
  Ceviche with Corn or Avocado 25

Corn Muffins 80
  Removing kernels 177
Coulis, about, 199
  Fruit Coulis or Sorbet 199
  Meringue Nests with Ice Cream & Fruit Coulis
    or Chocolate Sauce 198
Country Grain Bread 72
Couscous, about 99
  Coconut & Orange Couscous Salad 60
  Moroccan Vegetable Couscous 116
Cranberries:
  Banana & Dried Cranberry Muffins 82
  Cranberry Meatballs 154
  Orange Cranberry Torte 213
  Pear & Dried Cranberry Strudel 205
  Wild Rice Pilaf with Cranberries 114
Cream Gravy 139
Cream of Spinach Soup 42
Creamy Potato Salad with Peas & Parsley 52
Crème Caramel Flan 207
Crêpes, about 89
  Mushroom-Filled Crêpes 89
Crostini 19
Croutons, to make 40
  Rosemary Mushrooms in Croutons 181
Crudités 20
Cucumber:
  Chilled Minted Cucumber Soup 43
  Cucumber Herb Sauce 16
Cumin seeds, to toast 53
Currants:
  Cinnamon Buns 75
  Irish Soda Bread 65
Curry: Indian Lamb Curry 164
Custard: Baked Orange or Vanilla-Flavored Custard 206

Danish Baked Apple 203
Desserts, about 192
  Apple Crisp 204
  Baked Orange-Cinnamon Bananas 202
  Baked Orange or Vanilla-Flavored Custard 206
  Chocolate Mint Fondue with Fresh Fruit 197
  Chocolate Pears with Ginger Cream 201
  Chocolate Roll with Coffee Cream Cake 210
  Chocolate Truffles 219
  Crème Caramel Flan 207
  Danish Baked Apple 203
  Fruit Coulis or Sorbet 199
  Maple Orange Mousse 202

Desserts (cont.)
    Meringue Nests with Ice Cream & Fruit Coulis
      or Chocolate Sauce 198
    Mixed Fresh Fruit Salad 196
    Pear & Dried Cranberry Strudel 205
    Stewed Rhubarb or Rhubarb Sorbet 197
    Strawberry Shortcake 214
Dinner Rolls—Knots or Rounds 74
Dips:
    Chèvre Cheese Dip 21
    Cucumber Herb Sauce 16
    Lemon Mayonnaise Sauce 17
    Peanut Sauce 25
    Roasted Red Pepper Dip 21
Dressings. *See* Salad Dressings
Drinks. *See* Beverages
Duck: Grilled Duck Breast with Orange Wine Sauce
    & Skin Crisps 142
Dumplings: Feather Dumplings 77

Eggnog 33
Eggplant, about 178
    Grilled Eggplant or Zucchini, Tomato
      & Mozzarella Pizza 108
    Roasted Ratatouille 178
Eggs, about 83–84
    Asparagus or Snow Pea Frittata 88
    Basic Omelet 86
    Eggs Italiani 87
    Fried eggs 84
    Hard-cooked eggs 84
    Herb Omelet 86
    Mushroom-Filled Crêpes 89
    Poached eggs 84
    Scrambled eggs 84
    Smoked Salmon Omelet 86
    Soft-cooked eggs 84

Feather Dumplings 77
Feta Cheese, about 85
    Bulgur, Feta & Mint Salad 59
Fiddleheads, about 179
Fish, about 120–21. *See also* Seafood
    Baked Butterflied Fish with Spinach Stuffing &
      Caper Sauce 126
    Butterflying fish 127
    Grilled Fish Steaks 124
    Sole in Creamy Tomato Sauce 122
    Trout Meunière 123
Flaky Pastry 222
Flan: Crème Caramel Flan 207
Flour, about 61

Focaccia: Rosemary or Sage Focaccia 67
Fondue: Chocolate Mint Fondue with Fresh Fruit 197
Fresh Lime Chiffon Pie 228
Fresh Pea Soup with Mint or Dill 40
Fresh Tomato Salsa 23
Fresh Vegetable Tree (Crudités) 20
Fried Chicken: Southern Fried Chicken 138
Frisée Salad with Warm Chèvre 54
Frittata: Asparagus or Snow Pea Frittata 88
Frosting:
    Butter Frosting & Filling 210
    Chocolate Butter Frosting 216
    Cocoa Frosting 210
    Coffee Frosting 210
    Icing a cake 209
    Lemon or Orange Frosting 210
    Mocha Frosting 210
Fruit:
    Chocolate Mint Fondue with Fresh Fruit 197
    Fruit Coulis or Sorbet 231
    Fruit Stuffing 146
    Meringue Nests with Ice Cream & Fruit Coulis or
      Chocolate Sauce 198
    Mixed Fresh Fruit Salad 196
    Preparing varieties 196
Fudge:
    Chocolate Fudge Cake 215
    Fudge Peppermint Balls 218
    Mocha Fudge Tart 232

Garlic, about 179
    Removing skin 179
    Roasted Garlic 179
Gazpacho 41
Ginger:
    Candied Ginger Gems 217
    Chocolate Pears with Ginger Cream 201
    Ginger & Soy Marinade (for beef) 152
    Ginger Soy Marinade (for chicken) 135
    Ginger Tea Bread, 66
    Pear Ginger Almond Tart 229
Glazed Carrots 175
Glazed Fresh Berry Tart 230
Glazed Whole Ham 167
Gluten, about 61, 62
Golden Rice Pilaf with Cashews & Raisins 114
Gorgonzola Bruschetta 19
Grains, about 99
    Asian Short-Grain White Rice 110
    Barley & Mushroom Pilaf 112
    Golden Rice Pilaf with Cashews & Raisins 114

Grains (cont.)
Long-Grain White Rice 110
Moroccan Vegetable Couscous 116
Polenta 115
Risotto Milanese 111
Rosemary-Scented Millet & Quinoa Pilaf 113
Wild Rice Pilaf with Cranberries 114
Grated Carrot & Cumin Salad 53
Gravy:
Cream Gravy 139
Gravy 145
Great northern beans, about 100
Baked Beans with Aromatic Herbs 119
Greens, salad, about 48
Grilled Duck Breast with Orange Wine Sauce & Skin Crisps 142
Grilled Fish Steaks 124
Grilled or Pan-Fried Steaks with Caramelized Onions 151
Grilled Polenta 115
Grilling vegetables 168
Guacamole 23

Ham: Glazed Whole Ham 167
Herb Butter 156
Herb Omelet 86
Herbed Brown Rice 111
Homemade Pasta 102
Hot Chocolate 30
Hot Mulled Cider 30

Ice Cream: Meringue Nests with Ice Cream & Fruit Coulis or Chocolate Sauce 198
Iced Tea: Minted Iced Tea 30
Icing. *See* Frosting
Indian Lamb Curry 164
Irish Soda Bread 65

Jerusalem Artichokes with Chives 180
Juicy Beef Burgers 155

Kitchen Equipment 3–10
Kneading, breads 62
Knives 4–5
Kugelhupf 212

Lamb, about 160
Barbecued Boneless Leg of Lamb 160
Braised Lamb Shanks with Fennel 162
Indian Lamb Curry 164
Minted Lamb Shish Kebabs 161

Pan-Fried Lamb Chops with Cucumber Herb Sauce 163
Lasagna: Mushroom & Broccoli Lasagna 104
Leek & Potato Soup 42
Legumes, about 99-101
Baked Beans with Aromatic Herbs 119
Chickpea Patties in Pita Bread 118
Lemon Frosting 210
Lemon Mayonnaise Sauce 17
Lemon Meringue Pie 227
Lemon & Mustard Marinade 152
Lemon Pecan Meringues 216
Lemonade: Minted Fresh Lemonade 31
Lemony Pork Tenderloin Medallions 165
Lentils, about 99-100
Spicy Lentil Soup with Yogurt 38
Liver: Tender Pan-Fried Calf or Beef Liver 153
Lobster, about 121
Lobster with Clarified Butter 130

Macaroni and Cheese: Old-Fashioned Macaroni and Cheese 96
Mangoes:
Chicken, Mango & Grape Salad 57
Dicing 57
Fruit Coulis or Sorbet 199
Mango Ginger Chutney 125
Maple Orange Mousse 202
Marinades:
Balsamic Marinade 124
Ginger & Soy Marinade 152
Ginger Soy Marinade 135
Lemon & Mustard Marinade 152
Lemon & Oil Marinade 124
Mustard Marinade 135
Mascarpone Cream 231
Mashed Potatoes with Celeriac 186
Mayonnaise 51
Lemon Mayonnaise Sauce 17
Mayonnaise Provençal 51
Meat, about 147–49. *See also* Beef; Lamb; Pork; and Veal
Cooking methods 149
Testing for doneness 147-48
Meatballs: Cranberry Meatballs 154
Melba Toast: Homemade Melba Toast or Pita Wedges 14
Meringue:
Lemon Meringue Pie 227
Lemon Pecan Meringues 216
Meringue Nests with Ice Cream & Fruit Coulis or Chocolate Sauce 198

Mexican Tortilla Chicken or Beef Wraps 22
Milk, to sour 80
Millet, about 99
   Rosemary-Scented Millet & Quinoa Pilaf 113
Minestrone with Parsley Pesto 44
Mint: Bulgur, Feta & Mint Salad 59
Minted Fresh Lemonade 31
Minted Ice Tea 31
Minted Lamb Shish Kebabs 161
Mixed Fresh Fruit Salad 196
Mocha Frosting 210
Mocha Fudge Tart 232
Moroccan Vegetable Couscous 116
Mousse: Maple Orange Mousse 202
Muffins:
   Baking tips 62
   Banana & Dried Cranberry Muffins 82
   Blueberry Muffins 79
   Corn Muffins 80
   Orange & Raisin Muffins 81
Mushrooms, about 180-81
   Barley & Mushroom Pilaf 112
   Cleaning and cooking 180
   Mushroom & Broccoli Lasagna 104
   Mushroom-Filled Crêpes 89
   Mushroom Pâté 12
   Rosemary Mushrooms in Croutons 181
Mussels, about 121
   Beer-Steamed Mussels 131
Mustards, about 49
   Lemon & Mustard 152
   Mustard Marinade 135
   Mustard Pot Roast 150

New Potatoes, about 184

Oils, about 49
Old-Fashioned Apple Pie 225
Old-Fashioned Macaroni and Cheese 96
Olives, about 12
   Pitting 12
   Tapenade 12
Omelet
   Basic Omelet 86
   Herb Omelet 86
   Smoked Salmon Omelet 86
Onions, about 182
   Caramelized Onions 182

Orange Sweet Potatoes Gratin 187
Oranges:
   Baked Orange-Cinnamon Bananas 202
   Baked Orange or Vanilla-Flavored Custard 206
   Coconut & Orange Couscous Salad 60
   Cutting in segments 60
   Maple Orange Mousse 202
   Orange Cranberry Torte 213
   Orange Frosting 210
   Orange & Raisin Muffins 81
   Orange Syrup 213
Orzo Salad with Tuna & Vegetables 58
Oysters, about 121
   Oysters on the Half Shell 14

Pancakes:
   Cinnamon Banana Pancakes or Waffles 79
   Cinnamon Pancakes or Waffles 78
Pan-Fried Lamb Chops with Cucumber Herb Sauce 163
Pan Juices 141
Parmesan Cheese, about 85
   Tomato Bruschetta 18
Parmesan Veal Scallopini 159
Parsley Pesto 45
Pasta, about 98
   Homemade Pasta 102
   Mushroom & Broccoli Lasagna 104
   Orzo Salad with Tuna & Vegetables 58
Pastry:
   Flaky Pastry 222
   Making and baking tips 194
   Sweet Tart Pastry 224
Pâtés:
   Chicken Liver Pâté with Brandy 13
   Mushroom Pâté 12
Peanut Sauce 25
Pears:
   Chocolate Pears with Ginger Cream 201
   Pear & Dried Cranberry Strudel 205
   Pear Ginger Almond Tart 229
   Poached Pear with Roquefort Salad 55
Peas, about 183
   Buttered Peas with Mint 183
   Fresh Pea Soup with Mint or Dill 40
Pecans:
   Brussels Sprouts with Pecans 173
   Lemon Pecan Meringues 216
   Toasting 173
Peppers, sweet, about 183
   Broiled or Grilled Sweet Peppers 183

Pesto 108
    Parsley Pesto 45
    Pesto, Sun-Dried Tomato & Goat Cheese 107
Phyllo Pastry, about 205
    Pear & Dried Cranberry Strudel 205
Pies and Tarts, 194. *See also* Pastry
    Flaky Pastry 222
    Fresh Lime Chiffon Pie 228
    Glazed Fresh Berry Tart 230
    Lemon Meringue Pie 227
    Mocha Fudge Tart 232
    Old-Fashioned Apple Pie 225
    Pear Ginger Almond Tart 229
    Pumpkin Pie 226
    Sweet Tart Pastry 224
Pilaf:
    Barley & Mushroom Pilaf 112
    Golden Rice Pilaf with Cashews & Raisins 114
    Rosemary-Scented Millet & Quinoa Pilaf 113
    Wild Rice Pilaf with Cranberries 114
Pine nuts:
    Frisée Salad with Warm Chèvre 54
    Spinach with Pine Nuts 188
    Toasting 54, 188
Pita bread:
    Chickpea Patties in Pita Bread 118
    Homemade Melba Toast or Pita Wedges 14
Pizza, about 106
    Grilled Eggplant or Zucchini, Tomato & Mozzarella 108
    Onion, Sausage & Black Olive 107
    Pesto, Sun-Dried Tomatoes & Goat Cheese 107
    Tapenade, Fresh Tomato & Asiago Cheese 108
    Thin-Crusted Pizzas 106
Poached Pear with Roquefort Salad 55
Polenta 115
    Grilled Polenta 115
Popovers & Yorkshire Pudding 76
Pork:
    Glazed Whole Ham 167
    Lemony Pork Tenderloin Medallions 165
    Pork Chops with Apple & Sauerkraut 166
Potatoes, about 184
    Baked Sweet Potatoes 187
    Creamy Potato Salad with Peas & Parsley 52
    Leek & Potato Soup 42
    Mashed Potatoes with Celeriac 186
    New Potatoes 184
    Orange Sweet Potatoes Gratin 187
    Potatoes au Gratin 185

    Roesti Potatoes 185
    Stuffed Baked Potatoes 184
    Warm New Potato Salad with Tarragon 53
Pot Roast: Mustard Pot Roast 150
Poultry, about 132. *See also* Chicken; Duck; Turkey
    Cooking tips 132
Pumpkin:
    Cooking fresh 226
    Pumpkin Pie 226
Puréed vegetables:
    Broccoli—Plain or Puréed 172
    Puréed Butternut Squash 189

Quick Breads. *See* Breads, Quick
Quinoa, about 99
    Rosemary-Scented Millet & Quinoa Pilaf 113

Raisins:
    Cinnamon Buns 75
    Irish Soda Bread 65
    Orange & Raisin Muffins 81
Raspberry: Fruit Coulis or Sorbet 199
Ratatouille: Roasted Ratatouille 178
Red Cabbage Braised with Wine 174
Rhubarb: Stewed Rhubarb or Rhubarb Sorbet 197
Rice, about 99
    Asian Short-Grain White Rice 110
    Golden Rice Pilaf with Cashews & Raisins 114
    Herbed Brown Rice 111
    Long-Grain White Rice 110
    Risotto Milanese 111
    Wild Rice Pilaf with Cranberries 114
Rice paper wrappers, about 24
    Vietnamese Salad Rolls with Peanut Sauce 24
Ricotta cheese:
    Mushroom & Broccoli Lasagna 104
Risotto Milanese 111
Roast Boneless Turkey Breasts with Pecan-Orange Crust 143
Roast Chicken: Herb Roast Chicken with Pan Juices 140
Roast Fillet of Beef with Herb Butter 156
Roast Turkey with Fruit Stuffing & Gravy 144
Roasted Garlic 179
Roasted Ratatouille 178
Roasted Red Pepper Dip 21
Roasting meat 149
Roasting vegetables 168
Roesti Potatoes 185

Rolls: Dinner Rolls—Knots or Rounds 74
Roquefort: Poached Pear wtih Roquefort Salad 55
Rosemary or Sage Focaccia 67
Rosemary Mushrooms in Croutons 181
Rosemary-Scented Millet & Quinoa Pilaf 113
Roulade: Cheese Soufflé Roulade with
    Spinach Filling 92

Sage: Rosemary or Sage Focaccia 67
Salad dressings:
    Balsamic Vinaigrette 50
    Basic Vinaigrette 50
    Mayonnaise 51
    Mayonnaise Provençal 51
    Vinegars, oils and mustards for dressings,
        about 48–49
    Yogurt Dressing 50
Salads, about 46–49
    Bulgur, Feta & Mint Salad 59
    Chicken, Mango & Grape Salad 57
    Coconut & Orange Couscous Salad 60
    Creamy Potato Salad with Peas & Parsley 52
    Frisée Salad with Warm Chèvre 54
    Grated Carrot & Cumin Salad 53
    Greens 48
    Mixed Fresh Fruit Salad 196
    Orzo Salad with Tuna & Vegetables 58
    Poached Pear with Roquefort Salad 55
    Warm New Potato Salad with Tarragon 53
    Wilted Winter Salad 56
Salsa: Fresh Tomato Salsa 23
Sangria Blanca 33
Sauces, savory:
    Caper Sauce 127
    Clam Sauce 109
    Lemon Mayonnaise Sauce 17
    Peanut Sauce 24
    Pesto 108
    Summer Tomato, Basil & Mint Sauce 105
    Tomato Sauce 103
    White Sauce 93
Sauces, sweet:
    Chocolate Sauce 200
    Fruit Coulis or Sorbet 199
Sauerkraut: Pork Chops with Apple & Sauerkraut 166
Scallops, about 128
    Ceviche with Corn or Avocado 25
    Chinese Lemon Sea Scallops with Broccoli
        Stir-Fry 128
Seafood, 120. See also Fish
    Beer-Steamed Mussels 131

Chinese Lemon Sea Scallops with Broccoli
    Stir-Fry 128
Lobster with Clarified Butter 130
Shrimp Creole 129
Shrimp with Cucumber Herb Sauce 16
Shish Kebabs: Minted Lamb Shish Kebabs 161
Shortbread 221
Shortcake: Strawberry Shortcake 214
Shredded Green Cabbage with Caraway Seeds 174
Shrimp, about 121
    Ceviche with Corn or Avocado 25
    Shrimp Creole 129
    Shrimp with Cucumber Herb Sauce 16
    Vietnamese Salad Rolls with Peanut Sauce 24
Smoked Salmon Omelet 86
Snow Peas: Asparagus or Snow Pea Frittata 88
Sole in Creamy Tomato Sauce 122
Sorbets:
    Fruit Coulis or Sorbet 199
    Stewed Rhubarb or Rhubarb Sorbet 197
Soufflé, about 93
    Cheese Soufflé 91
    Cheese Soufflé Roulade with Spinach Filling 92
Soups, about 34
    Brown Stock 35
    Chicken, Rice & Tofu Soup 45
    Chicken Stock 36
    Chilled Minted Cucumber Soup 43
    Cream of Spinach Soup 42
    Fresh Pea Soup with Mint or Dill 40
    Gazpacho 41
    Leek & Potato Soup 42
    Minestrone with Parsley Pesto 44
    Spicy Lentil Soup with Yogurt 38
    Three Sisters Bean Soup 39
    Tomato Soup with Herbs 37
    Vegetable Stock 36
    Vichyssoise 43
Spaghetti Squash with Tomato Sauce & Parmesan
    Cheese 190
Spicy Lentil Soup with Yogurt 38
Spinach, about 188
    Cream of Spinach Soup 42
    Spinach Filling 94
    Spinach with Pine Nuts 188
Squares. See Cookies and Squares
Squash, about 189
    Puréed Butternut Squash 189
    Spaghetti Squash with Tomato Sauce
        & Parmesan Cheese 190
    Summer Squash with Summer Herbs 189

Steaming vegetables 168
Stew: Beef Stew with Roasted Vegetables 157
Stewed Rhubarb or Rhubarb Sorbet 197
Stir-Fries:
    Chinese Beef & Green Bean Stir-Fry 158
    Chinese Lemon Scallops with Broccoli Stir-Fry 128
    Mushrooms 180
Stir-Frying vegetables 168
Stocks:
    Brown Stock 35
    Chicken Stock 36
    Vegetable Stock 36
Strawberries:
    Fruit Coulis or Sorbet 199
    Strawberry Shortcake 214
String Beans with Browned Butter 170
Strudel: Pear & Dried Cranberry Strudel 205
Stuffed Baked Potatoes 184
Stuffing: Fruit Stuffing 146
Summer Squash with Summer Herbs 189
Summer Tomato, Basil & Mint Sauce 105
Sweet Peppers: Broiled or Grilled Sweet Peppers 183
Sweet Potatoes, about 187
    Baked Sweet Potatoes 187
    Orange Sweet Potatoes Gratin 187
Sweet Tart Pastry 224
Syrup: Orange Syrup 213

Tapenade 12
    Tapenade, Fresh Tomato & Asiago Cheese
      (for pizza) 108
Tarragon Chicken Breasts 133
Tarts. *See* Pies and Tarts
Tea, about 28
    Minted Iced Tea 31
    The Perfect Pot of Tea 28
Tender Pan-Fried Calf or Beef Liver 153
Thai Chicken and Coconut Curry 137
Thin-Crusted Pizzas 106
Three Sisters Bean Soup 39
Tofu: Chicken, Rice & Tofu Soup 45
Tomatoes, about 191
    Bulgur, Feta & Mint Salad 59
    Caramelized Baked Tomatoes 191
    Fresh Tomato Salsa 23
    Seeding 59
    Summer Tomato, Basil & Mint Sauce 105
    Tomato Bruschetta 18
    Tomato Coconut Chutney 125
    Tomato Sauce 103
    Tomato Soup with Herbs 37

Torte: Orange Cranberry Torte 213
Tortillas: Mexican Tortilla Chicken or Beef Wraps 22
Trout Meunière 123
Truffles: Chocolate Truffles 219
Tuna: Orzo Salad with Tuna & Vegetables 58
Turkey:
    Making turkey stock 145
    Roast Boneless Turkey Breasts with
      Pecan-Orange Crust 143
    Roast Turkey with Fruit Stuffing & Gravy 144

Veal, about 159
    Parmesan Veal Scallopini 159
Vegetable Stock 36
Vegetables. *See* individual varieties
    Cooking methods 168
Vichyssoise 43
Vietnamese Salad Rolls with Peanut Sauce 24
Vinegars, about 48
    Basic Vinaigrette 50
    Balsamic Vinaigrette 50

Waffles:
    Banana Cinnamon Pancakes or Waffles 79
    Cinnamon Pancakes or Waffles 78
Walnuts, to toast 55
Warm New Potato Salad with Tarragon 53
White Bread, 68
White Sauce 93
Whole Artichokes with Lemon Mayonnaise Sauce 17
Whole Wheat Bread 70
Wild Rice Pilaf with Cranberries 114
Wilted Winter Salad 56
Wine, about 26–27
    Wine with appetizers 11
    Wine with fish 121
    Wine with menus 233–37
Wraps: Mexican Tortilla Chicken or Beef Wraps 22

Yeast, about 62
Yogurt:
    Yogurt cheese, to make 16
    Yogurt Dressing 50
Yorkshire Pudding: Popovers & Yorkshire Pudding 76

Zucchini:
    Eggplant or Grilled Zucchini, Tomato
      & Mozzarella (pizza) 108
    Summer Squash with Summer Herbs 189